The Man Who Made the *Monitor*

ALSO BY OLAV THULESIUS

*Harriet Beecher Stowe in Florida,
1867 to 1884* (McFarland, 2001)

Edison in Florida: The Green Laboratory (1997)

*Nicholas Culpeper: English Physician
and Astrologer* (1992)

The Man Who Made the *Monitor*

A Biography of John Ericsson, Naval Engineer

OLAV THULESIUS

McFarland & Company, Inc., Publishers
Jefferson, North Carolina, and London

LIBRARY OF CONGRESS CATALOGUING-IN-PUBLICATION DATA

Thulesius, Olav.
   The man who made the Monitor : a biography of John Ericsson,
naval engineer / Olav Thulesius.
      p.   cm.
   Includes bibliographical references and index.

   ISBN-13: 978-0-7864-2766-6
   softcover : 50# alkaline paper ∞

   1. Ericsson, John, 1803–1889.   2. Marine engineers — United
States — Biography.   3. Monitor (Ironclad) — Design and
construction.   I. Title.
VM140.E75.T48   2007
609.2 — dc22   2006038049
[B]

British Library cataloguing data are available

©2007 Olav Thulesius. All rights reserved

*No part of this book may be reproduced or transmitted in any form
or by any means, electronic or mechanical, including photocopying
or recording, or by any information storage and retrieval system,
without permission in writing from the publisher.*

On the cover: John Ericsson ©2006 clipart.com; *Monitor* and *Merrimack*,
March 9, 1862 (Library of Congress)

Manufactured in the United States of America

McFarland & Company, Inc., Publishers
   Box 611, Jefferson, North Carolina 28640
      www.mcfarlandpub.com

Acknowledgments

John Ericsson came alive for me not only through my childhood experience at the place where he was born and now rests, but also through the many people who helped me trace his path in Sweden, England and the United States.

In the U.S. I would like to acknowledge the help of Mr. Kjell Lagerstrom, former chairman of the John Ericsson Society; Mr. Leif Brisfjord, chairman of the John Erricsson Society; Mr. Sten Sture Nordin, New York; and the librarian at the New York Historical Society, Ms. Alyssa Slinly. Special thanks go to Mr. John Broadwater, manager of the *Monitor* National Marine Sanctuary at the Mariners' Museum, Newport News; Ms. Doris A. Oliver at the Special Collections of the Stevens Institute of Technology, Hoboken, New Jersey; Director Richard Waldron and curator Margaretha Talerman of the American Swedish Historical Museum in Philadelphia; Ms. Ann Hassinger, U.S. Naval Institute, Annapolis, Maryland. Ms. Kathleen Golden, Smithsonian Institution, Washington, D.C., and many others. In England my friend John Kennedy Melling guided me to special locations.

In Sweden I want acknowledge the help of the librarian at the Royal Library, Stockholm Mrs. Eva Björling; at Tekniska Museet, Stockholm, Mr. Peter Larsson; at the Nobel Foundation, Stockholm, Mrs. Camilla Hyltén-Cavallius; in Riksarkivet, Stockholm, Mr. Rolf Linde; John Ericsson Sällskapet i Sverige, Karlstad Göte Göransson; Björn Albinson, Landsarkivet, Lund and Mrs. Elisabet Reuterswärd.

Last but not least, I would like to thank my dear wife, Layla, for her continuing support.

Table of Contents

Acknowledgments v
Preface 1

1. Miner and Canal Boy 5
2. Soldier and Inventor John 11
3. To England 19
4. Locomotion 29
5. John Bull 37
6. Propulsion 42
7. The New World 49
8. The *Princeton* Disaster 56
9. The Age of Caloric 67
10. Naval Blockade 81
11. The New *Merrimack* 87
12. Lincoln's Raft 91
13. The *Monitor* 102
14. The Right Track 114
15. Happy Experience 118
16. The Monitor Boys 126
17. Tragic End 133
18. Monitor Craze 139
19. The *Destroyer* 146
20. Solar Energy 151
21. Centennial Exhibition 160

22. Alfred Nobel	166
23. Manhattan	173
24. The Man	181
25. Family and Friends	196
26. Home Again	211
27. Ericsson Remembered	218
28. Lost and Found	227
Chronology	235
Chapter Notes	237
Bibliography	249
Index	253

Preface

All history becomes subjective, in other words there is properly no history, only biography.
                                    Ralph Waldo Emerson, *History*

We probably remember the *Monitor*, the famous Yankee ironclad, that during the Civil War defeated the *Merrimack*, renamed *Virginia*, in the decisive battle at Hampton Roads, Virginia. The memory of this famous ship has recently been revived by the discovery and recovery of the wreck near Cape Hatteras, North Carolina. The ship now is again also in the minds of many who read the book *That Anvil of Our Souls* by David Poyer, the most famous living author of American sea fiction. But who knows about the story of the interesting man, John Ericsson (1803–1889), who designed the *Monitor* and who was a pioneer of solar energy and inventor of the ship's propeller?

Because I grew up and attended school in Filipstad, Sweden — the birthplace of Ericsson and where he is buried — he is a natural part of my life. In Filipstad everybody was proud of him; he was considered the icon of ingenuity. I remember the frightful experience of going to the cemetery where he is buried in a magnificent mausoleum on a hill overlooking lake Daglösen, with the white burial church on the other side. When we went up the hill my mother used to lift me up to a window where I saw the big, dark sarcophagus of the great man. I preferred to go down to nearby *Kanon-udden*, a miniature Battery Park, and sit on one of the huge, cold soda-bottle cannons on the shore of the lake and have my picture taken. These guns John Ericsson once donated to be fitted into the first Swedish monitor class of ship he designed for the Swedish navy.

With these memories in mind I wanted to find out more about the man when I came to America. What happened, where did he live and work, and in particular, who was the man behind the story? What was he like and was he really a genius? Was he the first to come up with the idea of a ship's propeller? I had some experience when I wrote my book on the great American

John Ericsson and his inventions (courtesy of the artist, Göte Göransson).

inventor Thomas Alva Edison.[1] We all know that he is the celebrated inventor of the electric light bulb, but the man behind his inventions can best be found in the private atmosphere of his home and laboratory in West Orange, New Jersey, and Fort Myers, Florida, in the company of his caring wife, Mina, and his kids. I wanted to do the same with John Ericsson: find the face of a man behind the inventions of war and peace.

This is the life story of the brilliant and stubborn Swedish-American naval engineer who lived 50 years on Manhattan after his early years in Sweden and a remarkable inventive career in England, where he introduced the ship's propeller. He dedicated his life to a number of important inventions he hoped would improve the conditions of life and win the freedom of four million slaves during the Civil War.

Preface

This book explores John Ericsson's work as an ongoing battle against technological conservatism, his personal life and relationships to contemporaries such as Alfred Nobel, and his complicated love stories. It also reveals the result of searching for the wreck of the *Monitor* on the ocean floor off Cape Hatteras.

In writing a modern biography about John Ericsson, I felt it was my duty not only to describe laudable perfection but also his weaknesses and to show the extent of the man's character, his personal life and discover his real genius.

1

Miner and Canal Boy

How foolish those behave who attempt to create artifices without the true knowledge of mechanics and its laws.
— Martin Triewald, 1734.

In Värmland, a mountainous region of Sweden, at the mining settlement of Långbanshyttan near Filipstad, John Ericsson was born on July 31, 1803. The time of his birth started a highly technological age. It was the year John Dalton, born and raised in the hilly Lake District of England, proposed his atomic theory of matter, which would later explain that as temperature rises, gasses expand, and the cause of *aurora borealis*, the Northern Lights, visible in Sweden. The same year the mining engineer Richard Trevithick in England invented the steam locomotive; these were all events that lit the path for John.

Seeing the Light

Both of his parents, Britta Sophia and Olof Ericsson, came from respected families with a long technical tradition in the mining industry.[1] Father Olof had studied at the gymnasium in Karlstad. He was a good mathematician and draftsman and in 1799 succeeded Britta Sophia's father, Johan Yngström, as head of the local iron-mines. It involved taking over the ownership after assuming a debt of 3700 crowns. He and his wife moved into a house overlooking the Hytt-lake at Långban and there the Ericssons had three children, Anna Carolina born in 1800, and two boys, Nils in 1802 and Johan (John) the year after.

Legend has it that long before the birth of the Ericsson children, an old herdsman serving Johan Yngström shortly before his death predicted: "In the house on the lake two boys will be born who [will] become famous in this country and the world over."

For the two young lads the road to fame started in the beautiful mountainous nature of Värmland and a stimulating environment their parents had created. Mother Britta Sophia was a very gifted person who by her father had

John Ericsson's birthplace near Långbans lake. Here a memorial stone was raised in memory of the famous inventor (*Ny Illustrerad Tidning*, 1867).

been trained in foreign languages, and during her whole life she enjoyed books. She taught her children reading and writing and father Olof took care of arithmetic and the basics of drawing. He loved to make practical demonstrations of his own little inventions such as using a glass tube connected to a coffee kettle. This device sucked water out of a barrel after a fire burning inside the kettle was suddenly extinguished by closing the lid. John always remembered this, thinking: what was the mystical force that could act as a pump? How can it be used in practice to power a machine?

The boys were supposed to follow in their father's footsteps and were brought up hearing stories about Christoffer Polhem (1661–1751), the brilliant Swedish pioneer of technology, called the "Archimedes of the North." It was Polhem who first suggested building canals in Sweden. Admiringly, Olof Ericsson often told stories about how this man established a mechanical workshop to construct the first elevators for iron and copper mines powered by a system of long rods which transferred motive energy from waterwheels driven by nearby streams of water. He also invented tools for metalwork and pumps to drain water-logged pits, all things the boys could see working in the mines of their father. One of Polhem's motivations to invent mechanical devices and produce metalwork was the fact that he hated to see Sweden buy these things from abroad at high prizes when his own country produced top grade raw material of iron, copper and silver.[2]

Father Olof painted a rosy picture of a future when technical innovations would make mining easier and more gratifying. He also praised the pioneer of fire- and air-machines, Marten Triewald (1691–1747), who he said was the first Swedish engineer who had studied abroad. At the age of 25 he came to England and together with Thomas Newcomen set up a steam engine to pump water from a pit in a coal mine near Newcastle. When he returned to Sweden he introduced the first "fire engine" at the Dannemora mine near Uppsala. It was not a success, probably because of difficulties getting men competent to work it and to do necessary repairs. A few years later the mine owners reverted to the use of horse whims for pumping. Was it the story of these two mechanics that inspired young John to go abroad to study and eventually construct a better engine to work daddy's mines?[3]

John used to follow his dad to look at the deep shafts down the rocky mines and the towers above to which an elevator was hoisted. From the very beginning John, when playing, showed a special talent and interest in mechanical devices of mining equipment such as water pumps and windmills. He loved what he saw and soon was absorbed with his ambition to create his own little world, excavating the ground near his family's home and building miniature mines. When the family went to social events he liked to stay behind, busy making drawings with circles, lines and squares, creating sketches of mining machinery.

New Future

In 1803 Olof Ericsson resigned his position at the iron mines because of economical hardship and a conflict with his workers. The following years were politically difficult, business was bad, and many were ruined, including Olof, who had invested in a silver mine that did not succeed. In 1807 he was forced to sell his comfortable house and the family had to move to a small nearby cottage. The happy life at the big house in Langban finally ended. Also, 1808–09 were the years of war with Russia in which Sweden lost the big province of Finland.

Now Olof was looking for a new job in the biggest industrial project of its time, the establishment of a canal across the country from west to east, connecting the North Atlantic with the Baltic Sea. Olof was an expert in explosives used in his mines and now got a position as engineer in charge of excavating the canal and its locks by blasting rock. He was assigned a job on the first part of the project, to connect the two biggest inland waters of Sweden: the Vätter and the Väner lakes. In 1810 he was hired by Captain Jacob Forsell, who was in charge of the Göta Canal project at Forsvik.[4]

One year later the rest of the Ericsson family moved south to Forsvik. It was a nice wooded area near a small lake that was going to be connected with a canal to the Väner lake. The project involved not only excavation but also building locks and bridges on the seemingly endless waterway. The great enterprise was performed by 7000 men of the Mechanical Corps of the Swedish Navy and a platoon of defected Russian soldiers under the direction of Count Baltzar von Platen.[5]

Much later, after John had moved to the USA, the count's son, Baltzar Julius, who had met the Ericsson boys at the canal project, was chosen as Sweden's marine minister and became a fervent supporter of John in his plan to introduce low-draft monitors in the Swedish fleet.

Wonder Boy

The new environment of building a canal with locks and bridges, pumps and cranes became an exciting place for the Ericsson boys. John was eight years old and eager to learn when he began his new education at the construction site. To start with, the brothers had a governess, Mrs. Malmborg, who had come from Värmland, and later several private tutors, Johan Olof Afzelius (Latin), the Reverend Lampa (French) and the head of construction, director Pohl, for architectural drawings. Dr. Afzelius plagued them with Latin grammar, but John preferred his advice on how to mix colors bought from a druggist for little money to make professional designs. He also made his own drawing instruments and a compass of birch twigs with his mother's sewing needles at the end of the legs, and converted a pair of tweezers into a ruling pen. He colored the drawings with brushes made of hairs plucked from his mother's sable cloak. After completing one of his drawings John went on to design a complete working miniature saw-mill powered by a water-wheel. He developed a superb fluency at the drawing board and his pen spoke eloquently. All his life this was the best way to express himself, not by words.

In 1814 Nils and John were accepted as cadets of the Mechanical Corps of the Swedish navy responsible for construction. Now their training changed from a home school organized by their ambitious parents and private tutors to the stimulating environment of an engineering school in Tåtorp, run by experienced professionals such as Lieutenant Brandenburg and Captain Pentz.

In the same year the school was visited by the famous Scottish bridge builder Thomas Telford, who was the original adviser of Count Baltzar von Platen when he started construction of the canal in 1810. Telford was the foremost pioneer in canal construction who built the Caledonian Canal and soon gained continental reputation. Therefore he was invited to Sweden to make plans for the construction of the Swedish waterway. He brought with him two Swedes, Captain Johan Edström and Gustaf Adolf Lagerheim, who had studied engineering in Britain. These men were employed for the design of the various projects of the Göta Canal and came as new teachers for the Ericsson boys.[6]

The boys received practical instruction in design and were tutored in small groups, encouraged to work on their own. Their education became very much a hands-on affair comparable to modern "problem-based learning" methods in which students themselves are encouraged to find solutions to practical problems. The approach was just right for John, who much preferred this type of instruction to that of a college or university because "then [I would] have had such a belief in authorities that I would not have dared to develop originality."[7] During his practice John had the opportunity to learn English from a British controller of the works at Hajstorp station and further was able to chat with other Englishmen employed on the canal.[8]

John was a bright boy, the pride of his teachers and parents. When only eleven years, he learned to be a surveyor using leveling techniques and was assigned outdoor practice to determine distance and elevation of the ground to prepare contour designs. At the time he was so short that he had to be lifted up by an attendant on a stool in order to reach the height of the eyepiece of his leveling instrument. Soon John gained so much skill that before he was fourteen, six hundred troops labored under the direction of the boy cadet. He also was taught how to make mechanical drawings using the modern art of drafting with shading and colors and today some of his wonderfully exact designs have been in exhibitions at Forsvik and Långban. Finally, he was employed on the survey of the eastern new stretch of the canal at Norsholm.

Break-up

In 1817 the ambitious canal project nearly came to a halt because of economic difficulties. Voices in Parliament in Stockholm were raised to stop further construction, but von Platen pleaded for the importance of his canal for shipping freight and passengers across the country. He also believed in the strategic importance of the waterway for the defense of Sweden and the creation of a special fleet in the archipelago of the Baltic Sea with access to the canal to protect the capital, Stockholm.

In the end it was decided that the project should go on but on a limited scale. Father Olof lost his job but was given the opportunity to establish a quarantine station in the western archipelago outside Gothenburg. Here the incoming ships from the Far East, like the China trade, were to be detained and their crews isolated. Unfortunately this meant separation of the family because it was unwise to bring wife and children to an isolated island on the North Atlantic coast far away from their place of training. Therefore, mother Britta stayed behind and continued her own business of a catering service for the engineers and officers at Göta Canal.

In the summer of 1818 Britta Sophia was suddenly called to her husband, who had become seriously ill. Tragedy came to the Ericsson family because shortly thereafter father Olof passed away, only forty years old. John was devastated when he read the letter from his mother and immediately responded:

> What a sting in my chest I had when I saw that Papa was dead, I could not image such a misfortune could happen. Oh, if we could help Mama, that would be our highest wish in this world. Yesterday I woke up in the middle of the night and I could not go back to sleep, Papa was always on my mind. God shall know how sad it is for us to be separated from him,—but we should be comforted to know that we with God's mercy may meet again and talk to each other in a better world.[9]

According to contemporary law, the orphaned boys had to have a stepfather as legal guardian. The choice fell on the warm-hearted Captain Johan Edström, an experienced canal builder who early on realized that Nils and John were gifted boys and helped them in every way possible. Already in 1815 it was he who had commissioned John to make drawings for the archives of the Canal Company and appointed him as assistant surveyor.[10] Edström also played an important role for John's future career in England, where he himself had been trained. John was always very grateful to his stepfather and kept in touch with him for the rest of his life.[11]

2

Soldier and Inventor John

An invasion of armies can be resisted, but not an idea whose time has come.
—Victor Hugo, *Histoire d'un Crime*, 1852

At seventeen John decided he had enough of building canals and wanted to do something else. Not satisfied with only measuring heights of the ground to find out how much was needed to excavate a ditch, he realized that eventually the waterway would be finished, and what then? When listening to the animated talk of the engineers, such as the famous Scotsman Thomas Telford and his collaborators at his mother's table, ideas were passed on to him and he sensed the enormous potential of the power of heat and steam to turn pistons and drive wheels. Did he anticipate something of the limited role to be played in the future by inland canals as means of transportation? John looked beyond his present occupation with higher aspirations for the future, realizing that he needed new boots to go from there.

Enlisted

The ambitious young boy was looking for a challenge and thought, why not join the army? He already had obtained a basis of practical education and discipline combined with skills in drawing and sciences but lacked the prestige of a university degree or military title that would have opened the door to better pay and more satisfying jobs. Joining the military with the aim of becoming an officer could guarantee a secure position in life. He knew many men who had made a successful career in the army or navy without wearing arms, including his own bosses, Johan Edström and Baltzar von Platen.

When one of his teachers, Major Hans Adolf Pentz, resigned his position at Göta Canal to seek employment as a military surveyor in Jämtland, a northern province of Sweden, John was tempted to do the same. Here topographical work was in great demand and the government did everything to attract competent military cartographers by offering them higher salaries. It was part of a big project to survey every portion of the kingdom, especially the northern districts that were as yet poorly investigated. The officers in command of the royal troops and bureaucrats in Stockholm felt new detailed charts were not only of strategical importance, but contour lines of elevation and topography also served to display geological structure and property rights of the crown and private owners.

Such a career seemed to be a clever choice. John, being very fond of drawing and with his experience in charting from the construction of Göta Canal, decided that it would be an attractive challenge to become an officer in the army with the added position of an official cartographer. Why not try such a brilliant combination with double pay? Armed service looked like an easy job since way up north in Jämtland, with its long and dark winter days, military exercises were limited to only seven weeks in the warm summer and many months were left to surveying. The short period of military exercise also had to do with the Swedish type of conscription of part-time soldiers, who the rest of the year tilled the soil of their small farms allocated by the government. For ambitious Ericsson this seemed to be an ideal arrangement because here, near the Polar Circle, in summer the sun hardly ever set. Ten hours of service still left ample opportunity in the evening for other activities, like his own designs and construction.[1]

Captain Lukander, an officer at the canal, encouraged John in his plans and said that he would help him to enlist. John therefore made up his mind to join the army and to become a surveyor after passing necessary tests. It was a big step and not an easy one because his boss, the domineering Baltzar von Platen, hated to lose a competent leveler and resisted him leaving the job he so successfully had started on the new eastern section of the canal. When John asked for permission to leave and join the army, von Platen became angry and wanted to persuade Ericsson to stay.

John, however replied: "Dear Count! This decision is in total agreement with my inclination and since I did not engage in an academic career, and I do not want to be pursue a trade, I therefore consider a military career as the best option to make a living and if I stay with the canal until it is finished my best time will have passed, at least during which it is essential to make a decision for the future, moreover, canal construction is not a safe future employment."[2]

Von Platen was very upset but did not realize what a strong will his young employee had. He finally gave in, saying: "Then go to hell."

After obtaining satisfactory certificates and references as a cadet in the Mechanical Corps of the navy, he was recruited as an ensign on July 17, 1820, and enlisted at Frösö camp the following summer in the 23 Regiment of the Royal Rifle Corps in Jämtland. In August 1821 he wrote to his stepfather, Captain Edström: "Our seven week military service is over and I am really happy to have escaped the fetters of the canal."[3]

The next year John became an officer when he was promoted to the rank of lieutenant on November 5. To become a surveyor with an additional salary was the next challenge for ambitious John. After special training in trigonometry and mathematics in Stockholm, he passed the surveyor's examination on March 27 of 1822. Initially together with Major Hans Adolf Pentz, he started making his first drawings. During four year's service he managed to produce 120 charts in 4 different parishes. These meticulously made graphs with nice ornamental decorations caught the attention of his majesty, Napoleon's former general and now King Carl XIV Johan, who wanted him to do maps of his own military campaigns in France.[4]

Military Career?

The headquarters of the Royal Rifles was on Frösön, near Östersund, the capital of Jämtland, close to the Arctic Circle. It was a mountainous region with forests, green valleys and blue lakes. In this environment John was cut off from the stimulating canal-construction site led by international engineers, but here, when on his own he began a new life and had time to let his imagination run free.

Lieutenant John Ericsson of the Jämtland Rifle Corps (Church, *Life of John Ericsson*, 1890).

Military service was musketry, gunnery and marching but also gymnastics and swimming, important tasks for the athletic John. As an officer he hated the rules of stupid drills and blind discipline. Instead he tried to stimulate and encourage his enlisted men to meaningful bodily exercises. With characteristic enthusiasm and vigor he practiced wrestling, leaping, swimming and lifting. John had the strength of two men and his zeal was even greater so that he once hurt himself while leaping bars, but difficulties never discouraged him. However, on one occasion, while in garrison, he lifted a cannon weighing six hundred pounds, an effort that was too great. He hurt his back, an injury that in later years sometimes gave him trouble.

John introduced Per Henrik Ling's new school of gymnastics to his regiment. Ling in 1813 had started his program of calisthenics in Stockholm. Ling originally was a poet who promoted his idea of a healthy body and soul. His exercises comprised movements of the arms, trunk and lower limbs, so that every muscle of the body could be brought into play without the use of any tools. The Ling System later became very popular in England and America, were it was called Swedish Gymnastics. For the rest of his life Ericsson was stuck to this type of exercise together with ablutions in cold water.

Ericsson excelled not only in physical feats but he also devoted himself seriously to becoming an expert as an artillery draughtsman. He gained experience from handling eighty-pounders, used on Baltic Sea gunboats. In reality John's attempted "military career" never became a serious matter of climbing the ladder of promotion, but the army gave him ample opportunity to develop his favorite ideas and tinker with fancy gadgets. When not busy with compilation of topographical charts, he was drawing designs of his own.

Military service in the North was also the time when he started his life as an inventor. Despite his double job as an officer and cartographer, John still had time left over to devote to his own creative work, designing machines and building models in the barn of the farm he was given as his dwelling. Here he gathered the necessary tools, a drawing table and turning lathe. Some of these implements are still on display in a Jämtland museum.

The first invention was the construction of his own engraving machine, to be used for making cartographic prints. Since the time as a canal surveyor he had been fond of exact construction drawings that needed to be engraved to reach a wider public. Together with his teacher, Major Pentz, Ericsson had planned an illustrated edition of the edifices of Göta Canal. After moving to Jämtland he continued with this project and later took his drawings with him to Stockholm while sitting for his surveyor exam. Here he tried to learn the technique of engraving in a printing studio but the owner refused to share his secrets. Therefore, John simply went ahead and made his first invention: a machine for making prints. He printed a huge water-wheel and another design was that of a complete stationary steam engine. It had all the essential parts such as a boiler with chimney, cylinder, working beam and a big fly-wheel.

The next enterprise was to realize old ideas from early childhood. One of them was a hot-air or "flame engine" he had been inspired to develop by his father. To little John it had seemed as a miracle when Daddy demonstrated a coffee-kettle "fire engine" with which he could suck water from a pail. He also remembered the pumps that had been used in his father's mines to draw water from the flooded deep shafts. These had been cumbersome contraptions

2. Soldier and Inventor John

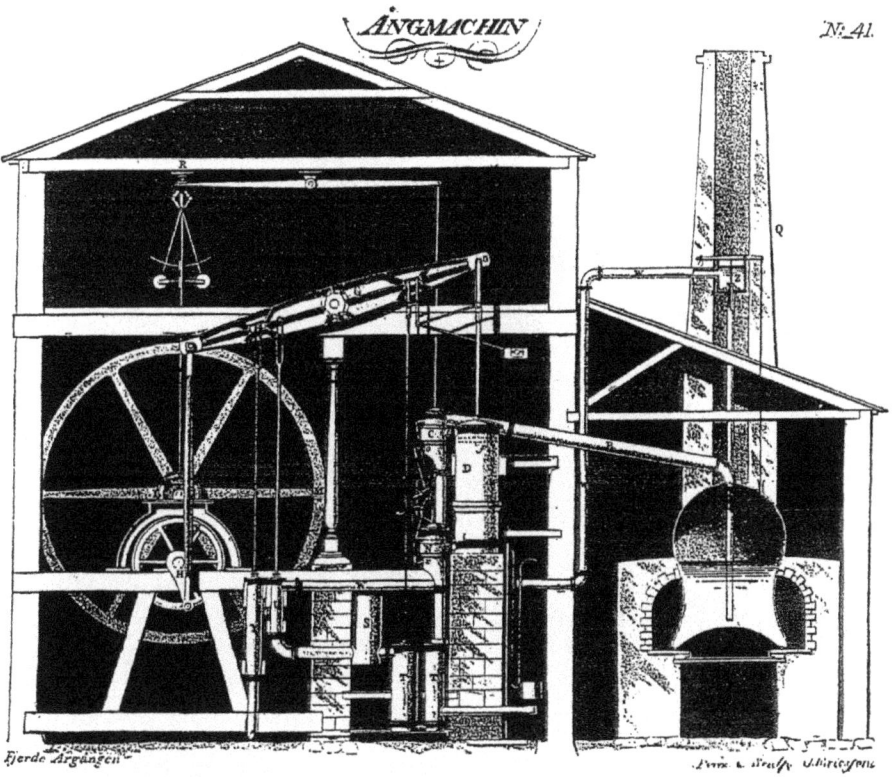

Engraving of a stationary steam engine by John Ericsson at age 18, 1821 (Church, *Life of John Ericsson*, 1890).

driven by water wheels or horse-power. Therefore, John now reasoned, why not use hot air to power pumps? In 1823 he produced his second invention, a flame engine.[5]

His neighbors had noted that he was hammering every evening when he was not out dancing. This time he was working to construct an engine that powered a water-pump. One day when he had finished military drill he tried it out. It was a metal barrel-formed container, inside of which were two pistons that moved a fly-wheel. He started the engine by heating the lower cylinder with a wood fire. Since there was no well on his own farm (John had to fetch water from a little creek), he went to his neighbor's and attached the engine to a pump of their well and—alas—a big stream of water was being sucked out onto the yard. The farmer was frightened, became angry and stopped the successful experiment. John, however, was excited. He knew that his idea worked and feverishly he continued his design to improve the engine that appeared extremely promising. He had demonstrated that it was possible to run a highly efficient engine only on wood fire and without steam from a dangerous boiler.[6]

New projects of immense practical importance emerged. He wanted to develop draining pumps driven by his machines for mines not only in Sweden but other countries like England, Wales and Scotland. His fire-engine certainly could be the solution; he would show that in the future motive power could be developed much cheaper and easier than with the clumsy and dangerous steam engines. Brimming with enterprise, he was eager to obtain a Swedish patent.

On April 8, 1826, in Stockholm, he applied at the Department of Commerce for the exclusive privilege or patent for a "fire engine" and in his application he specified: "A natural power and which from the mechanical point of view is capable of exerting greater efficiency than steam engines, powered at the same cost."[7]

When Ericsson managed to build his first flame engine he was happy, but being a lad of tremendous energy and ambition he eventually saw new opportunities abroad. He realized that a patent for his engine in Sweden was not sufficient, he had to demonstrate its superior working performance abroad. He thought England was the place to be because there was a long tradition of exchange of ideas and trade between the two countries. Sweden provided iron but England had huge coal mines and was the heartland of technological progress.

At the time information about technological innovations was not yet propagated quickly by technical magazines, but rather slowly by personal contact and word of mouth. So, who had inspired John to develop his new ideas and to go to England? There are many possibilities; one of them could have been the English engineer Samuel Owen, who in 1806 came to Sweden and in Stockholm established a foundry to build steam engines. Another link certainly must have been the Scotsman Thomas Telford, who was not only responsible for making drawings of locks and bridges for Göta Canal but also introduced a steam dredge to facilitate work. He belonged to the international team of instructors working on the project and therefore must have come in contact with Olof Ericsson and his boys when he arrived in Forsvik in 1814.[8]

After his successful work in Sweden, Telford was fêted as a public benefactor and the king conferred on him the Swedish order of knighthood, honors of a kind never bestowed on him at home. In 1818 Telford was one of the founders of the British Society, (later the Institute of Civil Engineers) and its first president.[9]

Tragic Love

Military service offered many opportunities to a young man full of muscle and lust. It was not only drills and shooting or making inventions in the evenings. No, he also enjoyed dance and love. While doing his charting jobs John traveled the countryside and met many pretty girls who were attracted to the good looking young man with his curly hair and charming behavior. He not only courted the girls but also wrote poems praising their beauty.

During one of his surveying trips in 1823–24 he was a boarder in the house of the nobleman and retired Captain Jakob G. Lilljeskold at the beautiful settlement of Side. It was a romantic place near Jämtland's biggest lake with a view over the mountains. Here he passionately fell in love with the youngest daughter of the house, Carolina Christina. He was so moved that he wrote poems to his sweetheart and the affection was indeed serious. Secretly they became engaged and when John asked for her hand in marriage, Carolina's father's reply was: "Never will I give my daughter to a commoner without a future."

In no uncertain terms he told John never to return. After he left it was found out that Carolina was pregnant, she was quickly and secretly sent away to Stockholm to conceal the scandal brought on to the family. John, who at the time did not know the facts, never saw her again but kept writing ardent letters to her. Carolina did the same but sadly, the correspondence was confiscated by her parents.

On November 24, 1824, Carolina in Stockholm gave birth to a son, Hjalmar, who was supposed to be adopted by unknown people in the province of Dalarna. She, however, secretly contacted John's mother, Britta Sophia, who agreed to take care of the child under the assumed name Hjalmar Elworth. Fortunately Hjalmar was raised in the family of John's sister, where mother Britta lived. In 1835 Carolina married a lawyer, Carl J. Schlyter, in Uppsala. They eventually moved to Lund where Schlyter was appointed professor of law.[10]

After John's unsuccessful courtship and unfulfilled fatherhood he was deeply depressed. Throughout his life he never recovered from his loss and the event left a deep emotional scar. Keeping busy in the evenings was a way to lighten up his fate, but in his mind he was looking for an escape and when the opportunity came he quickly made up his mind.

Swedish Lobby

Soon his superiors understood what was going on in the barn next to his house where he had established a mechanical workshop. They could only admire the unusual abilities and achievements of their young lieutenant. He seemed to succeed in everything he touched. It started with his drawings and the construction of his own engraving machine. A number of his exquisitely drawn charts and pictures reached the Royal Castle in Stockholm and here they were much appreciated by the monarch, King Karl XIV Johan. Up North he also had been engaged in a project to build bridges and houses.

There was a rumor among the locals that the handsome young officer had constructed a mysterious fire engine that was said to be a *perpetuum mobile*. Could it be that he had succeeded with the age old goal of inventors to construct a machine that without external interference could work forever and with 100 percent efficiency? Such a machine was expected to revolutionize industry and over the years Ericsson's reputation as a skilled inventor spread past the boundaries of Jämtland.

When he finally expressed a desire to leave his command in order to visit England, his wish was not met with opposition. On the contrary, everybody, including his superiors and his majesty the king, supported and encouraged him in his plans. The problem was only that he had no money to travel. An officer friend said that he could not bear the idea of his genius being wasted in Jämtland, and when he heard of his attachment to a poor girl, he considered him lost to the world if he should decide to settle here. He seriously advised him to go to England and offered to lend him the necessary money to travel. Ericsson accepted and soon had a check for 1000 crowns.[11]

In order to succeed in England it was necessary to have the convincing backing of influential people in Stockholm. Therefore, his superior, Colonel John Boy, volunteered to write two letters of recommendation, one to a high military official, Count Taube, and the other to a member of government, Baron af Wirsén. He pleaded to make proper arrangements that Ericsson should be received at the highest level in London. Therefore the first step was an introduction to the British ambassador in Stockholm, General Blomfield.

Ericsson was cordially welcomed at the British Embassy and there he met a very important man, Count Adolf Eugéne von Rosen, who was to become a life-long sincere friend and supporter. Von Rosen, a very outgoing and amicable person with a vivid imagination, had the best connections in England. Very interested in shipbuilding like Ericsson, he had started as a cadet in the Swedish Navy's Mechanical Corps and later served in the British Navy.

It was good fate that brought these two young, ambitious men together. Without von Rosen's help Ericsson probably would not have succeeded the way he did. Working closely with him in England during the years 1826–1828, von Rosen returned to Sweden to climb the ladder in the Navy and at one time was in charge of Motala shipyard, where he supervised construction of Swedish monitors of Ericsson's design. For the rest of their lives the two men stayed in contact with a lively correspondence.

3

To England

He who has never failed somewhere, that man can not be great.
—Herman Melville, *Hawthorne and His Mosses*, 1850

John Ericsson arrived in London on Friday, May 18, 1826, together with his friend and supporter, Count Adolf von Rosen. It was at a time when Britain was at the beginning of the Industrial Revolution and conservative Englishmen were speeding with bumptious optimism into the machine age. Their country, with coal mines and shipping connections to all corners of the world, was the center of technological development. Ericsson had come with the intention to show to a wider audience the breadth of his engineering ideas, but most of all he wanted to find necessary support and financial backing for his work. He hoped to come at the right time to a city that offered an eager market for profitable patents and a fertile ground to materialize inventions. Having achieved this goal, he planned to return to his native Sweden, but that was not going to happen and we will see why.

A New Life

As soon as the two men arrived in London they established a network of necessary contacts. The next step was to find a suitable place to live and buy fashionable clothes so that they could appear properly dressed in society. Von Rosen introduced him to many influential people he knew could benefit from his friend's ideas and support his projects. One of them was the mechanic and entrepreneur Charles Seidler, who through his own knowledge and family was to become another important life-long friend. Seidler came from Germany where he in 1816 had introduced steam propulsion on the river Rhine.

Ericsson's first practical project was to promote his hot-air engine which, carefully packaged, he had brought with him from Sweden. Shortly before he left Stockholm, after having obtained a Swedish patent for his machine, he sent a description to the newly established Institution of Civil Engineers in London. This brochure was translated into English, published in 1826 and distributed to its members. It was entitled: "A Description of a New Method of Employing the Combustion of Fuel as a Moving Power."

The steam engine of those days was costly and wasteful and could be dangerous if the boiler exploded, but nobody had yet been able to improve it. Therefore Ericsson was very optimistic about the prospect of his steam-less engine and believed in its success. A meeting with the London engineers had been scheduled and he was asked to make a live demonstration of his machine at one of their regular sessions at 15 Buckingham Street on the Strand. We do not know who first introduced him to the British civil engineers, but it must have been his former stepfather, Captain Johan Edström, a member of their institution. Ericsson probably also had the support of Thomas Telford, one of the founders of their society and its first president. At the time the Scotsman Telford had moved to London and from 1820 lived in a Georgian house at No. 24 Abington Street. As we have seen, Telford for his work at Göta Canal had been awarded a Swedish knighthood. He appreciated ambitious Swedes such as young John, whom he had already met as a boy at Forsvik.

As always, John was full of optimism and looked forward to the event, and when the day arrived the little engine was put on a stand for everybody to see. Critical eyes in the country of James Watt were curious to see what the curly-haired twenty-three-year-old Swede could achieve with a device that looked simple enough. It had no boiler, no water, no steam, only a firebox, and two cylinders with pistons, one driven by the expanding heat, the other sucking incoming air. The curious visitors were told that a flame was enough to make it run. So, when a fire was lit everybody in the audience was excited to witness when after some time it actually slowly started moving and then picked up speed. A beam converted the reciprocating movement of the cylinders into rotary motion by a crank attached to a fly-wheel. Unfortunately the impressive action did not last very long, because suddenly with a swishing sound and burning smell it all was over; the curious little contraption stopped and every effort by Ericsson to make it moving again failed.

What went wrong? The answer is that the engine was designed to run by the combustion of resinous wood. When John made his demonstration, anthracite coal was used instead, and this became a major problem. First it took a while to ignite the coal and since there were no flushing hot flames from the fire-wood to immediately start the engine, it was slow in starting. After a while when intense red heat developed in the furnace under the power cylinder it nearly melted and destroyed the engine.

In London the friendly admiration he had received in Sweden turned into cynical criticism and what was worse, now he could not expect backing from the civil engineers and of course, the planned British patent application was presently out of the question. Ericsson had to face a grim reality. Sadly, he packed up and took his creation back, firmly determined to modify the machinery. This was Ericsson's first great failure — and certainly not his last, but he never gave up.

The unsuccessful trial of the flame engine was by no means the end of Ericsson's career in England. Von Rosen remained confident, fully believing in his genius and ability to construct new, revolutionary machines that could be sold; the design of two more inventions already developed in Sweden were now accepted at the London Patent Office. These had, as one would have expected, nothing to do with Ericsson's flame engine.

The first one was a method to boost the performance of the conventional steam engine by a system of forced draft. This was achieved by a double-acting piston-operated air-pump connected to an ingenious furnace and tubular boiler. Before their departure von Rosen on April 1, 1826, had submitted an application for a British patent for this contraption. It was filed for "John Ericsson, a Swedish citizen, living in Ternland (Jämtland)." The patent (No. 5398) was registered on August 5, 1826, under the name of his friend. The entry was entitled: "Engine for communicating power, to answer the purpose of a steam engine."[1] The other was a water-suction pump, operated by compressed air. This application was also filed from Sweden and eventually registered on December 20, 1826 (No. 5437) under the name of his new friend in London, Charles Seidler.[2]

Polar Ventures

Although Ericsson's hot-air engine flopped the good thing was that at the demonstration he met another young and aspiring engineer, John Braithwaite, a capable entrepreneur with an office in Fitzroy Square and owner of a mechanical workshop in the North of London near Regent's Canal. Braithwaite built boilers, and coolers for London breweries and distilleries and in 1820 he was known to have ventilated the building of the House of Lords by means of air-pumps.

The two soon came to an agreement and became business partners, an excellent arrangement of a bold and enterprising businessman and a brilliant engineer who always shrank from the commercial side of his inventions. They rented a construction facility at Limehouse near the Thames.

Ericsson was happy; now he had the opportunity to do most of his construction work on models for new inventions in a reputable, well-equipped mechanical workshop and foundry. Over the years Braithwaite and his partner worked on many very successful projects, such as a machine for the production of files and a hydrostatic weighing machine. In 1830 alone four new patent applications were submitted: "An apparatus for making salt from brine," "Engine for communicating power for mechanical purposes," "Locomotive engines" and "A steam turbine." Many more were to follow and a number of these were filed jointly with his collaborators. Their construction projects were not limited to England but also stretched to Belgium and France in collaboration with John Cockerill, who was a leading industrialist in Liège.[3]

Through Braithwaite's business relations with the London breweries, Ericsson in 1827 came in contact with the wealthy gin magnate Felix Booth, who was a good customer of Braithwaite's distilling equipment establishment. The following year Booth approached Braithwaite and said that his friend, a captain of the Royal Navy, John Scott Ross, needed help with a marine steam engine and that he was willing to pay for it.

When Ross came to meet Ericsson at the Braithwaite foundry they immediately hit it off, discovering that they had much in common. Both were stubborn and vain, and while refusing to admit mistakes, they were willing to learn from them. Ross spoke Swedish since he had been in Stockholm and served in joint Anglo-Swedish naval operations in the Baltic. He also was interested in steam propulsion and had written about such odd subjects as steam power and phrenology (shape of the skull and mental faculties). Moreover, he subscribed to the then unfashionable opinion that steam would be the future of the Royal Navy, a notion that was famously ridiculed by Lord Melville, the first Lord of the Admiralty.

Previously the British Admiralty had offered a large sum of money (£20,000) as a prize for the adventurous sailor who could establish a sea route across the northern part of Canada that would make it possible to travel more quickly from the Atlantic to the Pacific Ocean. In 1818 Ross led an expedition to find the Northwest Passage, but he only got as far as Baffin Bay and did not succeed to discover the crossing. In subsequent years he was widely derided for not continuing his search but now, on his own and without the support of the Royal Navy, he had secretly arrived at the outrageous idea that steam propulsion would be the key to success in finally conquering the icy passage to India and finding the North Pole.

In Liverpool he purchased a packet-ship, ambitiously named the *Victory*, and brought her over to London, where she was taken in hand at Limehouse for strengthening the hull and fitting her with new powerful machinery and paddle-wheels. Felix Booth agreed to sponsor Ross and offered to outfit the *Victory* with a totally new system of propulsion: A steam engine with horizontally acting cylinders, two of Ericsson's recently patented high-pressure boilers, and a "surface condenser." The condenser was a very useful machine that could save freshwater at sea by shooting jets of cold water into a steam-containing cylinder. At sea in salt water it was vital to use boiler water over and over again by condensing exhaust steam. Surface-condensation also helped to overcome troubles arising from boiler-incrustation, i.e., deposits of lime-scale in marine boilers. Without it or the jet condenser a steam powered vessel could scarcely have sailed out of sight of land, for it could carry only a limited amount of fresh water.

At the time Ross did not disclose the purpose and destination of his ship because he feared that some other explorer might get there ahead of him if the news of his voyage leaked out. Braithwaite and Ericsson were told only that the vessel was being fitted for "experimental purposes." Their reasonable assumption, with their customer being a naval officer, was that the *Victory* would be fitted to be an experimental warship. Therefore, Ericsson suggested that the sensitive machinery all be placed below the water line. To this arrangement Ross agreed when he said, "So as to be out of reach of shot." When finally informed about his real plans, the pair had no time to try to adapt the machinery for the lonely polar region and its freezing waters.[4]

Before the departure of the *Victory* from the dock in Limehouse many invited visitors came on board. One of them was another arctic explorer, Captain John Parry, who admired Ross' ideas and said, "The application of steam as a moving-power to this object of the NW-Passage offers in my opinion, a very great hope of its accomplishment and as Ross has attended a good deal to both subjects I really think he has a better chance of succeeding than any of us."

But at the same time, he cast a warning note on the gadgetry: "I think, however, there is in the whole thing, rather too much that is new and untried, and this is certainly not the kind of service on which novelties of that sort first ought to be tried." Nevertheless having spent a day aboard Ross' ship he declared himself, "much gratified…. It is a bold, public spirited undertaking!"[5]

On May 23, 1829, the *Victory* with destination North Pole left the dock in Limehouse with a heavy cargo of equipment, coal, food and crates of Booth's driest gin. It was a pity that Ericsson at the time was not ready with his propeller because this type of propulsion definitely would have been superior to ice-clogged side-wheels in the waters of the North Pole.

Soon the *Victory* was surrounded by ice. Unfortunately the new installations did not work properly in the arctic climate and therefore Ross concluded: "Our engine entirely failed not in consequence of the principle on which it was constructed but owing to the very inferior materials of which the boilers were constructed."

He therefore during the months of October and November 1829 unceremoniously dumped the machinery, engines and boilers on the icy shores of Felix Harbour. Here to this day still lie the remnants of Ericsson's forced-air boiler and surface condenser.[6] The reasons for the failure of the *Victory* were many, not only untried new gadgets but also a totally inexperienced crew, not used to steam engines and mysterious blowers.

From 1830 to 1832 the *Victory* was enclosed by ice. Ross was furious, he never found the Northwest Passage but abandoned ship and continued on sledges to explore the Arctic. In order to thank his sponsor, he named a new found island "Boothia," for the famous London gin tycoon. After all the struggle finally Ross and his men had some luck. James Ross, the nephew of John Ross, made an important discovery. On May 31, 1831, he stumbled on the magnetic North Pole when he saw that the needle of his compass stopped moving and instead its tail pointed right up to the covering glass.

On his return to England Ross was received as a hero, became "Sir John Ross" and was promoted to rear admiral, but Ericsson only received criticism. Ross put the blame for not finding the Northwest Passage with the *Victory* on his London engineers and leveled serious allegation at Ericsson, saying that his engines were inefficient and responsible for the failure. Ericsson defended himself vigorously and argued that he was under the impression he was building an experimental warship and "in experimenting, complication is not regarded, since the intention generally is to ascertain facts and effects never known, for guidance in future practice." He charged Ross with "utter forgetfulness and candor." The matter became so serious that at one time there was a risk of a duel.[7]

Water Squirts

In 1828 Braithwaite and Ericsson started on an initially little appreciated invention, a revolutionary steam fire engine, built for fire brigades in big cities. The engine was a high pressure, ten horsepower steam engine fed by a blower, driving a water-pump, equipped with flexible suction and delivery hoses. The steam fire engine was mounted on a frame with wheels suspended by springs. The machine was capable of throwing 2 tons of water per minute, jets that could reach the highest buildings of London. It burnt coke and got up steam in 20 minutes. When completed, Braithwaite and Ericsson offered their engine for free trials to the London Fire Brigade.

This new engine's debut became a spectacular show when it was used to extinguish the fire at the Argyll Concert Rooms off Oxford Street. It happened on a cold winter day in February 1829. The hand-operated engines summoned to the scene froze up in the low temperatures, but the steam fire engine continued to function for 5 hours until the conflagration was put out. Despite the big success, the conservative firemen of London opposed the machine because they felt it threatened their jobs. The managers rejected it on the grounds that, "it would not be desirable to use, as the quantity of water thrown might be injuriously applied and cause mischief," and it "required larger supplies of water than could be obtained in London."

Braithwaite & Co. soon constructed four more engines of larger dimensions and in 1832 the fire engine found an eager customer in Frederick William III, king of Prussia, who bought one for Berlin. The harbor authorities of Liverpool also successfully adopted the new method to extinguish fires. One engine was sold to Constantinople, but the Turkish firemen had the same opinion about the machine as their London counterparts. The pasha became

3. To England

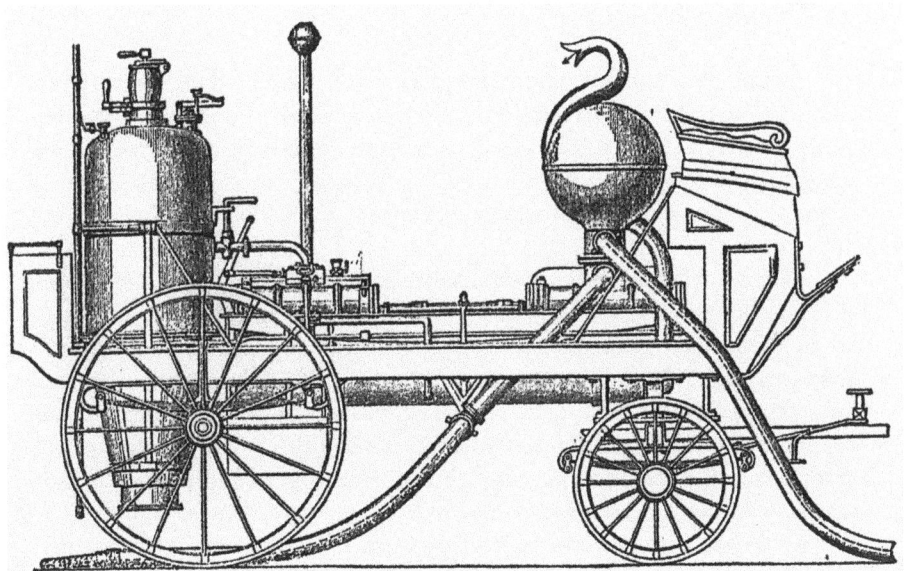

Braithwaite and Ericsson's steam fire engine, London, 1829 (Church, *Life of John Ericsson*, 1890).

excited and exclaimed, "Mashallah! Very good, but it will require a sea to supply it with water. It won't do for us, for there is no sea in the middle of the city."

So the pasha decided not to use any squirts, and to follow the custom of letting the fire spread until the wind changed or it could find nothing more to destroy. After his arrival in the U.S., Ericsson's invention was immediately embraced as a step forward in a more appreciative environment and a modified version was built in 1841.[8]

When Ericsson joined his partner at his workshop near Regent's Canal he soon realized that clumsy side-wheel tugboats had a problem pulling barges on inland waterways and he decided to do something about it. At first he designed and patented a steam-traction system with two rollers and friction rails along canals upon which heavy cargo vessels could be pulled. But as always his head was full of new ideas and he therefore also tried another method that operated "movable shutters," resembling Venetian blinds. Soon, however, he abandoned these cumbersome projects and instead concentrated on designing other means of propulsion, such as marine screw propellers. This was the important beginning of Ericsson's research on the ship's propeller and his first patent in this line was the 10 October 1834 entry entitled "Machinery for propelling vessels."[9]

To Cornwall

Flooded mines in the mountains of his native Värmland had been a lively childhood experience of young John. Water accumulating in the pits often made work impossible in his father's mines and as a boy he had witnessed the struggle of bailing the water-filled deep shafts with buckets on long ropes. As he grew up, one of his ambitions was to invent a machine that could do the job.

When during his military service he heard that Sweden's only coal mine at Höganäs was seriously flooded and needed a pump, he went to his drawing-board and cracked his brain for a solution. It was a difficult task nobody yet had achieved successfully before in Sweden, to design an efficient deep well water-pump, driven by a steam engine or his own more economical hot-air engine. Ericsson offered his invention to the Swedish mining company but never received a response, because who could trust a young unknown lieutenant from the wilderness in the North?

Why was Ericsson now so keen to push this invention in England? It was because he was convinced that his design was much more practical and fuel efficient than existing pumps. Skeptical British mine owners were of the opinion that to build a monstrous fuel gobbling steam engine required the iron ore from one mine for pipes and engines to build it plus the coal from another to run it. In certain areas of Sweden regulations already prohibited using wood to fuel steam engines since experience had shown that forests near mines and industries became devastated.

Efforts to drain mines with a variety of engines was nothing new. Already in 1702 Thomas Savery installed a steam pump in Cornwall. He had much in common with John Ericsson, being a military engineer with a fondness for mechanics and "natural philosophy." He also devoted much time to inventing paddle wheels for propelling vessels and made demonstrations on the Thames trying to secure their adoption by the British Navy, but met with no success. The surveyor of the Navy dismissed him, saying:

"What have interloping people, that have no concern with us, to do to pretend to contrive or invent things for us?" The pioneer work of Savery was continued by Thomas Newcomen and James Watt, who developed piston-operated steam engines to drive pumps.[10]

Ericsson's new system was quite different from that of his predecessors. It was based on the use of compressed air as a moving power to expel water through long pipes. His design envisaged an intricate pneumatic system powered by a hot-air engine driving a force-pump which through copper tubes transmitted pressure down to the bottom of the pit. Here the pressure emptied water from a cistern and pushed it through wide-bore tubes to the surface. He had built models in Braithwaite's workshop and purchased expensive material for his engine and long copper pipes — but was this really worth an expensive investment?

Ericsson was confident of his success and already from Sweden he had submitted an application for a British patent, entitled "Drawing water out of mines, wells, pits and other places." When he came to London he thought that approval would only be a matter of formality. Great was his surprise when he was summoned by the attorney general to the patent office, where he was told that a certain Mr. George Bodmer had submitted one for a similar purpose.[11]

Bodmer was a Swiss-German ordnance expert and a captain in the German artillery who in 1824 had established a mechanical factory in Manchester. After some deliberations the problem was resolved, probably because the rival scheme was not as technologically advanced and had to be run by a span of horses. Ericsson's patent was finally accepted and registered on December 20, 1826, under the name of his friend Charles Seidler.[12] Ericsson's further collaboration with Braithwaite resulted in an avalanche of twenty smart inventions.

Ericsson and his team had great expectations for their invention because most mines had problems with flooding, so there was a potential for a worldwide market. It was known that an Anglo-Mexican silver mine at Valenciana was looking for help and Ericsson submitted an estimate to their London office. In an optimistic mood, he wrote to his mentor in Sweden: "When I finish with this project I will return to Sweden or I go to warmer countries." He probably already saw himself working in the nice climate of Mexico.

At the same time he also established contact with the Carnon tin mine, near Truro in Cornwall, the southernmost part of the British Isles and far away from London. Drainage of pits was a special problem in Cornwall since many mines there were sunk along the coastline and extended out under the sea. The Carnon mine had a serious flooding problem and Ericsson offered to help. The water not only limited access to the ore but also had become a cause of ill health. The Cornish mines were notorious for their health hazards to workers that later were found to be caused by intestinal hookworms that had a favorable breeding ground in the watery shafts. The parasite produces an enormous number of eggs in the gut of infected workers, and the eggs pass with the stool into the water and mud. Here embryos developed and in the unsanitary conditions present at the time, the new breed gained access to the miners through their skin — usually the feet. Hookworm infestation was a serious disease because of its high mortality and because of the number of persons prevented from working by the debility it caused.

Although the Cornish mine was far away from London, that did not prevent Ericsson from making plans; here he saw a good opportunity to test his invention and hopefully to make some profit. One important merit of Ericsson's hot-air powered drainage pumps seemed to be their economy. In this part of England coal was scarce and expensive and therefore Ericsson was welcomed to Cornwall. After finishing all the necessary arrangements, such as purchase of material and construction of parts, he shipped everything to Carnon and then left London on July 18, 1827, to stay away for four months.

The Cornwall project, like his first hot-air engine and Ross' steam engine, became a failure. The mine was 1500 feet deep, a much larger depth than his pump was calculated for. Therefore several relay stations down the shaft had to be made and that was difficult and costly.

Back in Sweden Ericsson was not successful either with his invention. Eventually the Anglo-Swedish inventor Samuel Owen of Stockholm in 1828 won the race and got a contract to install a steam-powered pump at the Höganäs mine that proved to be very effective and worked successfully for seventy years.[13]

Caloric Engine

The 1826 flame motor Ericsson had brought with him from Sweden basically was a hot-air engine. In 1828 Ericsson made an attempt of improving it and his untiring efforts led to a new version using coal. The power of this machine was estimated at 5 hp. Unfortunately it also was no success.[14]

In 1833 he finally submitted a patent application for his favorite child, now called the Caloric Engine. The official entry was: "Engine for producing motive power, obtaining an increase of power with a given quantity of fuel."[15] This time it was an impressive looking engine with a framework of gothic arches. It was carefully designed with a closed system of one hot externally heated and one cold cylinder and equipped with a "regenerator" in the form of a tubular heat exchanger.[16]

The new engine promised to be a great success and now stirred much interest in engineering circles. Even the famous Professor Michael Faraday, pioneer of modern electricity, who just had constructed the first electric motor, was much impressed and held a lecture at the Royal Institution on the "Physical Forces of Hot Air" in which he promised to explain the mysterious motive power that made the "caloric engine" run. Ericsson was thrilled when he heard that the most distinguished "natural philosopher" cared to engage himself with his machine, but even Faraday confessed that its action remained a mystery. Much later eventually James P. Joule showed that thermal energy is due to motion of particles and equivalent to mechanical energy.

In the end further work on caloric engines stopped because Ericsson left for America. We will see that in the New World he finally brought his invention to new fruition.

4

Locomotion

The richest boon to civilization yet attained by the application to machinery of those natural forces created by omnipotence for the benefit of the human race.
—Freeman Hunt, 1853

The nineteenth century was a period when due to the development of steam engines "locomotion," or the art of moving goods and people from one place to another, changed dramatically. It started with a network of canals, and better roads, and finally came the age of locomotives. In a wider sense locomotion was not limited to machines to haul trains on land but it also included new modes of propulsion in water and everything that made this possible. From the very beginning, Ericsson was part of this development, having been involved in the construction of canals and later during his career as an inventive engineer he became very much engaged in the innovative process on land and sea.

Full Steam Ahead

At the beginning of the century transportation in Britain had been improved by building an extensive turnpike system at a cost of £2,200,0000 so that now one could travel by stagecoach from Edinburgh to London in sixty hours. This was considered outrageous and stories were told of deaths by stroke as the result of traveling at the alarming speed of five or six miles an hour. Speed was suspect and in certain quarters an anathema. At the breakthrough of the technological age and a move to introduce steam engines on rails, a hard core of prejudice against such extravagances became obvious. The practicality of steam locomotion was doubted. This opinion also came into play when it was proposed to put such "devilish" engines into ships.[1]

In the 1820s a railroad between Manchester and Liverpool was projected but this was met with strong opposition which did not always stop at legal action and verbal attack, but sometimes led to a display of force. It happened that the surveyors were driven from their work by a mob armed with sticks and stones, urged on by land-proprietors and those with interest in coaches on the highway. Finally a bill to promote railroads had been carried through Parliament, but only after a very determined effort of coach-men and landholders to defeat it. During the debate at the House of Commons the major proponent, George Stephenson, was summoned and asked, "Suppose, now one of your engines to be going at a rate of 9 or 10 miles an hour, and that a cow were to stray upon the line and get in the way of the engine, would not that be a very awkward circumstance?" He replied, "Yes, very awkward — for the coo!"

(Later, American locomotives were equipped with a bell and heavy whistle and had a "cow-catcher," a metal frame placed in front to remove obstacles from the track). At the time a newspaper reported: "What can be more palpably absurd and ridiculous, than the prospect of locomotives traveling twice as fast as stage coaches? We would soon expect people of Woolwich to suffer themselves to be fired off upon one of Congreve's ricochet-rockets, as trust themselves to the mercy of such a machine going at such a rate."[2]

The Novelty

One of the secrets of Ericsson's success was that he never gave up even after failures, like the disaster with his hot-air engine in 1826 and Ross' *Victory* ship. Together with an immense ambition to improve, he had a remarkable ability to change focus; he shifted to the design of new versions of the conventional steam engine and succeeded at Braithwaite's factory to develop a compact, high-powered machine that could easily be used in locomotives and ships. The heart of these improved engines were his patents of 1826 and January 1829 for new high power boilers for "communicating power" and "of converting liquids into steam."[3]

At this stage success of the steam locomotive depended on the development of compact, high-pressure engines and boilers. James Watt's old steam engines were fuel guzzling monsters working slowly at low steam pressure and only useful for stationary purposes. It is curious to recall that due to risk of boiler explosions, Watt attempted to secure an act of Parliament forbidding the use of high-pressure engines.

The attempts to transmit traction through wheels on rails were first made in the coal mines of Britain by Richard Trevithick in 1804. In 1808 he built a circular demonstration track in London, with a locomotive called *Catch-me-who-can* that made 10 miles an hour and that people could ride for a fee. Later in 1813 William Hedley followed with his locomotive, the *Puffing Billy*. At the time a constant problem was weak and slow engines because of inefficient steam power, until George Stephenson and John Ericsson introduced new boilers and used blowers to stimulate combustion. The *Locomotion* constructed by Stephenson was the first to run on the Stockton and

Darlington railroad line that opened for public traffic in 1825. But it was not until the Liverpool and Manchester Railway was established that the vast possibilities of this new form of transportation were to be tested beyond doubt.

The directors of the newly built Liverpool and Manchester Railway initially wanted to operate the line by horse power or "rope hauling" through stationary engines. But in 1829 they were reluctantly persuaded to invite entries for a public trial to see for themselves how advanced locomotives had become. A prize of five hundred pounds was offered for the best locomotive that should meet stipulated conditions with regard to weight, speed and tractive power. At a meeting on April 20 detailed conditions for the participant engines were issued. At a later date in May it was added that it did not have to be a steam locomotive but could be an "Improved Motive Power," meaning horse-power.

Ericsson got to know about the contest through his new shipbuilding associate, William Laird in Liverpool, and decided to participate with his partner, John Braithwaite. At the time only seven weeks of the allowed twenty-two remained and hasty preparations were made to build a locomotive that they called the *Novelty*. The only experience of moveable steam engines they could count on was the spring-mounted steam fire engine on wheels they just had completed and a boiler design that came from the engine of the polar vessel, the *Victory*.

The *Novelty* was fully worth of its name, and completely different from the locomotives known so far. It was a low carriage with four wheels. At the back was a vertical boiler with a fire-box. Fuel was introduced on top of the boiler and from there the hot gasses flowed through multiple tubes inside the boiler and a horizontal barrel to the front, ending in a small chimney. Ericsson's locomotive was one of the first with a multi-tubular boiler, an internal firebox and a forced-draft system for developing high-pressure steam. Two cylinders cranked the front axle, transmitting movement to the wheels. The *Novelty* was the only one of the competing engines to carry its own fuel and water, without an extra tender, and therefore it qualifies as the first "tank locomotive."[4]

The main contender was the *Rocket* built by the already experienced team of George Stephenson and his son Robert. Their engine was put through extensive trials at Killingworth and necessary corrections had been made long before it was shipped south. Unfortunately Ericsson and Braithwaite did not have time to test their locomotive before the trial.

Rainhill Trials

The culmination of hectic preparations came in the morning of the 6th of October when a great crowd of thousands of people had assembled at Rain-

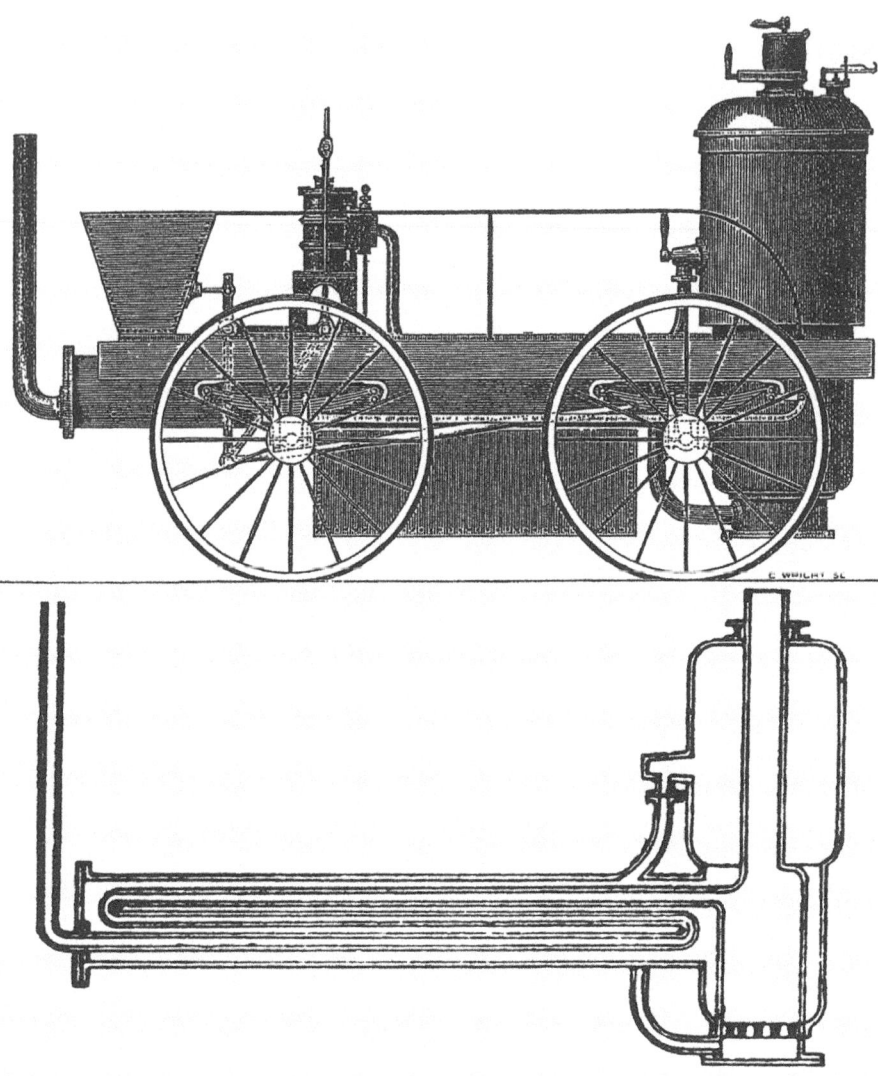

John Ericsson's locomotive, the *Novelty*, and a detail of the boiler with triple coil (C. Wright, London, contemporary illustration).

hill, near Liverpool, to witness a spectacle that, in the words of the *Liverpool Courier,* "would alter the whole system of our internal communications ... substituting an agency whose ultimate effects can scarcely be anticipated."

A large stand for visitors had been erected on a field near Rainhill Bridge. Flags were flying, a brass band played "pleasing and favorite airs" and the nearby Rail-Road Tavern was packed. "The race ground presented a scene of extraordinary gaiety and bustle. The day being remarkably fine, thousands of persons of all ranks were assembled," the newspaper reported.

It became an extraordinary race — a race, in fact without precedent in history, without the parading horses, jockeys or dogs, but steam locomotives. Instead of the race course there were two long lines of rail, stretching from the east to the west until they disappeared below a bridge. The London *Times* reported that 10,000 spectators were privileged to witness the contest and an assembly of "many scientific gentlemen and practical engineers" such as John Rennie and John Bourne, the constructor of the new London Bridge who had come wearing tall black beaver hats.

Below the grandstand on the Lancashire meadows were the railroad lines. Along the track, exactly 1½ miles apart, white posts had been erected as markers for timing. Here judges with "second-watches" were positioned to clock speeds. There was also a weighing-bridge to check the allowed weight and a blacksmith's shop, made for necessary repairs. Five entries had been recorded:

No. 1 "*The Novelty*," Messrs. Braithwaite and Ericsson of London.
No. 2 "*The Sanspareil*," Mr. Hackworth of Darlington.
No. 3 "*The Rocket*," Mr. Robert Stephenson of Newcastle.
No. 4 "*The Cycloped*," Mr. Brandreth of Liverpool.
No. 5 "*The Perseverance*," Mr. Burstall of Edinburgh.

The number 4 was a joke, because it was a carriage not propelled by a steam engine, but by two horses trotting on a treadmill, an idea that strangely enough cropped up again several times later. Increased speed was achieved by a transmission gear so that the horses were not driven too hard. The Brandreth "Cycloped" ran at approximately 12 miles per hour. This team was actually outside the terms of competition because its power output was too low to pull wagons. However, since its promoter, Mr. Brandreth, was a board member, his whimsies had to be indulged and his machine was allowed to trundle up and down the track to provide some light entertainment during the long intermissions brought by frequent breakdowns of the mechanical monsters.

Each locomotive had to pull wagons filled with stones as test loads for runs equivalent to the distance from Liverpool to Manchester and back. The tests were supervised by three judges. Because of mechanical failures many re-runs had to be done, therefore it took a full week to finish the contest for all four contestants.

The blue and copper *Novelty* of Braithwaite and Ericsson was the star attraction and considered "the beau-ideal of a Locomotive Carriage." At her throttle was John Ericsson's nineteen-year-old assistant, Charles Fox, who later became a famous engineer of the Crystal Palace exhibition hall in London and who maintained contact with Ericsson in America. Novelty performed exceedingly well, attaining a speed of 28 mph and later, according to one source, while running light, it covered a mile in one minute and 53 seconds, a speed record for the time. The *Mechanic's Magazine* reported, "The great lightness of the *Novelty*, its compactness, its beautiful workmanship, excited universal admiration."[5]

L. Rolt, the biographer of George and Robert Stephenson describes the promising situation for the *Novelty* on the first day:

> Braithwaite & Ericsson's *Novelty* was easily the favorite not only with the ignorant populace but also with that company of scientific gentlemen and engineers that, claimed the local press, was the largest ever assembled on one spot.... When the Judges arrived on the scene they found that the *Novelty* had already been showing her paces before an admiring crowd. Her royal blue livery with boiler, water tank and cylinders all clad with highly polished copper sheeting, she certainly made a brave sight. The apparent absence of moving parts also deeply impressed the spectators, only the tops of the cylinders being visible."[6]

The *Times* wrote that the speed at which it ran "surprised and amazed every beholder. It seemed indeed to fly, presenting one of the most sublime spectacles of mechanical ingenuity and human daring the world had ever beheld. It made one giddy to look at it, and filled the breasts of thousands with lively fears, and it seemed to fly, as it were, 'on wings of the wind.'"[7]

Unfortunately the *Novelty*, driven at maximum steam pressure at the end of the day was riddled by bursting of her blower bellows. The following day, when the damage was repaired, "she appeared again on the course, with the Director's carriage attached to her, in which were about forty ladies and gentlemen, and with which she moved along in beautiful style at almost incredible speed of 30 miles per hour!"[8]

Test-runs of the not so popular big *Rocket*, a John Bull on wheels, started on October 8. It was a heavy engine, weighing four tons, painted yellow and black with a horizontal boiler and a high smoke stack to induce good draft. Two cylinders placed high near the back of the boiler drove the two larger front wheels through diagonal pistons and connecting rods. This resulted in a vertical component of force that gave the engine an undesirable rocking action. (That, however, was not the reason for its name.) Driven conservatively, she averaged just under 14 miles an hour. But on the last day using full steam she finally thundered past the grandstand at 29 miles an hour.

The trials lasted eight days altogether and at the end of it, Stephenson's *Rocket* was the winner because of more reliable performance, although some people felt that had there been a railway near London where the *Novelty* could have been tried out, and perhaps improved before the trials, the result might have been different. The others fell out of the race early. So it happened that George Stephenson came into fame and has ever since lived in popular memory as the father of the locomotive. There was nothing new in his *Rocket*, except his good workmanship. He succeeded where others failed because he

The Rocket.

Novelty.

The *Rocket* and the *Novelty* (contemporary newspaper illustrations).

was a more experienced railroad engineer, or better combiner of sound principles into a working whole, than any of his rivals.

After the trial the *Liverpool Mercury* wrote:

> It is much to be regretted that the *Novelty* was not built in time to have the same opportunity of exercising that Mr. Stephenson's engine had, or that there is not in London or its vicinity, any railway where experiments with it could have been tried. — In withdrawing so honorably from the competition, Messrs Braithwaite and Ericsson have done themselves the highest credit and they may rest assured that the scientific world will do justice to their efforts.

We congratulate Mr. Stephenson but the grand prize of public opinion is the one which has been gained by Messrs. Braithwaite and Ericsson, for their decided improvement in the arrangement, the safety, simplicity, and the smoothness and steadiness of a locomotive engine; and however imperfect the present works of the machine may be it is beyond a doubt — and we believe we speak the opinion of nine-tenth of the engineers and scientific men now in Liverpool — that it is the principle and arrangement of this London engine which will be followed in the construction of all future locomotives."[9]

Despite losing the battle Ericsson, said: "After the Rainhill trials ... I designed another form of locomotive engine of very elegant appearance, two of which were built by Braithwaite, intending to astonish the world at the opening of the Liverpool & Manchester Railway." They were the *King William* and *Queen Adelaide* but unfortunately "they proved utter failures for the want of steam."[10]

Miss Kemble

One of the admiring spectators at the Rainhill contest was none other than the young and beautiful actress Fanny Kemble, who had lately achieved fame as Juliet on stage in London at Covent Garden. Now she was playing in Liverpool and had been invited by the directors to view the spectacle. (Miss Kemble later became John Ericsson's friend in New York when she approached him for help.) So captivated was she by what she saw that she made a trial trip on one of the "steam-carriages" and in a letter to her friend she wrote:

> We were introduced to the little engine that was to drag us along the rails.... This snorting little animal, which I felt rather inclined to pat, was then harnessed to our carriage, and, we started at about ten miles an hour. You can't imagine how strange it seemed to be journeying on thus, with the magical machine, with its flying white breath and rhythmical pace. I closed my eyes and this sensation of flying was quite delightful, and strange beyond description. When I add that this pretty little creature can run with equal facility either backwards or forwards, I believe I have given you an account of all her capacities."[11]

5

John Bull

... Bull, in the main, was an honest, plain-dealing fellow.... He was very apt to quarrel with his best friends.... If you flattered him you might lead him as a child.
— J. Arbuthnat, *History of John Bull*, 1712

In the beginning Ericsson was excited to be in England, which seemed to him like the center of the world with its vast financial resources and technical progress. This land of plenty was very tempting to a man who saw no boundaries for his creative work and who was blind to economic realities of spending. Living here meant many ups and downs and soon through his own experience he had to realize the painful aspects of envy and a harsh cut-throat environment.

Vagrant

Grim reality of the failure with his hot-air engine taught the initially confident young Swede to understand the competitive society of John Bull (a personification of the United Kingdom, equivalent to the United States' Uncle Sam). Already after four months in London the somewhat disappointed Ericsson wrote to a friend in Sweden: "Here you breath[e] coal-smoke, you live on roast-beef and bathe in porter. A good man by himself does not count, only how many pounds Sterling he weighs. Boxing for life and death — horse-racing — betting — games — cock-fights, dog-fights and hunting is entertainment here. The daily news are: murder, hanged, stolen. — Within a short time I had hoped to spell the death sentence for steam engines — and if not the Englishmen's devilish intentions put me to Hell I believe that I could part with some checks worth several zeroes. But I am not prepared to leave John Bull without five tiny squeezed rings behind the one."[2]

After more than a year in England Ericsson was so busy, he forgot that his leave of absence from the Swedish military had expired, thus making him, in a legal sense, a deserter. Therefore, great was his surprise when on October 3, 1827, he received the good news that His Majesty King Carl XIV Johan had intervened in his favor and not only granted him extension of his leave but at the same time promoted him to captain. When Ericsson was informed about his unexpected promotion he had just returned from the unsuccessful project at the Cornish mines and was without money and had no means to pay for the release of the original valuable Royal document. After the unexpected promotion Ericsson resigned from the army because he realized that his military career was over; however, he kept the title of captain for the rest of his life and was very proud of it.

When John and his friend Adolf von Rosen were looking for a suitable place to live they were moving from one location to another; during the thirteen years in London John stayed in five different places. The decision to move had to do with many factors, such as presence of friends, proximity to work and the cost of living. In the beginning they managed to rent a house at Kingston Upon Thames in Surrey, where they lived close to the rural countryside with fields and park land. Here they shared life with a Swedish friend, the artist John Way, who made a portrait of young Ericsson. They had fun together. His friends were impressed by John's "Nordic energy" and fun loving behavior and called him Arnliot Gelline after a hero in a tale by the Icelandic author Snorre Sturlason.

When Ericsson established collaboration with John Braithwaite's Limehouse workshop, which was just on the other end of London, he moved to 8 Albany Street, Regent's Park, near Braithwaite's residence. This was a fashionable area that just had been completed. But there was still space in the back yards to do some tinkering, as proven by his neighbor, Sir Goldsworth Gurney, an inventor who with his own hands in 1829 built a steam carriage which he tried out around the park, to the astonishment of the public and powerful opposition from horse-coach interests.[3] Later addresses in London were: Brook Street and Cambridge Terrace.

To Prison

Ericsson was single-mindedly occupied with his inventions and their possible successful application. Besides some profitable hits there were more and more expensive failures such as the caloric engine, water pumps for mines, the Polar ventures, the steam fire engine and costly locomotives. He soon had used up a fortune on designing models, and engines and payment of patent fees.

Already in the first year he had spent 30,000 Swedish crowns and run up debts not only in England, but he also had not repaid the money he had borrowed before he left his homeland.[4] Like his father he had absolutely no sense of economy and always spent freely on his projects and costly lifestyle. Despite efforts to secure profitable patents he did not succeed and had to take loan upon loan at high rates of interest. He plunged deeper and deeper in the minus and in 1832 he had accumulated a staggering debt of £14,750. No bank trusted him anymore. Finally he was caught by his creditors and confronted to pay off the debts he had accumulated in Sweden and England. When this failed he was put into debtor's prison.

On May 2, 1832, John Ericsson was admitted to King's Bench, an institution south of the Thames where many notable people had been jailed for debt. One was the famous Franco-American wizard and Thames Tunnel builder Marc Isambard Brunel, who went to prison when his business failed, and there was joined by his wife, who felt sorry for him.[5] Also Charles Dickens' father had been in debtor's prison. But in his *Pickwick Papers* the son tells us: "It strikes me, that imprisonment for debt is scarcely any punishment at all." Another famous victim was the polar adventurer and Ericsson's former customer Sir John Ross who 1846 was not allowed to return to Sweden and continue his job as consul general of Great Britain.[6]

The prison was a stately edifice with many small buildings inside a wall-enclosed large courtyard. In the early 19th century the place was known for the laxity of its rules and it had become "the most desirable place of incarceration in London." The courtyard thronged with life: there were tailors, barbers and even piano sellers. All kinds of delicacies such as oysters were sold there and drink flowed freely from 30 gin shops. Those who could afford it dined in style.[7]

Here Ericsson was held while court proceedings to file for bankruptcy went on. It is surprising and a testimony to his indomitable character that many months in prison did not kill his spirit. But simply being incarcerated must have been depressing. He did not, like many others, take comfort in free flowing alcoholic spirits and the only thing that kept his hope and ingenuity alive was the fact that nobody could prevent him from thinking and drawing. Ericsson continued making designs for new hot-air and compact steam engines and he was already formulating ideas about his most famous invention which would revolutionize marine propulsion, the ship's propeller. In fact, it sounds strange but being broke can be a powerful stimulant to creative endeavor and to Ericsson the only real relief in sight was the creation of profitable inventions. Therefore he worked on new patentable ideas that were sold under the name of companies and could be used to get him out of jail.

Despite certain liberties, imprisonment meant confinement to a small room and being deprived of freedom to move. A lid was put on his restless activity of working in the foundry and assembling his models. A most frustrating experience for him was when his new designs created at King's Bench for Braithwaite at Limehouse and Laird & Sons in Liverpool neared completion and he was unable to see and test the finished product and could make no modifications.

Finally, after a long confinement, in a letter to his friend von Rosen, now back in Sweden, Ericsson started complaining about "indifference and apathy." Fortunately, at Christmas 1832, brother Nils arrived to study canals and to visit John. With his help a deal could be worked out for the release of John. What happened was that all his assets and liabilities were collected to see if the case could be closed to the appreciation of his debtors. This was only possible because Ericsson during his prison term was able to be productive and after seven and a half months, he was finally freed. Returning home, Nils wrote to a friend in Sweden: "After my travel to England I have many reasons to be joyful and if the air-machine is successful I have a double reason to be happy, because without my arrival John probably would not have recovered from his depressed mood and only God knows what the end would have been for him in his unfortunate situation. In a few days I expect to receive John's request to file for patents for his air-engine in Sweden, Russia and Denmark."[8]

The joint business operation with John Braithwaite continued to be in serious trouble and eventually failed and the bailiffs now were again on the track of its junior member. So for a second time, Ericsson again "enjoyed the hospitalities" of prison, this time at the *Fleet Prison* as a foreign debtor. Here the living conditions in the filthy prison were bad. Fortunately, confinement was shorter because with the help of Count von Rosen and the financial help of the U.S. consul at Liverpool, Francis B. Ogden, a favorable agreement could be worked out. In the financially difficult time Ericsson took the benefit of the "act for the relief of insolvent debtors" and secured his discharge in bankruptcy.[9]

Freedom and Love

After the trying prison time Ericsson finally enjoyed his freedom. In order to secure a fixed salary he successfully applied for a position as senior consulting engineer at the Eastern Counties Railway in London. He worked in their office near London Bridge at a time

Amelia Byam Ericsson (Church, *Life of John Ericsson*, 1890).

when Isambard Kingdom Brunel was chief engineer at the other end of the Western Railways. They probably met and collaborated because Brunel was one of the first to realize the importance of Ericsson's propeller and helped to introduce it in Britain. (Isambard Kingdom was the son of Marc Isambard, who had shared prison life In King's Bench.)

Ericsson, the vigorous young man, again joined the company of the circle of his friends. After some time a more intimate relationship developed between John and a young girl he had met in 1827 when she was only ten years old. The connection was through Charles Seidler, his business associate he earlier met in London. Amelia, by John Ericsson called "Duck," was a relative of the Seidlers. She came from a respectable English family, being the illegitimate child of Edward Samuel Byam, son of Sir Charles Byam, who lived in Antigua. Amelia was the result of Edward Byam's relationship with a Spanish girl.

After Ericsson found out that his sweetheart, Carolina Christina in Sweden, had gotten married, the bonds with her were finally broken and he decided to marry Amelia. What was the attraction? As a girl Amelia obviously was cute. Later she was "the most fascinating he had ever seen ... intelligent, generous in disposition, cultivated and a very fine musician."

Amelia had two years before her marriage given birth to an illegitimate daughter, Ady, fathered by a rich London gentleman named Ellice. One reason John married Amelia probably was that he felt sorry for Ady and wanted to give her security, but he could never accept her as his daughter and John and Amelia did not have children of their own.

Amelia Byam was a teenager of 19 and Ericsson 33 when they married in London on October 15, 1836, at St. John's Church in Paddington. Referring to this occasion, John would later realize that these vows were difficult to keep.[10]

6

Propulsion

The component parts of all new machines may be said to be old.
— Robert Fulton

In 1832, while sitting in debtors prison, Ericsson was occupied with the idea of constructing a marine propeller. Ever since the 1829 disaster with John Ross' side-wheeler, the *Victory*, he had been thinking of how to improve propulsion of ships with steam engines. One of the many problems Ross had faced during his Arctic exploration was that the side-wheels of his steamer hit floating ice. This made Ericsson think that there should be something better than the clumsy paddle-wheels. Why not put wheels under water instead of above?

How to Propel?

During the following years Ericsson worked on various types of propellers for canal boats. The London haulage company Robins and Mills was very interested in the project and in 1835 agreed to sponsor construction. He first tried a design inspired by the movement of duck's feet under water because he realized they were thrusting the animal forward. When ready it became an underwater valve-like contraption mounted on an axle pushed to and fro by the cylinder of a steam engine. A tugboat called the *Annatarius* was constructed according to the new principle and when launched in the Paddington Canal it worked properly, making seven miles per hour. But when the boat failed to pull a heavy load, the sponsors backed out, leaving a disappointed and furious Ericsson with a debt of £2,000.[1] This, unfortunately, could have put Ericsson's future again in jeopardy.

The next design was a ship's propeller somewhat resembling the wings of a windmill. It became a wheel with multiple blades attached to the stern of a small experimental two-foot steamer with which he made demonstrations in a London public pool. People came running and watched in wonder a fast-moving ship without visible means of propulsion, no sails and no side-wheels!

The result was immediately very satisfying when the little boat steadily managed to run at a speed of three miles an hour. Initially Ericsson used a double screw on two shafts, one within the other, revolving in opposite directions, one carrying a right-hand and the other a left-hand screw. So the propeller could be used as an auxiliary power in sailing ships, Ericsson provided a way to lift it out of the water in order to eliminate the drag of the big screw when on sails. The first design therefore was a propeller mounted on a stage attached to the stern of a boat with a direct power transmission system — and it worked!

Ericsson's propeller had gone unchallenged until May 31, 1836, when a farmer, Francis Petit Smith, applied for a patent of a longitudinal Archimedes-type spiral screw to propel ships. Unfortunately Ericsson had failed to secure a patent until July 13, 1836, six weeks after Smith's application. Therefore, the British patent office refused to recognize Ericsson as the sole inventor.

Yankee Inspiration

During his time in England John was lucky to meet many interesting and stimulating people. One of them was an American from New Jersey, Francis B. Ogden, the other was the New York journalist and lawyer John Osborne Sargent.

After the War of 1812 Ogden went to England to follow his passion, to construct marine steam engines. In 1817 in Leeds, he built the first low-pressure engine with two cylinders with special cranks for which he had obtained a patent. James Watt, the nestor of steam engines, was impressed and said that it was "a beautiful engine." In 1829 Ogden became U.S. consul at Liverpool and in the same year at the Rainhill locomotive trials he met John Ericsson and friendship immediately took off. The two had similar interests and Ogden's first venture with Ericsson was an 1831 collaborative agreement to pay £20,000 for the U.S. right to a "steam-drum," a multitubular boiler with blowers to produce high pressure steam to power steam engines.[2] In 1835 they developed a sounding device for measuring depths at sea and in rivers. The instrument was based on the principle of determining the compression of air in an enclosed capsule. They obtained a patent and it soon became very popular and sold in the thousands both in Europe and the USA.[3]

During the time when Ericsson worked on the ship's propeller and marine engines he found in Mr. Ogden an attentive listener to his engineering ideas and a warm supporter of new projects. Ogden immediately realized the immense potential of screw propulsion and discussed with him the construction of a compact steam engine. In 1837 he helped Ericsson file a U.S. patent for his propeller in Washington. It included a connecting piece which allowed the propeller not only to move a ship forward, but also backward and in neutral. Ogden soon became to Ericsson "like the shadow of a great rock in a

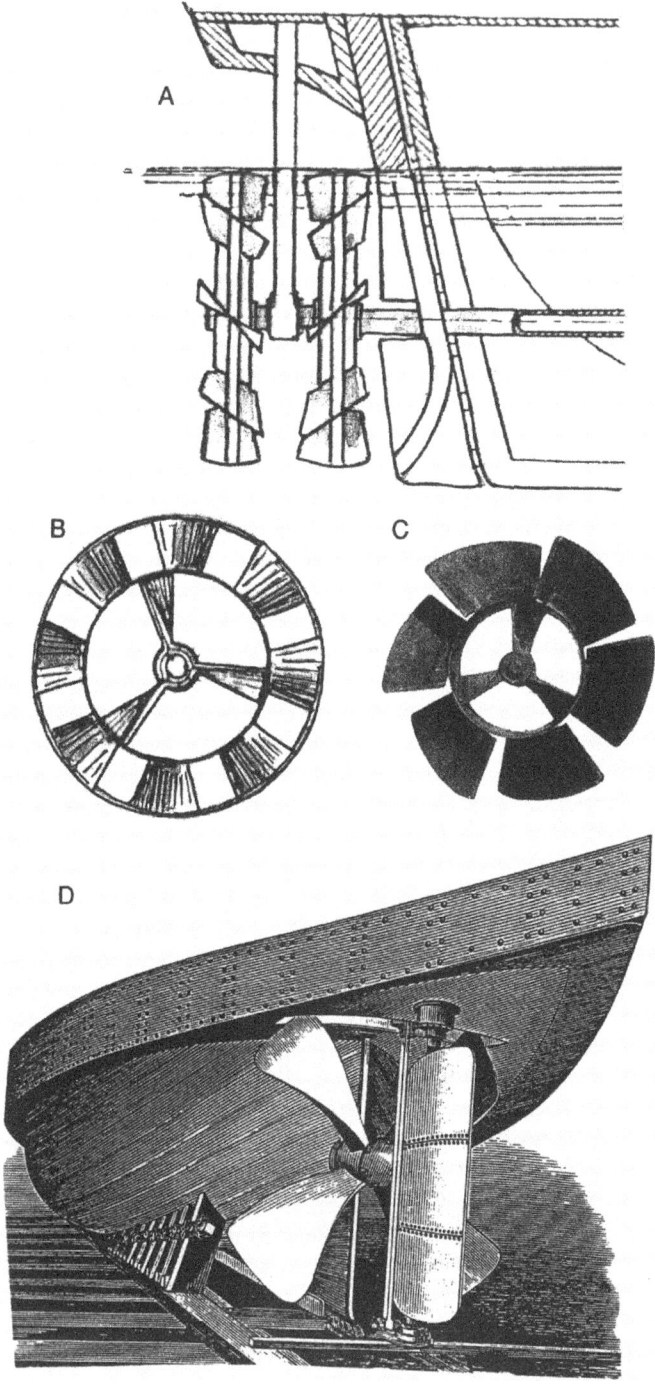

weary land." He encouraged and economically supported Ericsson to build his first full scale screw-propelled tugboat-steamer, the *Francis B. Ogden*, which was launched in the Thames on May of 1837. The steamer was 40 feet long by 8 feet wide. The propeller was double with two shafts being placed one within the other. On her trial trip the little steamer attained a speed of 10 miles an hour.

The Flying Devil

The Ogden tugboat became an immediate success; it towed the American packet-ship *Toronto* at a rate of five miles an hour. Because of the unseen "satanic powers" of propulsion the general public soon called her *The Flying Devil*.

The next step was to promote the marine screw propeller to the Royal Navy. Therefore, in the summer of 1837 Ericsson invited the lords of the British Admiralty for a demonstration of his propeller, offering them to be pulled by Ericsson's tugboat in their own barge on the Thames from Somerset House to Greenwich and back.

When the offer was gracefully accepted, John Ericsson and his American friend John Sargent picked up a delegation of the lords of the admiralty from the granite steps of Somerset House. On board the gilt-trimmed barge were four lords, including the polar explorer Sir William E. Parry, the hero of five expeditions to the Arctic seas; Admiral Sir Francis Beaufort, known for his classification of wind, zero to twelve from "dead calm" to "hurricane," and Sir William Symonds, surveyor of the Navy. The admiralty barge with her precious cargo towed by the *Flying Devil* glided smoothly like a gondola down the Thames at the rate of ten miles an hour towards Limehouse, where the Lords inspected "their favorite propelling apparatus" on another ship — a paddlewheel! During the trip Ericsson presented his drawings of his ship's rudder, propeller and steam engine and described the action of the propeller blades. The "scientific gentlemen" did not show the slightest interest, whereas ordinary Londoners along the Thames watching the strange convoy were spellbound by the sight.

After an uneventful and fast upriver tow back to Somerset House, Sir Charles Adams, the First Lord, "with a sympathetic air, shook the inventor by the hand thanking him for the trouble in showing him and his friends the *interesting* experiment." He added that "he feared he had put himself to too great an expense and trouble on the occasion." Although the speed attained

Opposite: Development of John Ericsson's screw propeller. A: twin screw of 1836. B, C: 8- and 6- bladed screws of 1838. D: 4-bladed screw used from 1850 onwards, here on the 1865 *Dictator* (sketch assembled by the author).

during the trial was far greater than that achieved by any paddle-steamer of similar size, the admirals were not convinced and after they had met and made up their minds Ericsson finally received a letter by Beaufort that informed him, their lordships had been very much disappointed with the result.

To Ericsson this verdict was a mystery, but it became evident that even before the trial started the Lords were violently prejudiced, and showed little courtesy to Ericsson. Later in a letter to Ericsson it was disclosed that "even if the propeller had the powers of propelling a vessel [which it had done with him in it] it would be found altogether useless in practice because the power being applied to the stern, it would be absolutely impossible to make the vessel steer."[4]

J.S. Carlton in his treatise on "Marine Propellers and Propulsion" is of the opinion that the reason for the British Navy's disappointment with the demonstration, which was good when judged by the standards of the day, was unclear.[5] It seems obvious that the real reason was that they did not trust the Swedish engineer because Sir William E. Parry made them believe that Ericsson had messed up Ross with a deficient engine on his Arctic adventure. That is understandable since Parry, the Navy's Arctic hero and friend of John Ross, was a very influential member of the admiralty, who recently had been appointed comptroller of steam machinery for the Royal Navy."

Obviously the admiralty's refusal to accept Ericsson's propeller was an excuse because after his successful demonstration on the Thames the admirals were eager to check out the performance of another screw propeller by Ericsson's rival, Francis P. Smith, on the Dover Coast. Smith had been supported by John Ross, who helped him build a steamer of 237 tons, aptly called the *Archimedes* (because it was equipped with an Archimedean screw). But when the ship was given a trial, Parry had to report: "Poor Mr. Smith's screw had no fair trial, the power applied being so much below what the engines ought to have produced."[6]

The problem with Smith's unsuccessful trial obviously was not only confined to the shape of his screw but also had to do with a weak engine. Smith's initially only developed six horsepower, whereas Ericsson's *Francis B. Ogden* managed twelve. But Smith did not give up; he had perseverance and finally with his *Archimedes* managed to circumnavigate England in 1840.

Simultaneously with his work on the ship's propeller Ericsson also embarked on the design of a suitable marine engine which had to be compressed into the smallest possible bulk. Like steam engines for locomotives, marine engines for Ericsson's propeller ships were powerful and small in size to be accommodated below deck and not like the huge above deck "walking-beam" engines of side-wheelers. Therefore he designed a compact two-cylinder engine. He did not limit his efforts to building it with vertical cylinders operating up and down, but soon developed a remarkably efficient rotary engine, patented on 16 February 1838. Most importantly, it was a direct-acting machine that could be placed right above the propeller shaft without a complicated system of gears as used by Smith.

Earlier he also had come up with the modern principle of steam-turbines, which are still used today driving the propellers of nuclear-powered ships. Some of these projects were done in collaboration with the Laird brothers, noted ship-builders in Birkenhead near Liverpool, who many years later built ironclads and Cowper Coles' gun-turret.

Ericsson's revolutionary ideas at first confused the minds of the average Englishman, who hated a thing merely because it is new. But as soon as the documents for the rotary engine were filed in the patent office, a Monsieur Rossiere from France appeared in London. He represented a Paris consortium which was eager to buy the whole system, propellers and engine for shipping on the Rhone. Rossiere had received recommendations from Mr. Laird and Francis B. Ogden in Liverpool. Ericsson, with no sense of business, immediately agreed to sell at a low price.

Things to Come

In 1837 through his friend Ogden, Ericsson met Captain Robert F. Stockton, a naval officer from New Jersey who had come to England to obtain support for his project to build the Delaware & Raritan Canal. It was the same year in May when Ericsson launched his new steamer on the Thames and made the conspicuous demonstration towing the large American packet-ship *Toronto* at the rate of five miles an hour.

Stockton was invited to accompany Ericsson in one of his excursions on the Thames on the *Francis B. Ogden*. Unlike the British admirals, he was impressed and immediately realized the importance of Ericsson's inventions for naval propulsion. A single trip from London Bridge to Greenwich was sufficient to convince Stockton. He also talked about ordering warships for the U.S. Navy, to be fitted with his steam machinery and screw propeller. A dinner at Greenwich ended their excursion and Stockton in a speech said: "I do not want the opinion of your scientific men, what I have seen this day satisfies me. We'll make your name ring on the Delaware, as soon as we get your propeller there." Before leaving he ordered a tugboat for his family's Delaware canal company from Ericsson.

The next time Stockton came to England his tugboat was being completed by Laird's shipyard at Birkenhead, near Liverpool. The vessel, named the *Robert Stockton*, an iron steamer, was launched on July 7, 1838, under the supervision of Francis Ogden. The London Times was on the spot and reported: "We were struck with the great regularity of the motion, not the slightest jar being perceptible. The engines consist of two cylinders, their construction is extremely simple and evinces a knowledge of steam machinery by the inventor which is calculated to give additional confidence in the success of his propeller in all the varieties of its application for the canal, river, or ocean navigation."

The vessel crossed the Atlantic in a stormy voyage that lasted 46 days "with no serious disaster except the loss of one seaman, who was washed off this little cockle-shell by one of the seas which were constantly sweeping her decks." It should be realized that the *Robert Stockton* became the first screw-propeller ship crossing the Atlantic, at fact that has not been recognized. Upon her arrival at the Battery she was visited by hundreds of curious persons, anxious to realize the possible truth of the nursery story about "the three men of Gotham who went to sea in a bowl." The *Stockton* was renamed the *New Jersey* and remained successfully in service for many years.[7, 8]

Born in 1795, Stockton had been a junior navy officer in the War of 1812 but with the ambition to advance. Before coming to England he wanted to be a pioneer in transforming the US Navy from sail to steam by proposing the construction of a paddle sloop, the *Mississippi*, but that did not materialize and now he had higher aspirations. Opposition to steam at this stage was not merely irrational sailing ship sentimentality. There were significant practical considerations, including the high fuel consumption of the inefficient side-wheelers, their vulnerability to enemy shot, and the reduction of broadside space for guns. Therefore, he thought that Ericsson's screw propeller and machinery below the water line could solve these problems.[9]

Stockton belonged to one of the most politically influential families of New Jersey. The city of Princeton was built on land that originally belonged to the Stocktons and his grandfather was a signer of the Declaration of Independence. He had ample financial and political resources at his disposal to materialize his ambitions, but without a background in engineering he needed the right professional assistance and Ericsson seemed to be the answer to his dreams. The feeling was mutual and Ericsson's eager mind constantly produced new ideas for what could be done to bring innovations to the U.S. Navy.

Stockton tried to convince Ericsson to join him across the Atlantic to start the new age of warships. Stockton said that he had the political power to appoint him as the designer and builder of a ship, with himself in charge of the project. He preceded Ericsson to America to set the necessary events in motion. After returning to the U.S., in a letter he told Ericsson that Congress had agreed to the construction of three warships. Two of these were to be equipped with paddle-wheels and the third was as yet undecided. That answer sounded promising and became decisive for Ericsson's future.

7

The New World

It will be seen that no talent or character of eminence runs any risk in the United States of not finding an opportunity for the exercise of all its powers.... Life in this country need never stand still....
—Fredrika Bremer, Letters 1853

On November 28, 1839, the *British Queen,* a new steam packet with giant paddle wheels and auxiliary sails, the pride of England, arrived on her first voyage in New York Harbor. On board was John Ericsson, tired and restless after a wild passage with autumn storms from Portsmouth across the North Atlantic. He was a naval engineer but not a sailor and hated the twenty-day passage of enforced idleness and sea-sickness in his dark cabin. He eagerly looked forward to setting his feet on land and having a new start.

Arrival

Approaching land Ericsson's first sight was a busy harbor and the round tower of Castle Garden, a center for popular entertainment that twenty-five years later New Yorkers called for a time "Monitor Garden" for its rugged resemblance to the turret of Ericsson's famous ironclad ship.[1]

The *British Queen* entered the East River and nosed her way towards shore by Pier 44 on the east side of Rutger's Slip, at the foot of Clinton Street. Here she moored and the young engineer took the ferry across the river to Brooklyn and the Navy Yard, for which he had a letter of recommendation by his sponsor, Captain Robert Stockton of Princeton, N.J., who had enticed him to come. Eager to start working, he set himself up in a nearby boardinghouse on 91 Washington Street and waited for orders.

From England he had brought the model of a naval steam engine with propeller and also sent a big iron gun of his own construction. After some time disappointing news arrived: plans of building a screw steamer for the Navy were postponed and Ericsson could not expect the promised financial support. Stockton had difficulty convincing the Committee on Naval Affairs of his project; instead he devoted his time and energy to the political scene in Washington. Meanwhile Ericsson did not waste time but worked on the prototype of the gun he had shipped from England for Stockton's future warship. Disappointed, he realized that he had to fend for himself and look for other opportunities in the private shipbuilding business.

Fortunately he was lucky to make the acquaintance of an understanding man, Samuel Risley of Greenwich Village, whom he told all about the many projects he wanted to start. At that Risley suggested Ericsson go to James Cunningham's Phoenix foundry on the North River because this company was specializing in fabricating marine machinery. There he met Henry Cornelius (Harry) Delamater, who later in 1842 took over the company with a partner.

Here, finally in the dark interior of the forges with the ring of hammers, the smell of charcoal, hot metal and the blazing fires, Ericsson felt happy. The meeting proved to be the start of a fortuitous teamwork because Delamater soon realized that the young man from Europe came with ideas of many promising projects and without hesitation and questions about immediate profit he placed technical resources at Ericsson's disposal. Ericsson did not come bare-handed but brought with him the working model of his propeller engine which he here put in operation. Collaboration with the Manhattan team soon started and proved to be fruitful and the foundry built, after his designs, some of the first propeller ships and the first steam fire engine in the USA.

Soon thereafter, at the recommendation of his American friend from England, the lawyer and writer John Osborne Sargent, Ericsson was advised to move to Manhattan to take up residence in the new fashionable five-story, three hundred room Astor House on the west side of Broadway between Vesey and Barclay Streets. The Astor House was at the time the nation's most prestigious hotel, built in Greek revival style with a doorway flanked by Doric columns. It featured such extraordinary new conveniences as gas lights in all rooms and baths and toilets on every floor with a supply of running water raised by steam pumps to a reservoir on top of the building. The hotel certainly was an excellent place for a fresh immigrant who looked for business connections, being the main watering place of businessmen, politicians and habitués such as Daniel Webster and Washington Irving and later Fredrika Bremer from Sweden. Even if expensive the move soon paid off. The location could not have been better, being at the hub of activities in the fashionable district west of City Hall. Here was the hub of travel and trade where omnibuses and streetcars connected with all the ferries and places of business and amusement, at the lower end of Manhattan and the commercial center of the United States. Everything was within easy reach — wharves on South Street and the sprawling new shipyards such as the Novelty Iron Works at the foot of 12th Street and East River, and the Phoenix Foundry on West and Vestry Street, near the North or Hudson River.

The American Way

Soon after Ericsson's arrival, in January 1840 the Mechanic's Institute of New York, alarmed by devastating fires, offered its great gold medal as a prize for the best plan of a steam fire engine. The institute had reasons to look out for new solutions, because only five years before, New York had been devastated by one of the biggest fires that any American city had ever experienced when more than 700 buildings were destroyed.

Ericsson applied with the design for the construction of a "goose-neck" steam fire engine, which was an improved version of the one he in vain had tried to promote in London and Istanbul in 1829. He won the gold medal for his scheme because of its obvious advantage over the ancient hand pumpers. Ericsson's engine promised to be a better device because it had the power of 108 men and could throw water as long as fuel held out and was not dependent on manual power. "This insured its success as an engine of the future even though initially held in resentment and even ridiculed by some of the city's firemen," one historian said.[2] The new engine also was capable of squirting a longer stream of water and could combat fires in taller buildings while allowing firemen to keep a safer distance from a blaze. The new engine got up steam in ten minutes and threw three thousand gallons of water a minute through a 1½-inch pipe to a height of one hundred and five feet. It became one of Ericsson's first ingenious ventures in America.[3]

He received his first orders for machinery and propellers from Russell and Stephen Glover, two New York captains and ship owners who had witnessed Ericsson's early trials of his propeller in England. They wanted him to build small propeller-driven steamboats mainly for use in canals, Lake Erie and the St. Lawrence River. Another important customer was the shipping magnate, Robert B. Forbes. At the Phoenix foundry Ericsson soon also designed machinery and twin propellers for the *Clarion*, the first ocean-going propeller-driven craft in the United States.[4]

John Ericsson was convinced that America was the land for him; finally he had come to the right place, a country that embraced the teachings of Adam Smith and his ideas of "liberal capitalism" and Tom Paine's beliefs of equality of rights and dignity of men. He fully subscribed to the opinion of another European observer of America, Alexis de Tocqueville, who said: "Here the entire world seems to be a malleable substance which a man can turn and shape as he likes. An immense field, of which not yet the smallest part has as yet been fully explored, lies open to human effort here. There isn't one man who can't reasonably hope to attain the comforts of life; there isn't one who doesn't know that if he loves hard work his future is secure."[5]

Despite the fact that Victorian England was the cradle of mechanical inventions, Ericsson found it very unreceptive to his ideas and much preferred the open environment of America. He also was much opposed to the elitism that suggested that the common man was incapable of understanding scientific concepts. He himself did not have a university education but he had become deeply involved in the concepts surrounding thermal energy.

He felt lucky to arrive here, a place where Yankees were not — like the Europeans — suspicious of machinery because they make possible the elimination of labor; no, they welcomed every improvement that facilitated life. The ultimate aim was the time when machines could do everything, and man would only have to see them work and enjoy the fruit of their labor. For some, a difficult problem was the fair division of production by these machines among those who believed that "all men are created equal," and have not only the right to "life, liberty, and the pursuit of happiness" but also work.

In England, almost everything old was held in high esteem. A business established a century ago was on a very firm foundation. In America on the contrary, it was novelty that gave success; here people really believed in progress and improvement. Why should they not prefer the new hotel, steamboat, machine or establishment of whatever kind? It was therefore not surprising that they also thought morals and religion to be subject to the "law of progress," and that the last-invented creed could be an improvement on those established centuries ago. This was a time when people believed in a positive moral evolution, parallel with technical advancement, a concept that inventors like John Ericsson and later Thomas A. Edison fully subscribed to.[6] For Ericsson it became part of his creed; he considered devotion to work more important than going to church.

In America he saw ample opportunities to find support for his new ideas and inventions, especially in New York City, the hot-bed of a booming industry and commerce. There was no need to stop or look back, it was just the right place for a self-made man looking forward. Soon Ericsson was able to establish himself as a successful mechanical engineer and shipbuilder and he wrote to a friend in Sweden: "I am very well satisfied with America, the people are much better than the travel books told me. I never felt better — my rheumatism has disappeared entirely."[7]

Amelia Comes

Amelia, by her family called Duck, arrived in New York in the winter of 1840 to join her husband. Her passage had been very stormy and after the ordeal she was happy to be in the arms of her beloved John. The couple first stayed at the Astor House where they often met Samuel Risley.[8]

Accustomed to the somber old buildings of London, Amelia saw everything in New York offensively new and cheap. One of the first things she saw was Barnum's Museum with its garish advertisements on Broadway, just opposite from the hotel. How could civilized people be interested in poor little dwarfs, bearded ladies and other freaks?

Soon, their accommodation proved to be very uncomfortable because the rooms they occupied were not only living quarters but also had become office space with piles of papers and models of ships. They needed more room and therefore, the following year, John rented a four story greystone mansion on lower Manhattan at 95 Franklin Street, close to the Hudson River. The street name was a good omen, since Benjamin Franklin shone in everything he touched, not the least mechanical inventions. In the beginning Ericsson had many house guests, one of the most notable of which was the author Washington Irving, who shared his interest in steamboats which he first had seen in France.

Initially John was extremely happy to be reunited with his wife, but soon problems surfaced. Amelia landed in the midst of strained activity connected with the renewed collaboration of her husband with Robert Stockton on the *Princeton* project, the building of a radically new warship at a shipyard in Philadelphia. This meant intense drafting activities at home and frequent travels to Philadelphia and to Stockton's estate in New Jersey.

John and Amelia's interest clashed. Men like Ericsson loved to be in a country where only achievement counted, a land that rewarded new ideas and hard work. Busy with Stockton, he rarely had time for his wife and friends and even in the evening at home he continued to work. Why did he work so hard? He simply was obsessed by it, not for the sake of earning money but to him it was a veritable ministry, which he followed like a pastor. Amelia, with her conservative English background, did not agree, she abhorred the fact that in New York a person was hardly judged by family background or rank but by his bank account. All the world over poverty was a misfortune, in New York it was a crime. To her, sprawling Manhattan was a Modern Babylon on account of its ostentation and dissipation and here she did not feel comfortable.

For her husband and most others, New York was the living gospel of work, the consecrated city of labor. Here one was ashamed to be caught doing nothing. Business, which in London was business merely, here was everything. She felt all around her the universal and compelling stress to "get out and hustle" and work, which in London was an unpalatable interruption of social life. It was said that the Englishman who does not succumb to New York in the first three months is a lost soul.[9]

Amelia soon strongly disliked America and found the social life of New York superficial and messy; she simply did not fit there. She walked the streets in her dark, conservative Victorian dresses which sharply contrasted with the colorful French style propagated by the leading fashion designer, Madame Ellen Louise Demorest, from her headquarters on Broadway. She missed her family circle and most of all her own daughter, Ady, left behind in London. In New York she felt pushed aside and was "jealous of a steam engine." Her appearance was described as "tall and being a bit masculine" and Samuel Risley, who had become Ericsson's secretary, said of her that she was "handsome and imperious." Soon she was desolate, surrendered her husband to his work and decided to return to England.

Yankee Doodle

About at the time when Amelia left, Ericsson was elected member of the Union Club, a fashionable meeting place for men, housed in a Florentine mansion on Broadway. The club was elegantly furnished and provided rooms for its members. A contemporary writer describes it as:

> A rich man's association. Its members are all men of great wealth. The club house is one of the handsomest buildings in the city, and its furniture and decorations are of the most costly description. Great care is taken in the investigation of the history of applicants for membership, and none but persons of good reputation are admitted. Members have all the benefits of an elegant hotel at a moderate cost, and are sure of enjoying the privacy which is so agreeable to cultivated tastes. They have constant opportunities of meeting with friends, and besides have a pleasant lounging place in which to pass their leisure hours.[10]

The Union Club was celebrated for its magnificent social entertainments and cultural offerings with balls, dinner parties, receptions and picnics. At this time Ericsson still appreciated joyous social events and in the company of his friends he joined to sing the quasi-national air, "Yankee Doodle Came to Town." Besides these diversions Ericsson now was happy because he did not have to worry about food and housekeeping. For single men it was a sanctuary, where they could dine in peace and here the vigilante feminine eye could not reach them. What counted much for Ericsson was also the fact that here he met an influential lobby that appreciated him; he could count on their support to materialize his outrageous ideas which he firmly believed would make a positive impact on present and future life. At this time Ericsson was still youthful in his appearance and dressed fashionably.

In a grateful letter to John Osborne Sargent, at whose recommendation Ericsson had been elected, Ericsson wrote: "You have added ten years to my life in calling my mind to generous living, by bringing me to the club. I can say with truth that I am now capable of undergoing twice as much labor as when I left the Astor House. The difference between living well and ill in this climate is in fact quite incredible. Men like engines, require food to keep up steam."[11] The lawyer and journalist Sargent assisted and counseled his friend and later tried to prosecute his unpaid claim against the government for construction of the *Princeton*.

7. The New World

It was at the Union Club that Ericsson and Peter Cooper met. He was a man of many gifts, and the owner of several iron mines and foundries, and the two had fun together. Another of his acquaintances at the club was the patent Lawyer Edwin Wallace Stoughton. Ericsson soon was invited into his house and met his wife, Mary. The couple was one of the few who were always welcome at Franklin Street.

Eventually John Ericsson applied and was granted U.S. citizenship in October of 1848. That was a certificate he prized most above all others.

8

The *Princeton* Disaster

Snug reefs and leeway will be things of another time, and in their stead, we tighten the screw, oil the machinery and poke the fire.
—John A. Dahlgren, 1838

When John Ericsson left England he hoped to escape the oppressive atmosphere of the conservative British Admiralty. Unfortunately in this respect his experience in America was not going to be better, on the contrary, it was worse because the U.S. Navy simply did not have the support in Congress that the Lords of the Admiralty had in Parliament. In the early nineteenth century design of warships and naval technology in the U.S. evolved slowly — the sea and the big sailing ships had made conservatives of the navy and shipbuilders.

No Navy?

What Ericsson met can be characterized by the experience of John Dahlgren, the tireless constructor of marine ordnance who is of Swedish descent. Best known for the massive iron Dahlgren cannon cast in the distinctive soda-bottle shape, he had to fight the Navy brass to convince them of the importance of innovation in marine engineering. Like Ericsson he had to face the conservative view about progress within the U.S. Navy as described by his biographer, Robert Schneller: "Senior officers showed contempt for new ideas. The pre–1815 generation ... tended to resist steam power. They detested the very thought of a navy dominated by cumbersome steam vessels that did not demand a high level of seamanship and created endless noise and dirt. They enjoyed the support of politicians such as Secretary of the Navy James K. Paulding and President Martin Van Buren."[1]

The idea to employ engineers as consultants in the naval bureau in Washington was an anathema. Only men of the line who had served before the mast were acceptable. Even the American pioneer of steam navigation, Robert Fulton, met resistance to completing his steam-propelled warship, the *Demologos,* later renamed the *Fulton.* She was the first paddle wheeler of the U.S.

Navy, designed in 1813, and had filled many sailors with horror because they believed it to be "a devilish contrivance." Therefore when finished she was soon decommissioned.[2]

As John Ericsson already had found out in England, before building the *Princeton* and during the Civil War, it was very difficult to convince the navy of technical innovations. He encountered active hostility; officers preferred sails and marine engineers believed for years that paddle-wheels were more practical and powerful than propellers. His New York friend, the pioneer of marine engines Harry Delamater, once told him: "You can never convince a sailor."

Planning

In the summer of 1839 New Jersey Captain Robert F. Stockton returned from England, where he had made the acquaintance of Ericsson and was much impressed by his revolutionary inventions of screw-propelled vessels powered by the new direct acting steam engines and equipped with modern guns. The ambitious Stockton returned with bold plans to modernize the U.S. Navy and was convinced that Ericsson and his ideas were right for him.

He tried to persuade the government of his plans to build a large steam-propelled warship according to Ericsson's design. His argument was that by introducing steam power and propeller propulsion with engines below the waterline out of reach of hostile shot, such vessels were better protected than side-wheelers. Moreover, huge side-wheels limited broadside armament with rows of cannon and during combat a steam-powered vessel could maneuver independent of wind and currents. He also proposed to arm his ship with new large-caliber Ericsson designed guns. But Stockton was met with skepticism and did not convince the conservative administration of President Van Buren, who was of the opinion that "this country requires no navy at all, much less a steam navy."[3]

After Ericsson had come to New York he was impatient and decided to act on his own. In September 1840 he traveled to Washington where he managed to get an appointment with the highest authorities. He told his friend in Sweden, Adolf von Rosen, about his meeting:

> I was very well received and the Secretary of War, Joel R. Poinsett, to whom I presented my plans of a canon-ship [*sic*], showed especial interest. My design was in every way accepted and I can inform you about the good news that it will be presented to Congress at their next meeting in December. This will be a revenge towards the lousy Stockton, because deep down I find him to be that way. Mr. Poinsett also accepted my gun-lock for coastal defense.
> The Ministers of War and the Navy, Mr. James K. Paulding and the chairman for Naval Affairs told me right out "we have the highest opinion of your new

propeller but we cannot bring our minds to approve of trying it on such a large scale as proposed by Captain Stockton."[4]

Unfortunately he was not lucky this time, but the following year suddenly the political scene in Washington changed. In 1841 Vice President John Tyler, a friend of Stockton, had to unexpectedly replace President William H. Harrison, who died after only one month in office. Stockton, who was a man of tremendous political influence and wealth, now saw his chance and managed to convince the new president and his secretary of the navy, Abel P. Upshur, to go ahead with his plans for a new warship. He succeeded in persuading the Navy Department and Congress to build the navy's first screw-propelled steamer with Ericsson's 12-inch wrought-iron gun he had brought with him from England. This meant that he desperately needed the help of the Swedish expert he had met in London and who now was in New York.

Stockton invited Ericsson to come to his family estate in New Jersey to start working on a vessel he would name the *Princeton*. Ericsson eagerly followed the invitation of his patron and took the ferry across the Hudson River to Jersey City. He was cordially received at the Stocktons' lovely manor house, Morven, near Princeton. At their meeting he was ordered to prepare drawings for a screw sloop of 600 tons and make an estimate of the cost. Ericsson was disappointed with such small dimension, so different from his original proposal of a big frigate, but Stockton convinced him that this was just the beginning. Once they had demonstrated the superior performance of their concept it would not be difficult to attract interest for more and far bigger vessels.

In his typical way Ericsson was immediately ready and unconditionally made a sketch on the spot. After a week detailed plans were quickly produced at Franklin Street and sent to Stockton. Now the question of remuneration was brought up in a letter to Ericsson: "I think you had better say to me in a letter what your charge will hereafter be if the experiment shall prove successful.... As this is the first trial on so large a scale, I am at liberty to use the patents, and after the ship is tried the Government may pay for their use in that ship whatever sum they may deem proper.[5]

Whenever it came to financial matters Ericsson was naive and modest and did not think of his own advantage. The prospect of achieving something worthwhile always was his primary concern. Therefore, in response to Stockton's letter, in good faith he replied on July 28, 1841:

> I have duly received your communication on the subject of patent right for the ship propeller and semi-cylindrical engine.... Should their success be such as to induce the Government to continue the use of the patents for the Navy, I submit that I am entitled to remuneration. But considering the liberality that enables me to have the patents tested on a very large scale, and the advantages which cannot fail to be derived in consequence, I beg to state that whenever the

efficiency of the intended machinery shall have been duly tested, I shall be satisfied with whatever sum you may please to recommend, or the Government see fit to pay for the patent right.[6]

In this letter Ericsson only mentioned possible charges for his patents and that payment for them was left to the generosity of the government. This was a big mistake, because he underestimated the cost of his own work and his efforts that became considerable. In addition to the master plan he made

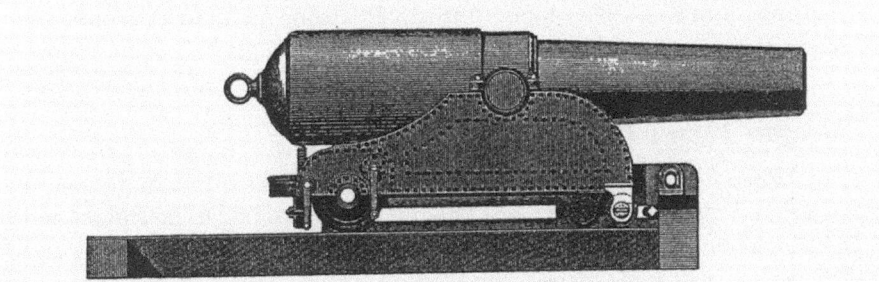

The first screw-propeller warship, the USS *Princeton*, and the Oregon, a 12-inch gun designed by John Ericsson (*Contributions to the Centennial Exhibition*, New York, 1876).

no less than 124 work-drawings with detailed sections and diagrams. The question about payment for his construction supervision, which occupied him for 2 years in Philadelphia and New York, was not raised.

The personal relationship between the two men had always been strained but as long as Stockton needed Ericsson he was keen to maintain an amiable co-operation. This is how Ericsson remembered his contacts with Stockton: "I brought an estimate of the cost of the steam machinery, made at his particular request. The maximum of the estimate was seventy-five thousand dollars. Captain Stockton told me he would put it down at one hundred thousand dollars, on which I remarked that it was too much; to this he replied: 'I want to make ample allowance for paying you for the use of patents,' ... Captain Stockton not only desired me to make the plans and superintend the manufacture of the engines, but he frequently complimented me as the only man in America capable of doing it."[7]

The keel was laid early in 1842 and the vessel was ready in 1843. The *Princeton* became a warship unlike any previously known. Not a large vessel, it had a length of 164 feet, a beam of 30½ feet, and a depth of 21½ feet. Her hull was of white oak. She had the most advanced construction of any warship: high-pressure boilers fed by forced draft and a compact two semi-cylinder engine, directly attached to Ericsson's six bladed bronze propeller. When launched the *Princeton* proved very successful as a screw steamer, attaining a speed of 13 knots, which then was considered remarkably fast. Equipped with a telescoping chimney and condensers, cooled by sea water, she became independent of fresh water. Stockton in a letter pointed out that the *Princeton* could attack "making no noise, smoke or agitation of the water."[8]

When launched in Philadelphia on September 5, 1843, the vessel was christened with American whiskey. At the inaugural party Stockton briefly praised the constructor and said that he had been all over the world in search of a man that could invent and carry out what he thought was necessary to make a complete ship of war; he at last had found that man. Later at the first trial run, Stockton called him: "Captain Ericsson, the most extraordinary mechanical genius of the present day."[9]

Oregon Versus Peacemaker

When Ericsson first came to New York he brought with him not only a model and plans for the *Princeton* but also drawings of other inventions and a 12-inch bore wrought-iron gun. This he had designed while still in England where it was cast at the Mersey Iron Works near Liverpool, and the unfinished piece which needed to be bored out was shipped as a "shaft" to the U.S. It had been forged of the very best material to withstand high pressure but still had the possible weakness of a forged gun, being strong lengthwise but weak transversely. When Ericsson made trial shootings at Sandy Hook, a long sandpit on the New Jersey side of the Hudson, he detected small cracks at the thick end of the gun, near the carriage supports. To prevent further cracks or bursting he used a technique later generally adopted to reinforce the breech with encircling iron-rings. After this modification in new test runs it had shown to be perfect in performance and safety.

Initially Ericsson called his gun the Orator, thereby expressing his wish that the threat of its fearful destructive power would speak for itself and induce the enemy to think twice before attacking. That name was very much in line with his later suggestion to name his ironclad ship the *Monitor* because it should "admonish enemies to beware of her dangerous power and come to terms without battle," an expression of a peace-loving inventor. All this happened at the time of the Oregon conflict between the United States and Britain when expansionists like Captain Stockton aggressively shouted, "Fifty-four forty or fight," insisting on taking all of Oregon above the 49th parallel (now part of Canada). Therefore he suggested naming the cannon Oregon which Ericsson dutifully had to accept.

Not satisfied with the perfect construction of the *Princeton*, the ambitious Stockton wanted more. He painfully realized that the vessel was not his brainchild but the output of a brilliant foreigner, a Swedish engineer. Therefore he decided to crown his project with a dramatic creation of his own — a gun, heavier and bigger than the Oregon. Full of anticipation of great triumphs, Stockton used the largest mass of iron ever brought under the hammer to produce his giant cannon, "forged of American iron ... here, where four years ago they could not forge an ordinary steam engine shaft!" When Ericsson heard of these plans he cursed himself for having turned over to Stockton the working drawings of his own gun and carriage. The effectiveness of his gun was not in weight and size alone but in the precision instruments he had designed controlling its operation. Ericsson also warned that improper forging could reduce the strength of iron to an alarming degree. He was pessimistic about Stockton's ability as a constructor and said he "lacks sufficient knowledge for the construction of a common wheelbarrow ... he never made a plan in his life."

Stockton ordered his gun to be manufactured at the Hammersley Works in Philadelphia with the assistance of two inexperienced assistants and then ordered it to be sent to New York for boring at the Phoenix Foundry with the help of Ericsson. When ready it was a 12-inch caliber monster, a foot more in diameter at the breech, with a weight of almost 10 tons but of inferior iron. Also, it was not fortified like Ericsson's gun with protective shrunk-on iron rings. Stockton called his great gun, The Peacemaker. He prophetically chose the name because, as he wrote to the secretary of the navy, he was confident that "the ocean may again become a neutral ground, and the rights of the smallest as well as the greatest nations may once more be respected."

Ironically, Samuel Colt's classic American firearm, the revolver, also became known as the Peacemaker because it was made for the demands of the frontier to kill "outlaws," Indians and Mexicans to impose law and order.

Display and Propaganda

The *Princeton* was a milestone in naval warfare; she became an immediate success, being the first screw-propelled warship in the world. After carefully arranged shows at the main ports on the Atlantic seaboard she arrived in New York for mounting her guns. There she made her first official appearance in a speed competition on October 19, 1844, with the "world celebrated Queen of the seas," the largest of all paddle-wheel steamers, Isambard Kingdom Brunel's *Great Western,* scheduled to leave for London. The huge vessel with sails set stirred up froth and full steam driving her paddle wheels. She came down the East River past the Battery and seemed unchallenged when suddenly the *Princeton* appeared from the North River without sails or smoke, propelled noiselessly as if in tow by a "subaquatic monster." The *Great Western* was soon overtaken and circled twice before the *Princeton* returned to the North River. Newspapers called the *Princeton* a "phantom ship" and hailed the event as "the great aquatic race — Great Britain against America, and America against the world."

After the competition Stockton could make extraordinary claims for his ship. Now it was proven: the *Princeton* could outrun the fastest ship and do battle with any vessel afloat, no matter how large. She could boast innovations that were the greatest since the invention of gunpowder. The *Princeton* was a maritime novelty, not a big ship but vastly superior in performance to anything built before. She was the first warship to carry a telescopic funnel that could be lowered to the level of the rail, out of the way of sails, and she used anthracite coal burning with hot smokeless flame, thereby avoiding the dense black clouds which revealed other war steamers. She also was the first to use blowers to force the draft into the furnaces and her screw propeller was directly coupled to the engine instead of using intervening cogwheels.

Two 12-inch guns, the centerpiece of her armament, could throw balls about a foot in diameter and weighing 225 pounds — guns that, when fired at a target from a range of 560 yards, could pierce fifty-seven inches of solid oak timber. They were so accurate that they would reduce the art of gunnery to mathematical certainty. They were said to have greater endurance and destructive power than any gun in service.

Members of the American Institute of Technology praised what they saw: "Nothing in the history of mechanics surpasses the inventive genius of Captain Ericsson, unless the moral daring of Captain Stockton, in the adoption of so many novelties at one time."

After the speed contest in New York harbor, Captain Stockton headed for the final important display of his vessel at the nation's capital on the Potomac. It was his goal to convince the government to modernize the navy by building several vessels like her, all based on the principle of qualitative superiority. To him "she would be a beacon of light to protect the country from danger."

When on a cold winter day the *Princeton* left New York for Washington it was agreed that Ericsson should come along. He walked to the chilly windswept slip at the foot of Wall Street. But here he was left standing with his luggage when his ship steamed out of the harbor. Now it was obvious, his help was no longer required!

The *Princeton* triumphantly steamed up the Potomac and anchored off Greenleaf Point. On 20 February 1844 Stockton invited members of both houses of Congress and other dignitaries to show the nautical wonder with a dinner and demonstration of his gun. Before firing, he said: "Now gentlemen, fellow citizens and shipmates, we are going to give a salute to the Mighty Republic. Stand firm and you will see how it feels. It is nothing but honest gunpowder, gentlemen, it has a strong smell of the Declaration of Independence."

One visitor was former President John Quincy Adams, who described what he met: "a war-steamer and sailing vessel combined, with the steam machinery of Ericsson's propeller, all within the hull of the vessel and below the water-line [and] the 'gimcrack of sundry other inventions' of Captain Stockton himself" (which could) "fire their souls with a patriotic ardor for a naval war."[10]

The press was enthusiastic and wrote about the "Flying Dutchman" coming to the capital: "The utter astonishment and amazement created among the inhabitants is not easily conveyed as they beheld the fairy phantom ship her onward way through the immense thickness of ice, ripping, tearing, breaking, crushing it with irresistible power. *Mirabile dictu!*"[11]

Although the whole ship and one of her guns, the Oregon, were designed by Ericsson, from then on Stockton deliberately took the limelight. Did he therefore want to take credit for everything?

Disaster Strikes

On 28 February 1844 in Washington, Stockton staged another gala event to show off the *Princeton* and her guns. This time he had invited a big crowd, including President John Tyler, cabinet members, foreign ministers, congressmen, senators, army and navy officers and their wives. Three hundred and fifty notables and a boat load of musicians thronged on board the *Princeton* for a sumptuous banquet and demonstration of the ship and her guns. Steaming down the Potomac, Stockton fired the Peacemaker twice to show off its power. The guests were startled by the roar.

After dinner someone asked him to shoot again. To this Stockton replied: "No more guns tonight!" But when it was revealed that the request had come from the Secretary of the Navy he conceded, went up and when for the third time firing his monster gun, the Peacemaker, with at least 25 pounds of gunpowder, a murderous blast occurred — a dense cloud of smoke enveloped the whole group on the forecastle. When this blew away a heart-rending scene appeared: the big gun had burst, at a point three feet from the breech, and scattered death and desolation. A chunk was thrown into the crowded deck killing six and injuring seventeen. Among the casualties were Secretary of the State Abel Upshur and Secretary of the Navy Thomas Gilmer. President Tyler was below deck at the time with his young fiancée, Julia Gardiner, who lost her father, David, in the accident. He consoled her in her grief and shortly after the accident married her.

In a message to Congress on the day after the explosion, President Tyler expressed his personal grief over the terrible loss of life and extolled the *Princeton* and "the merits of her brave and distinguished commander and projector." The same day the Naval Affairs Committee ordered an investigation and the Board of Inquiry concluded that the Peacemaker, a gun that had not been given the full U.S. Navy approval, was made of iron that was three-fourths the strength of Ericsson's British built gun and poorly welded.

A worse blow to Stockton's prospects after the grisly affair of the Peacemaker was hard to imagine. Despite a new investigations that followed not only exonerated him of any guilt or responsibility, but praised him for his handling of the traumatic incident. Later growing awareness emerged that there had been a massive cover-up headed by Stockton's good friend, President Tyler. Stockton on his part wrongly attributed all blame for the accident to his assistant, John Ericsson. At the beginning of the Civil War the former president joined the Confederacy.[12]

The tragic outcome crushed Stockton's proposal to build more ships like the *Princeton* or its guns. A further investigation of the remains of the Peacemaker at the Franklin Institute found it to be too light for its bore without additional reinforcement.[13] As the result of this disaster the maximum explosive charge was restricted to 15 pounds. This limitation remained until the battle between the *Monitor* and the *Virginia* in 1862, and probably caused the draw between the two instead of an outright victory for the *Monitor* with her powerful 11-inch Dahlgren guns, good for double the charge. The explosion of the Peacemaker was a disaster unparalleled in the history of American naval ordnance.[14]

Lost Opportunities

After the tragic explosion Ericsson was called to Washington for a hearing on the disaster. To this he answered:

Your request for me to come on immediately, whilst yet the funeral knell is piercing the air of Washington, you can readily imagine is not very agreeable.

How different would I have regarded an *invitation* from Captain Stockton a week ago! I might then have had it in my power to render good service and valuable counsel. Now I can be of no use. I must be permitted to exercise my own judgment in this matter. I have to state most emphatically that since Captain Stockton is in possession of an accurate working plan of his exploded gun, my presence at Washington can be of no use should an investigation of causes of the sad accident be deemed necessary.[15]

The refusal to attend was typical of Ericsson, who hated being questioned about anything that had to do with his work and particularly in Washington. Moreover, he knew that he was innocent. Although admonished by his friend Delamater, "This is ill-advised, John, it will irreparably damage your cause," he did not budge. His decision not only hurt his reputation but also deprived him of an excellent opportunity to dismiss accusations and clear his name.

Stockton was happy, he by no means wanted Ericsson in Washington to testify about the faulty design and testing of the Peacemaker nor did he want the authorities to know how little he had to do with the design and construction of the *Princeton*. As engineering expert and constructor Ericsson should have been subpoenaed, but Stockton saw to it that the Swede's denial to appear was honored. Ericsson's brilliance did not extend to understanding even rudimentary judicial matters. Now Stockton could without being contradicted easily fabricate a story which put the blame for the fiasco on the "ingenious mechanic." Simply refusing to appear would be interpreted as an expression of guilt and it did not help when he replied that he could provide written information about the production of the Peacemaker such as the quantity of metal used in forging and the boring procedure performed at the Phoenix Foundry.[16]

When four years later, the chief engineer of the navy without consulting Ericsson decided to replace the original propeller of the *Princeton,* Ericsson was furious. In a letter to Secretary of the Navy George Bancroft, he wrote: "I have understood that the Engineer in Chief of the Navy has recommended to the Bureau of Construction that my propeller should be replaced in the Princeton."[17] Ericsson was dismayed that he was not consulted, but in the end his own four-bladed propeller was installed.

New Era of Warships

The *Princeton* represented a totally new concept. She was the world's first propeller warship with engines below the water line. After some time it was realized that the *Princeton* as a warship was a great success and in the 1850s money was appropriated for the construction of six screw frigates, among them the *Roanoke,* the *Merrimack* (later to become the ill-fated *Virginia*), the *Minnesota*, and a number of screw sloops.

John Ericsson was dismayed by the lack of recognition and on February 18, 1857, he wrote to Congressman Bishop:

> The Court of Claims has refused to compensate me for services and expenses rendered in constructing the steam machinery of the *Princeton* many years ago.
>
> The *Princeton* was the first steamship of a class that has since been constructed in large numbers in the navies of France and England — and a few of them in our own service. I cannot therefore but be satisfied at the success of my labors, though they have been entirely unremunerated.
>
> It is now more than twelve years ago since I appealed to the justice of Congress in this regard — and the concurrent judgments of all the members of a judicial Bench expressly established that my claim was founded on legal rights.
>
> Pardon me, Sir, for soliciting from you, if practicable, such action as will secure the consideration of my case at the present session of Congress? My labors in my profession have always been of a nature to produce more benefit to the world than profit to myself."[18]

The *Princeton* disaster eventually faded in the memory of the general public and many responsible officials but Ericsson's part in the creation of the revolutionary warship was not forgotten by the chairman of the U.S. Naval Committee, Stephen R. Mallory. In 1858 after the successful construction of new frigates according to Ericsson's principle he pleaded to Congress for the payment of $13,930 to Ericsson: "The *Princeton* [was] made at great cost to Captain Ericsson. He exhausted every dollar he had on earth in making the experiment.... The quality which the *Princeton* had we have translated into every vessel, but we have never excelled her.... I ask you, when the country has reaped these great advantages, is it generous, is it just, is it magnanimous of the American people to refuse him this paltry compensation?"[19]

Mallory later became secretary of the Confederate Navy and adversary to his idol. Unfortunately his efforts were fruitless and Ericsson never received compensation during his lifetime. Only after his death payment was made to his estate.[20]

9

The Age of Caloric

Smoke of a steel-mill roof on a battleship funnel,
They all go up in a line with a smokestack,
Or they twist ... in the slow twist ... of the wind.
— Carl Sandburg, "Smoke and Steel," 1922.

John Ericsson's interest in hot-air and steam engines had already started when he as a little boy watched what was going on in the shafts of his father's mines. Here the big problem was how to drain the water that filled deep recesses of the pits, making it impossible to get at the iron ore. New machinery was tried to replace inefficient hand- or horse-operated pumps. This was at the time when revolutionary steam engines were introduced to do the job, but John had a dream, maybe he could invent something better, more economical and safer and that's how he came up with his first hot-air engine, originally called "flame engine" simply because a fire lit under the cylinder made it run.

Despite experiments in Sweden and the ill-fated demonstration of his flame-engine in London, Ericsson never lost his fixed belief in hot air or "caloric" as a useful working medium.

Hot Air

To convert work into heat is easy: you simply use muscle energy to rub an object and it gets hot. The reverse operation, to convert heat into work, is much more difficult. A noticeable effect of heat is that it makes matter move or expand (except ice). This is the principle on which all hot-air and steam engines are based.

When Ericsson first started working with his heat engines a mysterious concept of energy prevailed. The modern laws of thermodynamics were not yet established. At the time the cryptic term "caloric" was used loosely for a supposed driving medium of heat that moved the fly-wheels of these engines. Ericsson was inspired by the French scientist Sadi Carnot, who said that wherever there is a temperature difference, the possibility exists of generating motive power. In 1820 Carnot published his work *Réflexion sur la Puissance Motrice du Feu* ("Reflexions on the Motive Power of Fire"). In his treatise he offered brilliant insights into the force of heat as a generator of engines but the main purpose was to determine how heat could be used most economically for the production of work.[1] Ericsson, like others, initially followed Sadi Carnot's theory of heat, assuming that it was a weightless, indestructible, and highly elastic fluid that existed in all bodies. Although doubts had been cast on the truth of the theory it seemed to be reasonable and account for the phenomena of thermal expansion and heat of chemical reactions. Only the heat developed by friction could not be explained by calorists, as Count Rumford had demonstrated long before in his famous cannon-boring experiments of 1798, but nobody seriously realized the significance of Rumford's work until much later.[2]

In the nineteenth century the major development of heat technology was still about steam as motive power for engines. However, John Ericsson's credo was wider, he reasoned that the power of heat itself, without first generating steam, can move pistons and wheels, and to him conversion to steam was only an un-necessary detour. With his new thermometer, the "pyrometer," he measured temperature of air and found that an elevation to 480oF doubled its volume, meaning that there was a tremendous power to move heat engines.

It was finally realized that heat is the grand moving agent of the world because everybody could see for himself that it powered the great winds and ocean currents. Only at the end of the twentieth century we fully began to appreciate this truth and now propellers of aerogenerators are moving in the sky of California and the open plains of Denmark to generate electricity.

As we have seen, hot-air or "caloric" engines had been part of Ericsson's life even before he left Sweden. In fact, one of the reasons why he wanted to go to England was his ambition to further develop and promote his flame-engine. To the young hopeful inventor it was a big blow when he initially failed in London, but he always tried again. All his life Ericsson was busy improving the design of his pet and only temporarily abandoned it in favor of special steam engines because he knew how to shrink the huge monsters of James Watt and later George Corliss to make them more efficient and compact, especially for ships. He never lost track of the idea of an engine running simply with the power of expanding hot air instead of steam from coal-hungry boilers, a dangerous and expensive source of power. The construction of a new, more efficient hot-air engine still occupied him only a month before his death.

Over the years he had learned from his mistakes and introduced improved versions of his machines. Basically there are two types: open-system engines in which air is heated, moves a piston and thereafter the air is discharged at each stroke. The other is a closed system where the same volume of air is used over and over again, alternately being heated and cooled.

Ericsson worked with both types. In 1826, while still in Sweden he started with a "flame engine" which belonged to the first category. It had two separate cylinders and pistons: one for power and the other for air supply. The products of combustion passed through the engine at each stroke. The engine used a lot of firewood or coal because the exhaust gasses were still hot.

In order to improve economy, Ericsson in 1833 designed a new engine, based on the closed system. In it he added an ingenious heat store, termed "regenerator" or "economizer," a system of small copper tubes skillfully arranged through which the exhaust air is directed. The cycle starts with the air above the furnace being heated so that it expands, pushing a piston up and the air out. But during the exhaust heat is absorbed in a heat store or regenerator. The next cycle begins with the incoming air being pre-heated while passing through small tubes of the regenerator, then it expands again. The idea is that heat can be moved to and fro between the heat store and the

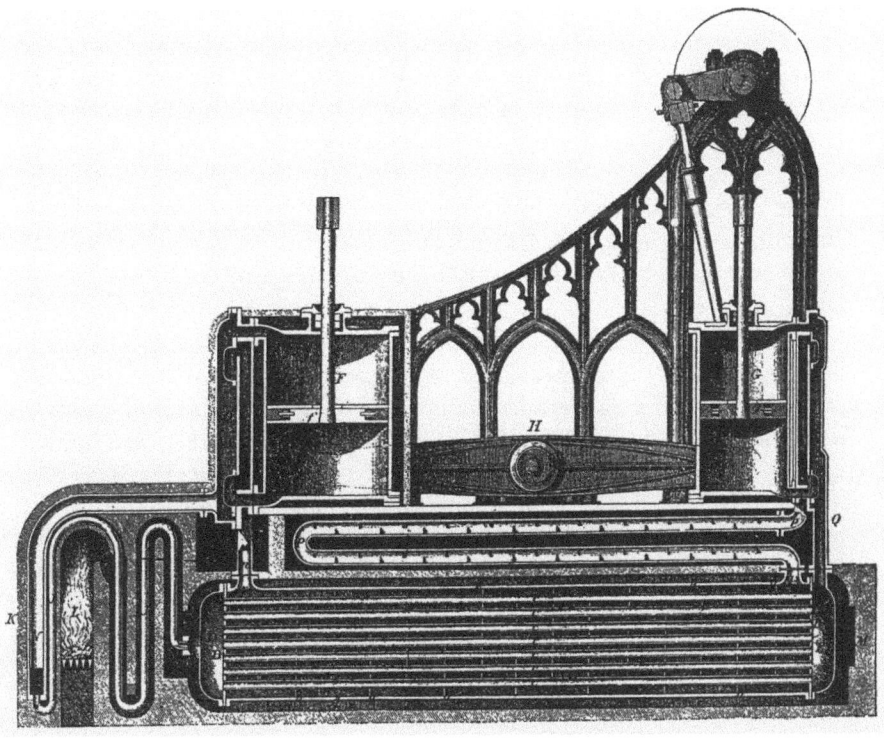

John Ericsson's "Caloric Engine," London, 1833 (Church, *Life of John Ericsson*, 1890).

air in the cylinder. With ever improved versions of Ericsson's energy-saving regenerators it became possible to use the initial intense starting heat over and over again, but in reality there was always heat loss. After the fire was extinguished these engines continued working for long periods of time so that some people had the vain hope that it verged on "perpetual motion."

The successful development of ever more powerful machines culminated in 1850 with the huge engine used for a "caloric ship," the *Ericsson*.

Caloric Ericsson

America was first in steam navigation with its pioneers John Fitch, John Stevens and Robert Fulton. Fulton's peculiar gifts manifested themselves early and started with steamships built in Europe. After faint success abroad in France and Britain, he returned to the U.S. and in 1807 on the Hudson launched the first commercially successful steamboat, the *Clermont* with an engine built by James Watt in Birmingham and shipped to New York. Thereafter side-wheelers for passengers and freight became a common sight on American rivers.

The steamers were, however, not without problems because of frequent breakdown of machinery. Most dangerous was the boiler when it was fired up to produce high pressure to increase speed. While a mechanical failure might stop the engine, malfunction of the boiler was much more consequential and could cause an explosion resulting in horrendous scaldings and death. In England Ericsson himself had experienced an explosion on his second propeller driven steamship, the *Robert F. Stockton*, before her delivery to the U.S. Fortunately nobody was hurt but the boiler had to be replaced before the vessel crossed the Atlantic in May 1839 as the first propeller steamer.[3]

Cracks and the inside build-up of scale made boilers susceptible to breakdown, particularly if overheated. At the beginning of the Civil War officers on steamers were more afraid of boiler explosions than enemy fire. Other problems had to do with the high cost of running the engines and limited space for storing coal on board. When Fulton designed his *Ambinavigator* that was intended to carry coal from Newcastle to London, the public joke was that his ship would consume the cargo before reaching her destination.[4]

Wonderfully cheap were they, Ericsson's latest wonder machines, the calorics, consuming only one fifth of the quantity of fuel required for a steam engine of similar capacity. They were safe because heated air had an advantage over high-pressure steam: an explosion was impossible. In addition his caloric engine was easy to operate because there was no water condenser and no boiler pressure to control.

Such was the situation in the 1850s when transatlantic crossing with big steamers without the help of sails was becoming popular. Now it seemed that the time was right for a "caloric revolution" at sea. The public considered steam engines dangerous and expensive and boilers of ships were a constant threat not only to engineers but also to passengers. In the early years of American steamboats, roughly half of all vessel losses were due to boiler explosions, and most were accompanied by fatalities. The public outcry resulted in one of the first instances of government industry regulations: a steam boiler inspection law of 1852.[5]

Therefore Ericsson reasoned: "Why not venture out and use safe caloric engines for the propulsion of ships?" Successful in the construction of his machines and the perfection of a new principle of "safe and cheap energy," he could now seek the backing of wealthy businessmen to build a big ship with his engines. He soon was lucky to attract a consortium of many hardy capitalists who took the risks of financing construction of a promising caloric ship. One of the sponsors was Gazaway B. Lamar, a New York businessman, who eagerly invested in Ericsson's idea. He was particularly keen because he had lost his wife and six children with 140 others in a steamboat explosion off the Carolina coast.[6] In order to attract interest of the public, Ericsson already in 1850 had started to design an experimental 30-horsepower model that could be used as a caloric ship engine. It was put on display at the Phoenix Iron Works. Before that he had built an engine that propelled his friend Delamater's private yacht, the *Vermland*, moored across the North River in the New Jersey port of Hoboken.[7]

The patent lawyer Francis B. Cutting at a meeting in the Union Club encouraged Ericsson and said if he was sure of being able to produce a rate of five miles an hour, he should not hesitate, reminding him of Fulton and his first attempt. John B. Kitching, a young man of wealth and enterprise, became Ericsson's principal investor. Previously he had been a backer of Samuel Morse, the inventor of the Morse Code, and telegraphy and later he helped finance the first transatlantic cable. Now Ericsson also gained the support of the popular daily press and few would dispute the contention that caloric propulsion was the way to go. The media frenzy surrounding accidents and deaths linked to steam engines and testy finger pointing on unsafe steamship lines turned the public's focus to "caloric safety." Publicity campaigns were under way not only in America but also in Europe. The *London Daily News* wrote: "The caloric ship will be all gain and no loss. As sure as water will find its level, the use of the caloric engine will force its way."

After these encouraging developments Ericsson, who initially was hesitant was swept away with all the fanfare of promotions nurtured by financial gurus. The daily newspapers like the *New York Times* echoed the general positive opinion and expressed the view "The event will be held memorable in the ages yet to come." Now he decided to go ahead. He wanted to give it a try and construction of the vessel started across the East River by Perrine and

Stack of Williamsburg, Brooklyn. She became 250 feet long and 40 feet wide and had a draught of 17 feet with a tonnage of 2,000. The huge engine was constructed at Delamater's foundry along the Hudson. The keel was laid in April 1852 and only five months later amid a huge crowd Ericsson launched his caloric ship, modestly named the *Ericsson*.[8]

The sponsors insisted that this ship with caloric engines should not only be a technical wonder but also a luxury liner. Therefore it was reported that

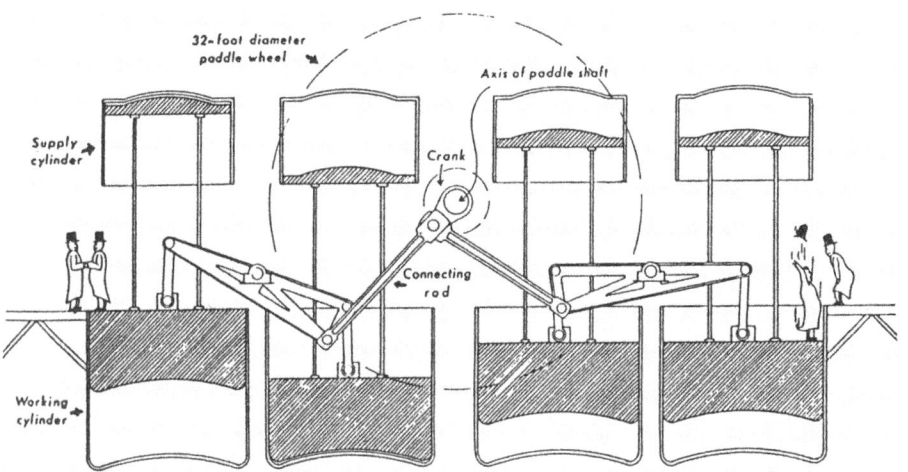

The caloric ship *Ericsson* and her four-cylinder hot-air engine (*Scientific American*, 1853).

"no ship sailing out of this port will surpass the *Ericsson* in beauty and completeness of interior appointments."

Ericsson's hot-air power plant consisted of four colossal working cylinders over furnace fires. An air-supply cylinder was located above each of them. The enormous working cylinders measured fourteen feet across and had a piston downstroke of six feet. She was equipped with an ingenious heat regenerator system to save energy.

A strange feature of the new ship, however, was the fact that she was not driven by Ericsson's own propeller but instead by two 32-foot conventional paddle-wheels. One has to ask the question, why was this anachronistic combination of the latest principle of power supply together with old fashioned paddles built by the inventor of the screw propeller? The reason was simple: Ericsson's caloric engines were so bulky that they could not possibly be squeezed down to the propeller shafts; moreover, transmission from the slow-moving engines would have required a system of complicated and space consuming gears.

Her first trial was on 4 January 1853. For the inaugural trip invitations had gone out to editors and reporters of all the New York newspapers and according to the *New York Daily Times*, "a few gentlemen whose scientific abilities render them amply qualified to pronounce judgment upon a project fraught with momentous results." The event was a great success. The big white ship pulled slowly away from her berth at Manhattan's Battery Park to a point off Fort Diamond in the Narrows, about seven miles distance, and returned. On board were some sixty curious friends, financial backers, and newspaper men.

On her maiden voyage the invited guests were led to the salon where Ericsson, using a paste board working model, explained "in a very persuasive manner" how the engine worked and why. They were also offered a grand selection of food and drinks and invited to the engine room. A popular entertainment for the visitors was standing on top of the engine and there being jumped up and down on the slow moving open giant working pistons. "Our sensation on riding up and down on these huge pistons we shall not soon forget," wrote one guest.

The launching of Ericsson's revolutionary ship was followed by enthusiastic reports. She was "driven over the bosom of the waters by an agent hitherto unknown." Now the public was expecting to hear sensational stories and Charles A. Dana of the *New York Daily Tribune* proclaimed: "The age of Steam is closed, the age of caloric opens. Fulton and Watt belong to the Past. Ericsson is the great mechanical genius of the Present and the Future."

Everybody on board had been optimistic and there were only a few opponents who claimed that the vessel was "promoted by hot air." One of them, surprisingly, was Orson Munn, the young editor of the *Scientific American*,

Ericsson's favorite magazine, who expressed doubts and exclaimed: "Viva la humbug." Michael Lamm in his *Hot Air Era* wonderfully characterized the situation that unfolded with the launch of Ericsson's caloric ship: "To say the world was ready for the Age of Caloric understates the case — the public was irrepressibly keen for it. The drama — the operetta — unfolded, though, as if staged by Gilbert and Sullivan. All the ingredients were there. The plot had its hero, the great hardluck inventor, Captain John Ericsson. The villain was Orson Munn, pesky young editor of the infant *Scientific American*. There was also that enthusiastic and most necessary element, the chorus — the nation's leading scientific gentlemen and members of the working press."[9]

Initially the *Ericsson*'s maiden voyage was seen as a success. It proved that a hot-air engine could indeed power a big ship and the vessel traveled roughly ten times as far as a steamship on the same amount of fuel. The engines seemed to be safe, as the piston-riders had demonstrated.

In February 1853 the *Ericsson* sailed to Washington at the request of the secretary of the Navy, who asked the government to appropriate $500,000 for a caloric warship of 2,000 tons to be designed and built by Ericsson. Among the guests in the capital was Washington Irving, a personal friend of Ericsson who wrote about the event: "I went down yesterday ... to visit the caloric ship. In our party were two Presidents, Fillmore and Pierce, all the Cabinet, and many other official characters. The *Ericsson* seemed to justify all that had been said in her praise, and promises to produce a great change in navigation."

It is a truism to say that "ships change but the sea does not." After her appearance in the nation's capital nothing much was heard of the *Ericsson* until the following year when she foundered in a storm off Jersey City. After the disaster Ericsson was devastated and to his good friend John Sargent he wrote: "Your letter yesterday indicates that you expect some further details respecting the accident to the caloric ship. The men on the freight deck had opened two lower starboard ports to clear some rubbish. The tempest struck the ship so suddenly to bring those ports two feet below the water line. The men as far as we [know] became terrified and ran on deck instead of attempting to close the port[s]. No human fervor could after that save the vessel.... In the meantime I had lonely days.... Having succeeded tolerably and having given 10 years of attention to the matter I ought to be able to make something that will last."[10]

After raising the wreck it was discussed what to do. On her trips she had averaged a modest consumption of five tons of coal in twenty-four hours but on the other hand the speed was slow. The *Ericsson* made only eight nautical miles an hour versus the 14 knots that a similar sized steamship could achieve. This speed was not deemed sufficient for competition with the now fast operating steamers and the backers withdrew their support, so the engines were removed and boilers and steam engines put in their place, after which the vessel was operated for a year by the Collins Line and later in North Atlantic service to Bremen, Germany.[11] During the Civil War she was used as a transporter and ironically she ended up as a sailing ship until 1898, when she was driven ashore in a storm off the west coast of Canada.

Despite all the encouragement from eager investors John Ericsson from the beginning had his doubts. In retrospect he wrote: "I hesitated in undertaking the construction. But for the encouragement received from some of our leading commercial men who were consulted on the subject, the caloric ship would not have been built." At the same time Ericsson also confessed: "There was more engineering in that ship than in ten *Monitors*. I regard the hot-air ship as by far the best work, it was simply a mechanical marvel."[12] The *Ericsson* obviously was a commercial failure but a mechanical triumph of the day.

At this time another attempt at propelling ships with hot-air failed when he had to exchange the caloric engine in the *Vermland* with a steam engine in Delamater's private yacht.[13]

One of the enthusiastic customers of caloric engines was John Bigelow, the editor of the New York *Evening Post*, whose interest started after being invited with a group of editors to sail down the bay on the *Ericsson*. He ordered a big engine to run his new fast-printing cylinder press and was proud to announce in his paper that he was going to receive the first engine to be produced after the impressive maritime demonstration. When it was delivered Bigelow was disappointed because it did not work as he had expected and therefore he replaced it with a steam engine. Now he had to confess that it was nothing more than an ingenious toy.[14] In 1853 Ericsson also received an order of a 90 horsepower caloric for the Washington Navy Yard but we do not know if it performed satisfactory.

Domestic Engines

After the humiliating failure of his big calorics Ericsson resumed construction of steam engines for ships, but in his mind he never forgot his pet machine. The future showed that the hot-air principle was best applicable to small, stationary engines, but useless in big monsters for ocean liners, where it had proved to be great embarrassment to him.

Four years later he decided to give it another try. He reasoned that hot air might power economic and easy engines in small industry and to drive water-pumps on farms and in households. He returned to the drawing board and in 1857 started a struggle of meticulous drafting, construction and trials. Finally on June 27 after an intensive bout of six days he succeeded and in a letter to a friend stated: "It is the most rapid and successful planning I have yet had the satisfaction of recording in my thirty years of daily journal."[15]

When ready the new engine was an open-cycle machine with a single cylinder containing both power and supply pistons and fitted with valves. These calorics were produced in four sizes of 8 to 32 inch cylinders. Ericsson did not immediately apply for a patent for his "pumper" but waited until the engine worked to his complete satisfaction in terms of reliability, durability and simplicity. The arbiter of quality, he said, would be that "a greenhorn Irish girl could run the engine after being taught for not longer than ten minutes."[16]

Finally Ericsson's new caloric engine was described in *Scientific American* and put on the market. There were new but less ostentatious publicity campaigns. The *New York Times*' heading was: "Caloric Engine Again," thereby also inferring to the previous failure. Ericsson was not pleased at all and replied: "The heading implies a snear [sic] — any allusion to the 'error' of the inventor is simply stupid in one who wishes the thing well.... The vile and condemnating notice has made me sick — given me a dose that has made me put aside the caloric planning for this day."[17]

To the surprise of many the new small engines became an immediate success with thousands sold. The public and business community was excited and soon expected much more from these fail-safe economic machines than just pumping water. They were used in small industry, mines and as auxiliary engines on ships, yoked to hoisting gear in mines and mills, applied on farms to threshing and on plantations in the South to cotton ginning.

Ericsson received much fan-mail from all over the United States. A Swedish-American farmer in Keosauqua, Iowa, enthusiastically wrote in Swedish, "Please answer me immediately with prices if you have small engines of 2–4 horsepower for threshing grain. With deepest respect, your obedient servant, Peter Dahlberg."

Another by Edward Lish, Springfield, Ohio read: "Pardon me for troubling you as I know no other way of obtaining information which I desire. For some time I have been eager to know more of your Caloric Engine & what kind of work it is capable of doing to better advantage than the steam engine. More particularly I wish to ascertain whether it would not be the very thing for driving a rotary saw, for sawing wood on our rail roads here."[18]

The unfortunate, long Civil War interrupted Ericsson's work with his pet project but after 1865 he again was able to devote time to develop more compact hot-air engines together with Alexander K. Rider, who had been in charge of production at Delamater's Phoenix foundry. He was a capable craftsman and constructor who for many years was responsible developing models for Ericsson's projects and who built caloric engines. This became the start of a very successful collaboration and the establishment of the "Rider-Ericsson

9. The Age of Caloric

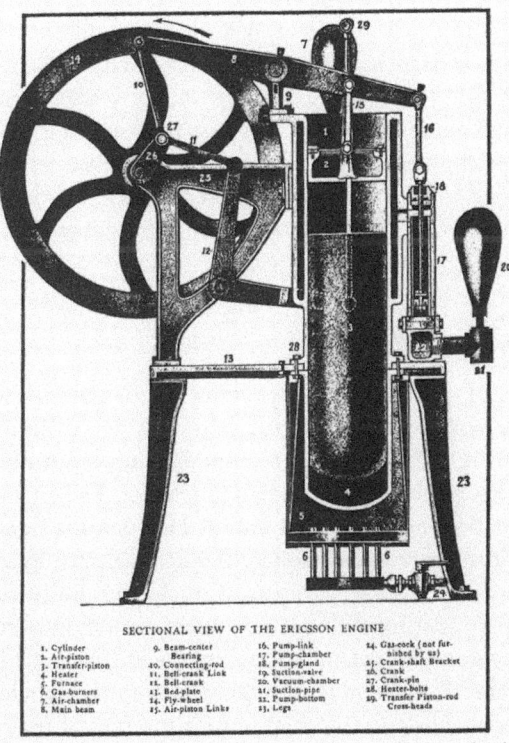

Ericsson hot-air engines in four sizes, patented in 1880 (Rider-Ericsson Engine Co. catalogue, 1906).

Engine Co." that later took over from the Delamater Iron Works with new manufacturing sites in Walden, N.Y., Great Britain and Sweden, and sales offices in New York, Philadelphia, Boston, Chicago and Sidney, Australia, and other places in Europe.

The design of later years was simple and sturdy: a single vertical cylinder with the furnace at the lower end, above it power and air-transfer pistons plus a fly-wheel. It could burn coal, gas or kerosene. In pumping-engines the top of the cylinder was provided with a cooling jacket, through which the water passed on its way from the well to the faucet or tank. This kept the upper cylinder cool, while the lower was heated. The up and down motion of the power cylinder was transferred to a revolving shaft on an axle with a fly-wheel. The operation began after lighting a fire to heat the air, which took a few minutes, then the engine was started by moving the wheel, giving it a revolution or two. The same air was used continuously in a cycle, being cooled, compressed, heated and expanded.

A Rider-Ericsson engine was also produced which was more like the Stirling motor, without valves. Therefore, it was very quiet in operation and became popular in churches to supply air to the wind-chest of organs. Many congregations preferred it to noisy choir boys with their feet tramping the bellows.

In the USA alone Ericsson was able to market some 10,000 before gasoline and electric motors replaced them. Most of the successful caloric engines in America were built by Delamater's iron works, but later also the Clute Brothers Foundry in Schenectady, New York, manufactured stationary engines.[19]

The Comforts of Rumford

A pioneer of modern thermodynamics was Benjamin Thompson (Count Rumford). He was an intelligent and practical man of limitless energy and resources, born in 1753 in Massachusetts. During the American Revolution he had to leave America because he had fought for the British, but he did well in Europe and became a Bavarian count. He took his new name from the town of Rumford (later called Concord) where he once lived.

In 1798 at a munitions factory at Munich, Rumford made an important discovery. Experimenting with boring a brass cannon in a trunk of water, he found that the vibrations generated heat that made the water boil. No amount of boring exhausted the supply of heat; therefore, he concluded, heat could not be a material substance but had to be a product of motion. Had it been matter, stored in metal, it would eventually have been used up, and no more heat would have been available. Rumford now challenged the caloric theory that was accepted by contemporary scientists when he found that "heat is motion." For nearly fifty years his findings were overlooked and he was mostly remembered for the construction of efficient heating stoves. He also had a nose for good business and he established the Royal Institution of Science in London and founded the Rumford Professorship at Harvard. In 1796 he endowed the famous Rumford Medals to be awarded for "improvements or discoveries in light or heat."[20]

In view of Ericsson's achievements in the technology of heat engines he was by many considered a good candidate for the Rumford Medal. He was first considered in 1860 for the improved model of his caloric engine with two pistons in a single cylinder and the previously used amazing heat regenerator. Nothing happened until 1862 when members of the Rumford Committee, initially divided in their opinion, finally on June 10 at the annual meeting agreed to award the gold medal to John Ericsson on account of "his improvements in the management of heat, particularly as shown in his caloric engine of 1858." These achievements were considered "particularly for the adequate enjoyment and comforts of life, especially in the lower and more numerous classes of society."[21]

Due to the Civil War the ceremony of the award was delayed until 1866. Now to everybody's surprise Ericsson declined to attend with "warmest thanks for your generous intention and kind invitation."[22] An invited guest for the ceremony was G. V. Fox, the former assistant secretary of the Navy in Washington, to whom Ericsson wrote: "My friends Sargent and Horsford put me in a very unpleasant position last week by inviting yourself and other great men, to meet an unwilling guest.... How can a sensible man commit such an act of impertinence and folly as to ask other sensible men to travel hundreds of miles to see a piece of metal cross from one hand to the other, I cannot understand."[23]

Another outstanding scientist, Michael Faraday, the pioneer of electricity, already in 1833 was so impressed by Ericsson's caloric engine that he made it the subject of a public lecture. Faraday actually worked at the Royal Institution, founded by Count Rumford.

Despite refusing to attend the ceremony Ericsson felt not only honored for receiving the Rumford Medal but he also became impressed with Rumford's teachings, which now were being accepted by the scientific community.

From 1852 with the advancement of physics, the modern laws of thermodynamics were gradually established by the work of the British physicists James Joule and William Thompson (later Lord Kelvin), but it took time before the new theory was generally understood and accepted even by Ericsson. These laws showed that heat is not a medium in itself such as the mystical "caloric" but a form of thermal energy. Now it was finally established that heat is not matter but rather motion of particles The First Law of Thermodynamics established that: "energy can be neither created nor destroyed but only converted from one form to another."

John Ericsson by no means claimed to be a mathematician or a theoretical physicist, but as an engineer he observed that heat is the product of motion because drilling on metal in Delamater's foundry or even rubbing together two pieces of ice from the Hudson River generated heat. He also realized that a heated body has the same weight after it is heated, hence heat could not be a material substance and initially was classed as "imponderable caloric." In other words, it was no mystical fluid that guaranteed "perpetual motion" and in the end it is interesting to realize that the regenerative principle is still widely used today in power plants with gas turbines.[24] In 1855 he wrote about his "regenerator" to a friend: "I yet contend that a mass of wire not greater than a common haystack will on this principle, some day, be found to yield more motive power than a mountain of coal." He now realized that a regenerator can utilize heat energy that would otherwise be wasted, but *no* heat that already had done work.

10

Naval Blockade

Let the navy blockade the southern ports. With rebellion isolated, it could then be crushed at leisure.
—Winfield Scott, 1861

When the Civil War started with a naval blockade of the South, Ericsson thought that finally his time had come to make a contribution to his new homeland. Now he did not have to offer his services across the Atlantic Ocean to France as when he in 1854 designed the Cupola Vessel for Napoleon but could design warships suited for coastal actions of the Union Navy. He was well aware of the fact that the U.S. Navy was outdated and there were no modern ironclads.

Anaconda Plan

In 1861 after the capture of Fort Sumter in Charleston Harbor by the secessionists it was realized that something had to be done. Therefore, the U.S. General-in-Chief Winfield Scott proposed "a strict blockade of the seaboard, so as to envelop the insurgent States and bring them to terms with less bloodshed than by any other plan."[1]

The purpose was primarily an economic blockade isolating the southern states and not a military assault on the Confederacy. President Abraham Lincoln followed the advice of his senior officer and on April 19, 1861, proclaimed a naval blockade against the ports of the seceding states, cordoning off the South's harbors and rivers. The proclamation specified that ships trying to enter or leave southern ports would be warned first, and in case of further attempts they were to be captured and confiscated. In addition, a fleet of gunboats was to enter the land up the Mississippi and estuaries of other rivers and a small army should advance downriver from southern Illinois.

It was an extremely ambitious plan to patrol a coast from Alexandria, Virginia, to the borders of Mexico on the Rio Grande with the few ships currently ready for action. The 3500 mile long coast was honeycombed with rivers, creeks, inlets and bays, including 185 harbors and river openings that might be used for commerce for the Confederate States.[2]

At the beginning of the conflict the Union Navy was not yet ready and there was only one vessel available for each 400 miles of Confederate coastline. Now the development of an effective fleet immediately became an urgent priority for both the Federal and Confederate states because the plan depended entirely on readiness for attack and defense by well functioning naval forces and the skills of engineers responsible for modernizing warships suitable for action in shallow waters. John Ericsson on Manhattan witnessed this development with great interest and was ready to make his contribution.

In the early exaggerated emotional state, unfortunately, it was believed that no threats or blockades would be effective in forcing a compromise with the South. People were too impatient for anything except quick action and with the battle cry "On to Richmond" demanded an invasion force to crush the rebels in their own territory. Nothing short of complete defeat would ensure the restoration of the Union and tragic massive military offensives with ground troops followed. The northern press ridiculed the Federal strategy as the "Anaconda Plan." Using the South American water snake anaconda as a metaphor for the early Union strategy was appropriate because the world's most powerful serpent is known for its ability to kill not quickly through the bite of poisonous fangs but by encircling its prey followed by slow strangulation.

Nevertheless, the anaconda concept of blockading the South, ultimately carried out in a modified form, became the cornerstone not only in the first phase of the conflict but continued to remain an important element throughout the long war and a strategy that eventually became decisive. In fact, it has been assumed by some historians that if the plan had been followed more closely, "with more reliance on the Navy to win by attrition, less on the army to capture territory as if it were playing a game of football instead of fighting an enemy, the Union would have won the war just as surely, but at far less cost in lives and money than actually was the case."[3]

Father Neptune

When the war started, the Union was unprepared to implement Lincoln's blockade of southern ports. Its navy essentially was a deep-water fleet, ill trained and not suitable for inshore and coastal tasks. The government had only partially followed Ericsson's early plans of the *Princeton* to build new steam-propeller warships and had at its disposal still mostly the old class of sailing frigates and sloops that were too large, and drew too much water to enter the shoal southern harbors and there act offensively.

Early in 1861 the navy consisted of eighty-nine ships of which on March

4, 1861, only 39 were in commission, and most of these were far away, assigned to five foreign stations. The duty of each foreign squadron was to look after and protect American interests within its area such as the Mediterranean and the African Squadron for the suppression of the slave trade, the Brazilian Squadron, the Pacific Squadron, and the East Indies Squadron to protect US commerce in South America, Japan, India and China. A limited number of the Home Squadron were based in northern ports and only eight of these vessels were ready for service, of which only four were steam-propelled. It took time to recall the ships from foreign stations, such as the *Congress* from Brazil for the Chesapeake Bay.[4]

On March 5, 1861, Gideon Welles was appointed secretary of the Federal Navy. He was a Connecticut newspaperman, an ambitious bureaucrat with no direct experience of the sailing navy but an impressive person with a long beard, wearing an ill-fitting wig, who lacked humor but proved to be one of the most capable, efficient and loyal members of President Lincoln's cabinet.[5] Lincoln jokingly called him "Father Neptune." The choice of assistant secretary fell on Gustavus (Gus) V. Fox, a businessman who had served in the navy. He was a man brimming with self-confidence, energy and enthusiasm and became *de facto* chief of naval operations during the Civil War. He despised "old fogyism" and learned to embrace innovative weapons and ships and became a good friend and supporter of Ericsson. Being a personable man and a lover of food and cigars, he was a boon dinner companion who during sociable sessions could attract supporters by explaining political imperatives to commanders and the navy's needs and limitations to politicians.[6]

Immediately Welles was faced with the task of enlarging and developing a new fleet for blockade duty. He started an the intense effort to purchase any steamship that would float and carry guns. Cannons were put aboard New York ferries and tugboats. The next step was an ambitious program to build gunboats suitable for coastal and inland waterways. In quick succession the Navy Department ordered 23 steam-powered vessels for coastal blockade, each displacing about 600 tons, armed with four to seven guns, and designed with shallow draft to enable them to work close inshore. From keel-laying to commissioning, each was completed in about three months — hence their nickname, "ninety-day gunboats."[7] For river services a collaboration with engineer James B. Eads of St. Louis was established. He was a wealthy businessman who supported the Anaconda Plan and constructed a fleet of seven armored "City-class" gunboats or "Pook Turtles" named after their designer, Samuel H. Pook. The project was prepared and smoothly run with the army in a "unified command with the navy" and helped in joint operations on the Ohio and Mississippi rivers.[8]

Initially the Navy Department at the advice of John Lenthall, chief of the Bureau of Construction, was not planning to build any armored vessels;

he considered ironclads to be a "humbug." But Welles and Fox, who had been informed about the ambitious program of the Confederacy to build such warships, now felt that this threat had to be taken seriously. They decided to inform Congress and leave the matter to their decision. Under pressure from progressive naval officers like Commander John A. Dahlgren, the pioneer of naval guns who had raised the issue of having properly armored vessels, Welles, on July 4, 1861, at a special session of Congress finally admitted that something had to be done because "much attention has been given within the last few years to the subject of floating batteries, or ironclad steamers. The period is, perhaps not one best adapted to heavy expenditure by way of experiment." This initially led to the decision to build two iron plated warships, the *Galena* and *New Ironsides* and later, as we will see after many turns, Ericsson's *Monitor*.[9]

Smart Mallory

For the Confederacy Stephen Russell Mallory was selected as secretary of the Navy. He came with extensive experience from his former post, having for over seven years been chairman of U.S. Senate Committee for Naval Affairs. Being a man of short stature, he did not have the imposing appearance as his northern counterpart and at first was underestimated for his ability to run the important job of creating a navy from nothing. But unlike most southerners, the farsighted Mallory was aware that "King Cotton" might not be a powerful enough monarch to force Great Britain to aid the Confederacy in breaking the blockade.[10]

Now he faced a seemingly impossible task. The South having no warships and lacked most of the important technical support of shipyards and heavy industry. The original seceding states impounded ten U.S. Navy ships carrying a total of 15 guns. They also seized private Northern vessels in southern harbors and purchased others from merchants. To this tiny fleet fell the task of defending the South's harbors and shipping.[11]

But that was just the beginning because Mallory had the ambition to build his own navy. The famous authority of naval science, Commander Matthew F. Maury, advocated building a fleet of 100 wooden steam gunboats, measuring 112 feet in length and drawing only six feet of water. Maury advocated the concept of "big guns and little ships" with the notion that "a large fleet of small steam-powered wooden gunboats, each armed with two rifled guns, offered the best defense for the South's rivers and harbors." The most attractive feature of the plan was that a large number of gunboats could be completed quickly, cheaply and in secrecy. At the beginning of the war some of these gunboats were laid down until the construction of ironclads put them into the dustbin of history.[12]

In his old job in the U.S. Navy Mallory had learned about the importance of ironclad vessels, screw propellers and modern ordnance. He was much more farsighted than his northern counterpart and soon realized that it would be a mistake to counter warships only with many guns. Therefore he dropped the gunboat program in favor of ironclads, built at home. He also tried to order warships abroad and backed the development of rifled cannons, mines, torpedo boats and submarines when he established a Torpedo and Submarine Bureau, originally advocated by Maury.[13]

After studying the development of the new ironclads in Europe Mallory wrote an important statement: "I regard the possession of an iron-plated ship as a matter of first necessity. Such a vessel at this time could traverse the entire coast of the United Sates, prevent all blockades, and encounter with a fair prospect of success their entire Navy. Naval engagements between wooden frigates, as they are now built and armed, will prove to be the forlorn hopes of the sea, but inequality of numbers may be compensated by invulnerability."[14]

The new secretary of the Confederate Navy and lifelong lover of ships had been an enthusiastic follower of the progressive Swedish-American engineer John Ericsson. As we have seen, it was he who during his time as chairman of the U.S. Naval Affairs Committee of the Senate always fought for his recognition and payment to him of still outstanding debts for the USS *Princeton.*

Mallory had reason to know what he could accomplish and Ericsson also respected the new secretary of the Confederate Navy and acknowledged his ability. He wrote: "Indeed, the utility of armor plating adopted by France and England proved to be better understood at Richmond than at Washington."

The Merrimack

In April 1861 when Virginia seceded from the Union, Gosport Navy Yard, located across the Elizabeth River from Norfolk, fell into the hands of the Confederates. As the U.S. Navy moved out and was unable to save all vessels, orders were given from Washington to scuttle and burn the remaining ships. Among them was the steam frigate *Merrimack*, commissioned in 1856 and built after Ericsson's principle of the *Princeton.*

When the Confederates took over the navy yard they found the scuttled remains of the *Merrimack.* She had been one of the best ships in the navy but was laid up for repairs with the engines dismantled. When Mallory and his men were unable to get the necessary steam engines for a new ironclad vessel, they suddenly remembered the *Merrimack.* Maybe her repaired engines could be used? Under the present conditions the best solution was go ahead without delay. Therefore, rather than build a new ship, why not build an ironclad shield on what was left of the hull of a refloated *Merrimack?*

Mallory quickly approved, and on July 11, 1861, he issued orders to reconstruct the vessel. The conversion of the *Merrimack* into the Southern ironclad took almost a year to complete. The vessel was trimmed down to the old berth deck and built over with a roof of oak and pine. This was plated with two layers of iron, making a total thickness of four inches. The pilot-house was forward of the smokestack and at the prow they attached a ram of cast iron, projecting three feet, like on ships in Roman times. The armament consisted of two pivot guns at the bow and stern and in the broadsides six nine-inch smooth-bore cannons.

On February 17, 1862, when re-launched, the ironclad was renamed the *Virginia*, but in the North she is still generally remembered by her original name, spelled without the final *k* and she was thus referred to by most of the contemporary press. With its roof-like structure covered with lard to make her slippery, she appeared like a "shining barn roof." The wheezing monster was able to make at the most five knots per hour with the same refurbished engines as before but still defective boilers and cylinders.

The *Virginia* proved to be an effective monster; she virtually decimated a Union fleet of wooden warships off Newport News on March 8 — destroying the sloop *Cumberland* and the 50-gun frigate *Congress*, while the frigate *Minnesota* ran aground.

11

The New *Merrimack*

I propose to adopt a class of vessels hitherto unknown to naval service.
—Stephen R. Mallory, April 26, 1861

At the beginning of the Civil War the Confederate States had no navy, only some seceding officers and able constructors but no warships. The Confederates, however, had selected a very competent secretary of the Navy, Stephen Russell Mallory, who soon found out how to tackle the problem and was of the opinion that "inequality in numbers may be compensated by invulnerability; and thus not only does economy but naval success dictate the wisdom and expediency of fighting with iron against wood."[1]

Southern Teamwork

In the South the build-up of a modern ironclad fleet started immediately but proved to be a difficult and expensive task. Mallory in his effort to build a modern navy was lucky to have a team of intelligent and experienced co-workers. One of them was John M. Brooke, who early in 1861 came with the idea to build an ironclad warship. He presented plans of a vessel with inclined iron-plated shields on a deck with submerged ends. Brooke, like his colleagues, was an exceptionally gifted naval officer, scientist and inventor of a useful deep-sea sounding instrument permitting accurate mapping of bottom topography. For his invention he had been awarded the gold medal of science from the Academy of Berlin by the king of Prussia. He also invented the "Brooke Gun," a rifled cannon made of cast iron.

In order to realize his plans Mallory in June of 1861 ordered the naval constructor John Porter and chief engineer of the Norfolk shipyard William Williamson to Richmond to consult with Brooke about the construction of the ironclad. Porter, an experienced draftsman, prepared a design of the vessel, which was to draw only eight feet of water to allow navigation in inland waterways.[2]

Now the main problem was where to get the necessary iron and engines for the vessel. First the men considered using the engines from the *Merrimack* for a new ship, but they found the engines were unsuitable for a vessel of low draft. They decided instead to rebuild the *Merrimack*. Williamson was to recondition the engines, Brooke to oversee the iron-plating and guns and Porter to remodel the hull and construct a shield.[3] The conversion of the *Merrimack* into the Southern ironclad cost $172,000. Construction was a difficult task in a country with scarce resources. Where should they get iron for plating? In the end it was decided to use flattened railroad tracks. In order to get the necessary 732 tons of iron, rails had to be stripped from the B & O Rail lines and for many months up to 1500 men worked on her. The pilot-house was covered with the same thickness of iron as the sides.

When re-launched in 1862 as the *Virginia* she became the flagship of the James River Squadron. The navy team was very optimistic: this could become the first big assault weapon of the Confederacy. In a letter to President Jefferson Davis, Mallory optimistically suggested that the *Virginia* steam up the Potomac and blaze away at the Union capital. Later he also expressed even more far-reaching dreams to her commander, Franklin Buchanan: "She can, I doubt not, pass Old Point safely, and, in good weather and a smooth sea, could doubtless go to New York. Once in the bay, she could shell and burn the city and the shipping. Such an event would eclipse all the glories of the combats at sea ... and would strike a blow from which the North could not recover. Peace would inevitably follow. Bankers would withdraw their capital from the city. The Brooklyn navy yard and its magazines and all the lower part of the city would be destroyed, and such an event, by a single ship, would do more to achieve our immediate independence than would results of many campaigns."[4]

The CSS *Virginia* as she looked on March 7, 1862 (*Century Illustrated*, March 1885).

Spying Information

Lately the North had also started building ironclads like the *Galena,* the *New Ironsides* and most recently had started the *Monitor*. Now a grim and fateful race had begun between the North and the South.

The conversion of the *Merrimack* at Norfolk had been closely watched in Washington by the press, spies and deserters such as slaves, often called "contraband" when escaping north. They would volunteer to bring intelligence with them to inform the North of what was going on. The slave Mary Louvestre, who was owned by a Norfolk ship's chandler, secretly copied the plans of the new warship, and convinced Welles of their authenticity.[5]

The South also was aware of what was going on at the Greenpoint shipyard and a month before the *Monitor* was launched the Confederates, through their own spies, had learned the exact condition of the vessel and the day on which she would probably be launched. Therefore, after the New Year in 1862 the number of workmen on the *Merrimack* was doubled. Not satisfied with the reports from the Gosport Navy Yard, Mallory sent Naval Captain Sidney Smith Lee, the brother of Robert E. Lee, with instructions that work be carried out by day and night. This extra energy made all the difference in the world, and doubtless gained the one day which enabled the Confederate vessel in the nick of time to commit great havoc without any effective opposition.[6]

That threat to the U.S. squadron at Hampton Roads was imminent became obvious after the report of Admiral David Porter, at the time a junior officer in the U.S. Navy, who witnessed the following event: "While standing on the wharf a decent looking mechanic landed from a small boat. He told that he had escaped from Norfolk, where he had been employed on the *Merrimack* which vessel was very formidable and nearly completed. His account of affairs was correct, but when the man was taken to Captain Von Brunt, commanding officer of the *Minnesota,* that officer questioned him fiercely and then roughly dismissed him, as if he considered him an impostor."[7]

No one in the Hampton Roads squadron seemed to anticipate any danger. But Porter took the message seriously and immediately wrote to G.V. Fox, urging him to hurry up work on Ericsson's ironclad.

In the meantime, according to secret information another threat had appeared. In the late summer of 1861 the Confederates were said to be building another "iron monster." Just exactly what it was did not become clear, but it was supposed to be formidable, something fierce that grew in proportion to the imagination of the reporter. The truth was that the Confederates at New Orleans were rebuilding under the name *Manassas* an old Massachusetts-built icebreaker-tug, the *Enoch Train*. It was a fearful looking craft with a cigar-shaped turtle-backed body, a "hellish machine."[8] Similar to the procedure on the *Merrimack*, all the upper works were cut away and replaced by an iron- coated convex deck, pierced by a single gun and topped with a smokestack. At the bow, invisible beneath the water was a ram that protruded fifteen feet. To repel boarders, provision had been made to throw scalding water and steam over the curved iron deck. This fearful looking turtle was propelled by a screw propeller that enabled her to move in only one direction: forward.[9]

What Mallory heard about Ericsson's *Monitor* made him understand that she would be an extraordinary opponent because he knew that he was dealing with the most experienced shipbuilder of America. Welles also was frightened of the big *Virginia* now nearly completed. But the Confederates did not know how the *Virginia* would behave once she came down the Elizabeth River entering Hampton Roads to face two hundred guns of the wooden armada. They had no idea of how seaworthy and maneuverable she would be. She was still an unproven vessel even to those who built and commanded her, not much different from the approaching ironclad whose designer had unshaken confidence in himself and his vessel.

Both the North and the South had high and totally unrealistic hopes for their new weapons. Stephen Mallory was toying with the idea of taking the *Virginia* north as far as New York. Likewise in the North, Gideon Welles had plans to dispatch the new ironclad to Richmond, hoping to provoke capitulation of the Confederate capital.

12

Lincoln's Raft

All I have to say, is what the girl said when she stuck her foot into the stocking: it strikes me there's something in it.
—Abraham Lincoln, 1861, on seeing Ericsson's model of the *Monitor*

Within four months after the beginning of the war, thousands of workmen in the North were busy in shipyards and foundries building forty-seven new wooden vessels, ranging from 300 to more than 2000 tons. There was not much time to spare if the blockade of Southern ports was to be successful and before the Bureau of Construction had begun drawing up plans, Gideon Welles, the secretary of the Navy, also had ordered the purchase of various merchant ships suitable for conversion to blockade duty. But was that really enough? Welles had shown commendable energy in the rapid build-up of a blockading fleet, but he lagged far behind his Southern colleague, Stephen Mallory, in grasping the implications of modern ironclads. Now many were waiting for a decisive step: would the Union government agree to fund armored vessels?[1]

Shot-proof Ships

The first unsuccessful attempt to build an ironclad warship in the United States was begun in 1842. A ship was built after the plans of Robert L. Stevens of Hoboken, New Jersey, but never completed because of lack of government funds.

Since experiments with new guns of Ericsson's *Princeton* had shown that shots at a distance of 560 yards easily penetrated 57 inches thick timber, this had become a concern lingering with the U.S. government. Therefore, as if to calm their consciousness, in 1846 a Committee on Naval Affairs of the Twenty-ninth Congress asked for ideas on the "practicality of rendering an iron-vessel shot-proof." In response to this request Ericsson submitted a proposal of an ironclad vessel with low freeboard because he said that "a conventional iron ship so thickly armored would sink." His drawings showed a ship with guns mounted on circular rails (pivot guns) so that they could be aimed in any direction and engines protected by coal stowed above them in watertight bulkheads. His suggestion was filed in the Archives of Congress and thereupon he heard nothing more from Washington.[2]

In Europe it was the Crimean War of 1853–55 that finally started the trend toward armored warships. The transition was initiated by introduction of a new forceful artillery of shell guns, designed by the Frenchman Henri-Joseph Paixhans. John Ericsson was well aware that these shots threatened to be the death-knell to all wooden ships and therefore in 1854 he designed the first "subaquatic" ironclad, his *cupola* vessel. It was a revolutionary floating battery. Today we would call it a semi-submarine protected from hits by iron coating and equipped with a rotating globular gun turret. At its base the turret was surrounded by an iron "glacis," a protruding rim to protect its rotating mechanism. It contained a huge 20-inch gun and in addition to the turret gun the vessel was also equipped with an underwater attack system of "hydrostatic javelins" or torpedoes.

The idea of this raftlike warship had come to Ericsson while still in Sweden, where he observed the motions of lumber rafts on lakes. In a confidential letter to a friend he wrote: "The great importance of what I call the sub-aquatic system of naval warfare strongly presented itself to my mind in 1826."[3]

He later explained this further to Gustavus V. Fox: "I found that while the raftsman in his elevated cabin experienced very little motion, the seas breaking over his nearly submerged craft, these seas at the same time worked the sailing vessels nearly on their beam ends."

With no conflict in the United States, Ericsson decided to offer his design to France, at the time involved in the Crimean War with Russia, Sweden's arch enemy. In September of 1854 Ericsson sent drawings and a model of his vessel through the Swedish Embassy in Paris to Napoleon III, as a prototype for production. He received a polite reply:

> Monsieur:
> The Emperor has himself examined with the greatest care the new system of naval attack which you have submitted to him. His Majesty directs me to have the honor of informing you that he has found your ideas very ingenious and worthy of the celebrated name of their author; but the Emperor thinks that the result to be obtained would not be proportionate to the expenses or to the small number of guns which could be brought into use. Although not disposed to make use of your inventions the Emperor appreciates all their merit, and directs me to thank you for this interesting communication.[4]

Obviously Ericsson's ship was too advanced for its time and the main concern was the same as seven years later. How could one or two guns be effective weapons? The offer came when the French government already had

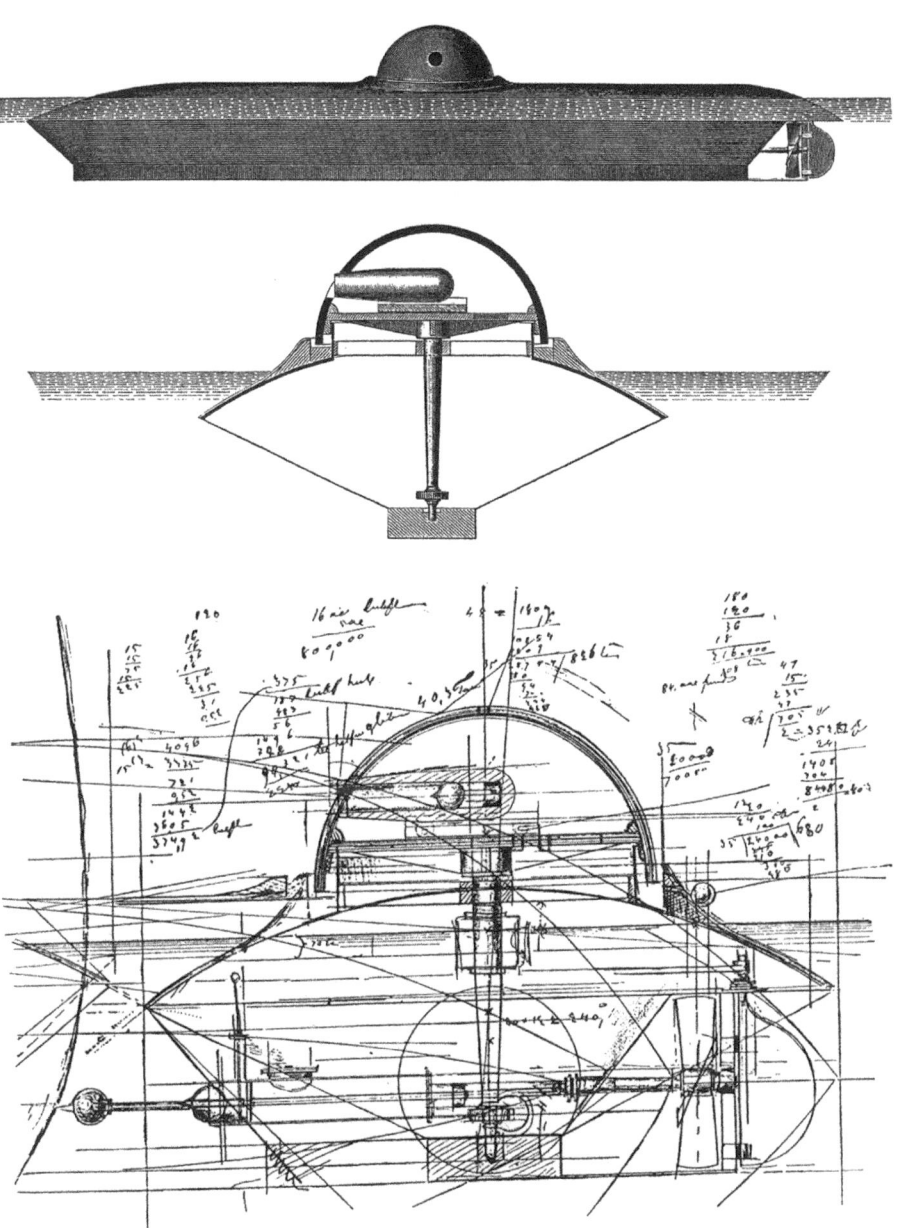

Top: Ericsson's iron-clad "cupola vessel," offered to Napoleon III, 1854 (*Contributions to the Centennial Exhibition*, New York, 1876). Bottom: Sketch of the cupola vessel with details of the turret, the propeller and a torpedo, 1854 (Church, *Life of John Ericsson*, 1890).

started building three ironclads; one of them was given the threatening name *La Dévastation*.

At the time the tradition-bound U.S. Navy was still not interested in ironclads, although there had been a slow transition from sail to steam a process John Ericsson had initiated with the construction of the *Princeton* the world's first screw-propelled warship. In seagoing vessels steam was still auxiliary to sail because engines were inefficient and required a heavy consumption of coal.

New Ideas

At the beginning of the Civil War when the Confederates had raised and started rebuilding the *Merrimack* in June of 1861, the North was still undecided about introducing modern warships. But at the extra session of Congress which convened on the 4th of July, 1861, at the recommendation of President Lincoln a report was submitted which explained that other governments were constructing armored vessels, and it recommended the construction of "one or more iron clad steamers or floating batteries, and to select, a proper and competent board to inquire into and report in regard to a measure so important."[5]

A month later Congress, as little excited as the secretary of the Navy (the bill passed the Senate by 18 votes to 16), authorized the creation of an "Ironclad Board of three skilful naval officers" to decide on new warships and appropriated $1.5 million for armored vessels. On August 3, 1861, Welles finally invited proposals for "impregnable" warships. For the board he selected Commodores Joseph Smith, chief of the Bureau of Yards and Docks, Hiram Paulding and Commander John A. Dahlgren, whose appointment was revoked at his own request on August 16 when Captain Charles H. Davis was chosen in his place. Dahlgren was the personal friend of Lincoln, who at the time was in charge of the Washington Navy Yard and may have taken part in discussions as to the value of the *Monitor* even after resigning.

On 7 August 1861 the Navy Department advertised in the major newspapers of the North for bids to construct "one or more ironclad steam vessel of war ... for either sea or river service to be no less than ten or sixteen feet draught of water.... The smaller draughts of water ... will be preferred. The vessel was stipulated "to be rigged with two masts, with wire rope standing rigging, to navigate at sea."[6]

At the outbreak of the war Ericsson had perfected details of his "Napoleonic" model and when he saw the for him highly interesting advertisement, he was jubilant. At the beginning of the conflict he was of the certain opinion that "victory will rest upon the side which holds possession of the seas, and I will offer my services to the Federal Government to assure that its navy will dominate."

Finally, after many painful years of misunderstanding and neglect, he thought that now his time had come to show what he could do to revolutionize naval construction and help his country win the war. The allowed deadline was very brief for a proper response. Who could possibly at short notice come up with a detailed design of an unconventional ship? But full of confidence and equipped with his model and design, he now had high expectations and replied both directly to the president and the Ironclad Board. On August 29, 1861, he wrote a letter that showed his dedication:

> His Excellency Abraham Lincoln
> President of the United States
> Sir:
> The writer, having introduced the present system of naval propulsion and constructed the first screw ship of war, now offers to construct a vessel for destruction of the rebel fleet at Norfolk and for scouring the Southern rivers and inlets of all craft protected by rebel batteries ... in making this offer I seek no private advantage or emolument of any kind. Attachment to the Union alone impels me to offer my services at this fearful crisis — my life if need be — in the great cause which Providence has called you to defend.

That Ericsson did not lack self-confidence is evident from this statement:

> Apart from the fact that the proposed vessel is very simple in construction, due weight, I respectfully submit, should be given to the circumstance that its projector possesses practical and constructive skill shared by no engineer now living. I have planned upward of one hundred marine engines and I furnish daily, working-plans made of my own hands of mechanical and naval structures of various kinds, and I have done so for thirty years. Besides this I have received military education and feel at home in the science of artillery. You will not, sir, attribute these statements to any other cause than my anxiety to prove that you may safely entrust me with the work I propose. If you cannot do so then the country must lose the benefit of my proffered services.[7]

Initially his letter also was supposed to contain designs of his vessel, but because he felt that this very important and secret message could be intercepted, he avoided including actual drawings. Therefore he added the following note of caution: "At the moment of putting this communication under envelope it occurs to me finally that it is unsafe to trust the plans to the mails. Your most obedient Servant." Ericsson's caution was justified because the letter never was delivered to the president.

The following days were filled with expectations and fear and Ericsson had many sleepless nights at his home on Franklin Street. He was anxiously waiting for a positive answer but never received a reply. Did the president and his secretary of the Navy outright reject his plan, like Emperor Napoleon? He also was very worried that his proposal had been lost or seized by southern spies. The letter, however, reached Washington, because later it was revealed that his written proposal was totally rejected by the navy's chief engineers, the dogmatic Benjamin Isherwood and the conservative John Lenthall, who always were jealous of Ericsson and considered ironclads as "humbug."[8] Although Lenthall later tried to do his best not to lose out in the move to build better warships, he still belonged to the old U.S. Navy which was opposed to radical innovations and refused to listen to the talk about ironclad ships with gun towers, rejecting with ridicule the idea of adopting them.

Another and probably the most important reason for not taking Ericsson seriously was the fact that since the *Princeton* disaster Washington was suspicious of Ericsson. Although he was in no way blameworthy, a stigma had been attached to his name.

Lucky Coincidence

On September 16, 1861, the Ironclad Board in Washington after admitting that they had "no experience, but scant knowledge in this branch of naval architecture," from the received proposals recommended two for construction contracts. These were given to Cornelius Bushnell of New Haven, Connecticut, for the *Galena,* and the second to Merrick & Sons, Philadelphia, for *New Ironsides;* both were conventional, masted and sparred iron plated broadside warships.[9]

Ericsson was disappointed and depressed when he did not hear from Washington but then something strange happened. In September at his home on Franklin Street he had an unexpected visitor. The businessman and entrepreneur Cornelius Bushnell urgently wanted to see him. He was the lucky one who was to build the *Galena.*

While in Washington to negotiate the contract for his vessel, Bushnell was met with critical reservations about his ship designed by Samuel H. Pook, who just had completed seven river ironclads for the army. The naval "experts" doubted whether the *Galena* would be able to carry the stipulated amount of 400 tons of armor on her topsides. Since everything about the planned vessel was new to him and the shipbuilders he had engaged, he wanted to consult a real expert who knew what he was talking about.

On the steps of Willard's Hotel by sheer lucky coincidence Bushnell met the New York shipbuilder Harry Delamater, who just came from the secretary of the Navy, to whom he had offered his services and those of his friend, John Ericsson.[10] When Bushnell asked Delamater for help, he said that he should consult with John Ericsson at New York, because "his opinion would settle the matter definitely and with accuracy." The next day he knocked at the door of the man he had heard to be the foremost expert on modern naval construction.

12. Lincoln's Raft

Ericsson happily received his guest with his question because it was a matter of great interested to him. Bushnell handed him Pook's drawings of his vessel and wanted to know if his *Galena* with all the massive coats of armor would be able to float and still be seaworthy and not top-heavy. Ericsson asked to have a look at the design to make some calculations. His answer would be ready the following day.

When Bushnell returned the next morning, he was happy to hear that there was no problem with the buoyancy of his vessel, and he could go ahead with construction. As he was ready to leave, Ericsson asked if he was interested in seeing his own plans for a totally new type of a low-draft ironclad vessel. Bushnell was immediately curious and agreed to have a look because this was the topic that had occupied his mind for the last months and, yes, why not? In fact, it might be a new project and business opportunity for him. Ericsson showed him the latest version of the model of his cupola vessel plus copies of drawings for his proposal to President Lincoln.[11]

The ship looked simple enough, a raft, flat as an ironing board with a gun turret in the middle. Ericsson said that it was absolutely secure to the heaviest shot and designed for action in shallow coastal waters like Hampton Roads and Southern rivers. He explained that even in narrow passages it could operate its guns in battle, since only the turret and not the whole ship needed to be turned. This sounded very promising and what was more, the vessel could be built quickly and cheaply.

To Washington

The proposition came during a critical period of the war when President Lincoln urgently needed armored warships for naval blockade. Therefore Bushnell urged that Ericsson speedily take his model and plans to Washington and present them to the secretary of the Navy. Ericsson was reluctant to go but when asked by Bushnell if he himself might take them to show, the secretary he agreed. Bushnell did not immediately go to Washington, but took the treasure to his old Connecticut friend, Gideon Welles, still at his home in Hartford before moving to Washington.

He came at the right moment because the new secretary of the Navy was worried. He had just been informed that since June the South had been pushing its work on the *Merrimack* in the hope of winning the mad race to produce the first ironclad. Welles therefore urged that the model at once be taken to Washington for further scrutiny by the Ironclad Board. Bushnell agreed and, knowing of the difficulties of dealing with these conservative officials and not being a stranger to pressures of patronage, he managed through personal connections to arrange an appointment with the president because he probably was aware of Abraham Lincoln's interest in ships and guns.

On September 12, 1861, Bushnell was received by the president in the White House. Lincoln immediately was impressed by the unique features of Ericsson's battery with her little raft-like design and guntower. The following morning at 11 A.M. Bushnell joined the president, who had called the board for an informal discussion and examination of the exciting model. When the members asked the president about his opinion, taking the model of the little turreted ironclad, he responded: "All I can say is what the girl said when she put her foot into the stocking: 'It strikes me there's something in it.'"

The next day the board held an official meeting to decide on Ericsson's proposal. The ship was so odd, so unlike anything they had ever seen before or even imagined, and the very mention of Ericsson's name made them suspicious. In the ensuing discussion, two members finally favored proceeding with the construction because it was inexpensive and could be ready in three months. However, the third member, Captain Davis, was the most negative because he did not understand the epochal innovation presented to him and because he did not trust Ericsson as a reliable constructor since he with his own eyes had witnessed the *Princeton* tragedy. He refused to endorse the proposition, handing back the model to Bushnell. Paraphrasing a verse from the Bible, he said: "Take it home and worship it. It will not be idolatry. It is the image of nothing in the heaven above, or the earth beneath, or the waters under the earth."

Bushnell did not give up; he was convinced of Ericsson's superior design and again discussed the matter with Welles. They agreed that the only way to sway the opinion of the board to a unanimous decision would be if they could convince Ericsson to come to Washington to give more specific information and plead his case.

The same evening Bushnell left for New York and decided to use a friendly trick to entice his ally. When he met Ericsson the next morning he tried to appeal to his vanity and said: "The Board has been very impressed by your ingenious floating battery but one member, Commander Davis, only needs some further explanation about your design before signing a contract, details I was unable to explain. Therefore Secretary Welles suggested you come to Washington to give a personal explanation." Ericsson, obviously flattered and extremely curious about the state of his project, agreed to leave immediately for the capital. The night train brought the two men to Washington.

On September 15 they stood in front of the board. Great was Ericsson's surprise when he heard that his plan had been rejected by the junior member, Captain Davis. When confronted, he said: "Your ship, Captain Ericsson, lacks stability." These doubts excited Ericsson's strong professional pride and with detailed knowledge and numbers he defended his design convincingly and pointed out that the low freeboard of his vessel in no way made it unstable, in fact, from his own experience with rafts in Sweden he knew that these in high seas only were washed over, but the body of the ship itself remained steady.

In the end he concluded: "Gentlemen, after what I have said, I consider it to be your duty to the country to give me an order to build the vessel before I leave this room." Davis in the ensuing meeting reluctantly recommended construction as a mere "experiment" or as a "trial battery." The positive decision was a stroke of happy intuition. Ericsson was asked to return in an hour and when ushered into the room of the secretary and as if to make up for earlier procrastinations, after only five minutes Welles said: "Go ahead and start building as soon as possible, don't wait for a formal contract." So, by a series of unpremeditated but providential events, Ericsson and his long-hidden ship were thrust into the forefront of the conflict to save the Union.[12]

Ericsson's battery was so contrary to all conventional ideas that Welles and those about him still were not positively convinced of the success of the floating battery, including the assistant secretary of the Navy, Gustavus V. Fox, who nonetheless later became one of Ericsson's biggest fans and a powerful influence on Gideon Welles. He once stated that he never fully believed in armored vessels until he, on 9 March 1862 sitting on the shore of Hampton Roads, witnessed the success of the *Monitor*.

After Ericsson left Washington the board had second thoughts and did not fully trust Welles who they thought "could not tell a vessel's stem from its stern" and since eager to protect their reputation, they proposed a humiliating contract. Therefore, on September 21, 1861, Commodore Joseph Smith wrote a letter to Ericsson in which he specified: "The Board reported favorably on your proposition for an Ironclad Gunboat, but as there seems to be some deficiencies in the specifications, and as some charges may be suggested and a guarantee required, you had better come on and see to the drawing of a contract if we can mutually agree. As no time is to be lost I suggest this as the quickest mode of settling the matter."[13] Ericsson, however, did not go back to Washington; instead Cornelius Bushnell managed the deal.

The agreement was similar to one with a money-back guarantee offered eight years before, on March 3, 1853, by Smith to Ericsson asking him to construct a 90 horsepower caloric engine for the Bureau of Yards and Docks. It stipulated that "if you want payment, you will be required to enter into contract with good and sufficient sureties for the full faithful performance of the work before stated." The engine was ordered for the Washington Navy Yard. Unfortunately, we do not know if Ericsson at that time was able to live up to the promises.[14]

The final document was issued on October 4, 1861. It also contained a deadline, besides specifications of technical details and payment by installments and performance. The contract for building "an ironclad, shot-proof steam battery" stipulated a money back clause if she proved to be a failure. Furthermore, it specified that the vessel was to be provided with masts and sails and that it should make six knots under sail. This clause is a mystery but shows that the board did not consider how rigging of the low draft steam battery could be done without limiting shots from the rotating gun-turret. Furthermore, it was agreed "that said vessel and equipment in all respects shall be completed and ready for sea in one hundred days from the date of this indenture." Then came the final threatening verdict, that if the vessel — the iron-clad-shot-proof steam battery of iron and wood — was no success, "the party of the first part would have to refund to the government all moneys received."[15]

In reality, recommending construction of Ericsson's battery was an act of great courage because the weight of contemporary professional experience and prejudice did not support it. The most advanced naval constructors of the day were against the decision and it required bold men to advocate the *Monitor* idea. With the final decision to go ahead a great responsibility rested on President Lincoln and his Navy Department.

Abe and Technology

Although born in a Kentucky log cabin and raised on frontier farms in Indiana and Illinois far from the sea, Abraham Lincoln had extensive experience in navigation of flatboats on the Ohio and Mississippi rivers. He not only had operated a ferry and navigated twice down to New Orleans, but he also was very keen on naval innovations and the only president who had been granted a patent. His invention was a contraption "that lifted boats over shoals by means of buoyant air chambers."[16] With his "Yankee shrewdness," as Nathaniel Hawthorne called it, he was not only a good judge of politics but also of practical matters like warships and ordnance.

Bruce Catton, who stressed the individual in history rather than nations or organizations, was of the opinion that "the decision to build the *Monitor* seems to have been made largely by Abraham Lincoln himself, who possessed less than normal allotment of orthodoxy." This is obvious considering the massive opposition Ericsson was facing, not only from officers but also the highest technical expert of the navy, John Lenthall, not an amiable man and who "looked with contempt on any innovation that intruded on his vision of stately sailing ships with well seasoned white-oak hulls."[17]

President Lincoln always looked for new ideas that promised to shorten the war and improve naval technology; therefore his word must have meant a great deal to counter criticism. The president had faith in Ericsson. He once said to Assistant Secretary of the Navy Gustavus V. Fox: "The *Monitor* was one of my inspirations. I believed in her when Mr. Bushnell first showed me

Ericsson's plans. Captain Ericsson's plain but rather enthusiastic demonstration made my conversion permanent. It was called a floating battery; I called it a raft. I caught some of the inventor's enthusiasm, and it has been growing upon me. I thought then and I am confident now that it is just what we want."[18]

New evidence shows that Lincoln was greatly influenced by his personal friend and favorite naval officer, John Dahlgren, commandant of the Washington Navy Yard. He was a man of similar interests and originally selected as a member of the Ironclad Board. Dahlgren, constructor of the massive smoothbore iron cannon cast in the distinctive "soda bottle" shape named after him, was the proponent for a modern navy. His biographer, Robert Schneller, described the attraction: "Lincoln simply liked gadgets, weapons, and munitions, and these things abounded at the Washington Navy Yard."

He often sought Dahlgren's opinion because Lincoln found him to be a man of "broad intellectual curiosity and of sound judgement." Dahlgren also frequently came to the White House and spent so much time with the president and his cabinet that Welles began to consider him a courtier.

Dahlgren belonged to the few officers who wanted to modernize the navy, not only technically but also in terms of organization and its system of promotion. In the beginning of 1861, when the secession of Southern states started, he tried to railroad several measures through Congress to authorize trials of ordnance against armor and recommended construction of an armored warship. Congress, however, at the time took no action.[19]

Shortly after the battle at Hampton Roads the president traveled to Fort Monroe and visited the *Monitor*. Lincoln no doubt was keenly interested in Ericsson's ship and at Hampton Roads, Paymaster Keeler described the situation: "He examined everything about the vessel with care, manifesting great interest, his remarks evidently shewing that he had carefully studied what he thought to be our weak points & that he was well acquainted with all the mechanical details of our construction."[20]

Later when the *Monitor* appeared at the Washington Navy Yard for repairs, Lincoln again came on board and studied her mechanical details. The same happened with the new monitor *Passaic* when in Washington, and her captain said: "The President went everywhere, crawled into places that Gerald or Henry would scarce have ventured in, and gave us a funny story or two in illustration of the incidents of the occasion."[21]

Lincoln was always fascinated not only by warships but also in new armament, and in June 1862, on an official visit to West Point, "he indulged his personal interest in ordnance technology" by taking an excursion to Cold Spring, New York, where he inspected the Parrot Foundry. There the most widely used rifled cannons in the Union army were made.[22]

13

The *Monitor*

No passion, all went on by crank,
Pivot, and screw,
And calculations of caloric.
— Herman Melville, "A Utilitarian View
of the *Monitor*'s Fight," 1866

The Civil War has an unshakeable hold on America's imagination and in all the story of Civil War coincidences, none is more remarkable than the one that brought the *Merrimack* and the *Monitor*, "designed, built, and commissioned in the very nick of time" into Hampton Roads, Virginia, within twenty-four hours of each other.[1]

A Race to Finish

As soon as Ericsson came back to New York he wasted no time but immediately started working on his "battery" because he thought he had succeeded in selling it to the government, although at this stage the project was still a private venture, financed by Cornelius Bushnell of New Haven, Connecticut, and two businessmen, John Griswold and John Winslow from Troy, New York.

By lucky coincidence construction began before Ericsson and his team received a contract from Washington, dated October 4. Had the involved parties of businessmen known the humiliating condition of "no success — no pay" beforehand, it is possible that the *Monitor* would never have been built.

Now Ericsson was under tremendous pressure but there was no doubt that he intended to live up to his promise and wanted to show Washington what he could achieve. Painfully aware that he was taking a calculated risk by accepting, he had acted impulsively, and he knew it. What he did not realize was that, without long consideration, or going through agonizing reflections, he had made the wisest decision of his life.

He immediately went to the drawing board in his office on Franklin Street. Fortunately, he had an excellent and dependable assistant in Charles

William MacCord, who since 1858 had been working in the design office of the Delamater Iron Works and there attracted the attention of Ericsson, who subsequently engaged him as his chief draftsman. MacCord later became one of the first faculty members of the Stevens Institute of Technology when in 1870 the college was founded at Hoboken, New Jersey. For many years as a professor there he taught Mechanical Drawing and Design.

The keel was laid on October 25, 1861, at Thomas Rowland's Continental Iron works, Greenpoint, Long Island, with slips on the East River. Here shipbuilding operations were carried out on a vast scale and work on the metal frame started immediately. The clang of hammers and the din of fabrication soon sounded from a specially built shed in which Ericsson's battery took shape.

A rush also happened to construct the revolving turret at the big sprawling Novelty Iron Works on the East River shore between 12th and 14th Streets in New York City. Delamater's Phoenix Foundry on 260 West Street got the contract for steam engines, blowers and other machinery. Countless components of bar-iron, armor plate, bolts and rivets were manufactured in dozens of foundries and iron mills from Buffalo to Baltimore. Ericsson always remained close to the job that called for fast planning and coordination to have all parts fabricated by the many different companies and people involved. Early in the morning and late at night he drew hundreds of detailed plans at home, traveling early every day by ferry across the East River to the Continental Ironworks to check on the progress.

Each part ordered from the different subcontractors had to fit properly and arrive on time. Building an armored iron vessel is a matter of much more exact calculation than a wooden ship, in which *ex tempore* modifications can be made on the spot. It

John Ericsson at the time of building the USS *Monitor* (Church, *Life of John Ericsson*, 1890).

took a perfectionist and mathematician to do the job and Ericsson controlled everything with a keen eye. Once started, work progressed endlessly, crews laboring around the clock on eight-hour shifts. Tireless efforts, coupled with the more adequate facilities in the North, rapidly ate up the time gap between the *Merrimack* and Ericsson's battery.

The author of *Lincoln's Navy*, Donald Canney, aptly describes the situation: "This little vessel, from concept through construction was a *tour de force* for John Ericsson. Certainly this ship marked the boundary of the possible in the technological milieu of the day, and only a monumental ego such as Ericsson's could have pulled it off."[2] For him the construction of his ironclad became the greatest challenge of his life. He wanted to convince everybody, including the doubting Ironclad Board, of the quality of his ship; then there was the time limit and the clause: "succeed or lose everything."

Floating Battery?

For obvious reasons, officially as little publicity as possible had been given to the construction of Ericsson's "battery," but perfect secrecy was, of course, out of the question. The spectacular turret of a vessel could not be hidden under a bushel, nor could the launching of an ironclad vessel be concealed from the public eye. But early in November 1861, *Scientific American* magazine ran an illustration of the craft, and the New York *World*, at the end of January 1862, published a complete description of the ship, giving all her principal dimensions. The press later speculated about the mysterious vessel while questioning her abilities.[3]

From the start some experts in the Navy Department remained prejudiced against the strange ship and so did their boss, Gideon Welles. But he promised to keep a watchful eye on the construction. He therefore appointed Commodore Joseph Smith to survey construction. Smith as the senior member of the Ironclad Board was very curious to follow every detail of construction because he felt that the decision to build Ericsson's battery rested on his shoulders. He kept sending inquiries to Franklin Street and sometimes personally appeared in New York. He put his nose into all details, closely following each step of the way, nagging about everything. In the background was the navy's chief engineer and Ericsson's rival, Benjamin F. Isherwood, who predicted that the work could not be completed in time and the battery was doomed to be a failure.[4]

One day Smith had his doubts about the turret and the next he thought that the ship would not float due to its weight of armor. Then came other worries about the workings of the ventilation system. Like all inventors Ericsson was proud of his work and touchy of criticism and became annoyed by the lack of confidence in his project. He simply was not left alone to do his job but constantly interrupted, having to soothe the doubts of Smith with long explanatory letters to Washington. Fortunately, he realized the importance of being diplomatic and tried to hold his mercurial temper. But when Smith's probing threatened to exasperate the hard-working inventor, someone in Washington reassured him and said, "The old Commodore is fidgety at times and may provoke you by his anxieties, but he has confidence in you, and he has no confidence in anybody else. So, give the old man his tether, and let him fret a little when he feels like it."[5]

The other representative selected by the Navy Department was Alban Stimers, a young engineer and expert on steam engines. In navy circles he was not popular because he belonged to the new generation of "navy mechanics" and had a reputation of being "abrasive, overbearing and disagreeable." When he arrived on the scene there was, however, immediately a good rapport between him and Ericsson, who hated to fuss with minor structural details. Now he could depend on Stimers and therefore did not always have to rush to the workplace, but could get back to his drawing board again. It is not difficult to understand why a negative epithet had been attached to Stimers; he was one of the few who was in tune with naval innovations, a view that clashed with the conservative elite in Washington. Later when he was given more responsibilities, however, it became obvious that he was overconfident.

The constant probing did much to delay completion. Another delaying factor was the late delivery of the Dahlgren guns. They arrived only on January 25 and 29, 1862. Instead of the planned bigger 12-inchers, two 11-inch guns were mounted in the turret. When finally the ship neared conclusion Commander David D. Porter was also sent to Brooklyn to examine the vessel and report to Washington on the status of Ericsson's battery and offer his opinion as to her ability to deal with an enemy. Ericsson was very upset of now having to deal with another "spy." But fortunately, after a thorough examination of all the details of the vessel, Porter telegraphed the Navy Department: "This is the strongest fighting vessel in the world, and can whip anything afloat."

Ericsson simply ignored the clause in the original contract which stipulated that "the vessel to be rigged with two masts, with wire rope standing rigging, to navigate at sea." At this point with the mounting threat from the Confederate *Virginia,* expected to be ready at any time, Porter agreed and disregarded the rigging clause. But when he returned to Washington a few days later he was laughed at by a high official who said: "Why, man, John Lenthall predicts that Ericsson's vessel will sink as soon as she is launched."[6]

In the end the navy had only one thing in mind, to get Ericsson's vessel out to sea, and was prepared to accept her under almost any terms even though the deadline for delivery had been exceeded and she was without sails. Besides, the government was partly to blame for the delay, since it had not kept its promise to provide the guns in time and was responsible for Smith's constant interference.

Everybody in Washington was anxious to see the completion of the unnamed and mysterious battery, but before launch Assistant Secretary of the Navy Gustavus Vasa Fox asked Ericsson if he would care to recommend a proper name for his vessel. To this Ericsson in a letter of January 20 replied:

> Sir: In accordance with your request I now submit for your approbation a name for the floating battery at Green Point. The impregnable and aggressive character of this structure will admonish the leaders of the Southern Rebellion that the batteries on the banks of their rivers will no longer present barriers to the entrance of the Union forces.
>
> The iron-clad intruder will thus prove a severe monitor to those leaders. But there are other leaders who will also be startled and admonished by the booming of the guns from the impregnable iron turret. "Downing Street" will hardly view with indifference this last "Yankee notion,"—this monitor. To the Lords of the Admiralty the new craft will be a monitor, suggesting doubts as to the propriety of completing those four steel-clad ships [The British ironclad frigates] at three-and-a-half million apiece. On these and many similar grounds I propose to name the new battery *Monitor*.
>
> Your obedient servant
>
> J. Ericsson

Ericsson sent a copy to his sponsor, John A. Griswold, who two days later replied:

"I return herewith the copy of your letter to G. W. Fox christening the Battery. My idea & preference was that the "Ericsson Battery" should be the name permanently adopted & this would have been my selection."⁷ But in the end the name "Monitor" won and was officially accepted.

During the whole period of construction the navy continued to be worried and was criticized for building the *Monitor*. Despite much ridicule and abuse and little encouragement expressed by officials to Welles about the novel "experiment" while in construction, trust in the success of the *Monitor* remained. In the public sphere confidence was unshaken, as expressed in a letter of April 25, 1862 to the editor of the *Herald*: "In your remarks on the administration of the Navy department in today's Herald you have inadvertently done the Secretary of the Navy great injustice relative to the construction of the *Monitor*. A more prompt and spirited action is probably not on record in a similar case."⁸

Ericsson's Folly?

The launch of the *Monitor* was an auspicious occasion that came 97 days after her keel was laid and 101 days after the contract was let. Throngs of

13. The Monitor

Launch of the *Monitor* on January 30, 1862, at Greenpoint, Long Island. The turret shown here was, however, not yet installed (*Harper's Weekly*, 1862).

people and reporters had gathered at the Green Point wharf. All were eager to witness what would happen. Naval experts had calculated that the *Monitor* would not float but sink or capsize. Was it therefore true that she could make one grand plunge and than disappear in the East River as predicted by some newspapers?

John Ericsson and his first crewmember, Samuel Dana Greene, a young enthusiastic volunteer, stood on her deck to prove that the craft would not dive to the bottom.[9] Ten minutes before ten o'clock on the morning of January 30, 1862, at high tide the *Monitor* slid slowly down the ways, stern first into the waters. Initially there was total silence and apprehension among the spectators. The watching crowd cheered as she rose buoyantly and floated in triumph, her deck barely eighteen inches above the water. Now a clapping crowd turned its attention to her designer, standing proudly on board.

The reaction to the successful launch was swift but mixed. The vessel was still considered unseaworthy but promising as a floating battery and the press came up with nicknames such as "Ericsson's Folly" and "Cheesebox on a Raft." The reporters roundly abused her constructor, denouncing Ericsson for wasting the resources of a country engaged in a struggle for its existence.[10]

She was far from being ready even though only seven days remained before her scheduled completion date. Mechanics continued to work on the interior and machinery after the launch. Trial runs were done to identify and repair any deficiencies. This proved to be very important since engine problems occurred. The first test run came on February 19 with a disappointing result because the top speed was only three and a half knots due to improper setting of engine valves.

The following week when she was put in commission and turned over to the government at the Brooklyn Navy Yard new problems were discovered, this time with her steering gear. The *Monitor* could not be controlled and rammed into the riverside near New York Gas Works, so she had to be towed back to her dock. There the Navy wanted to pull her into a dry dock and install a new rudder, but Ericsson did not agree and said: "Put in a new rudder? To Hell, the Monitor is mine, and I say it shall not be done. They would waste a month in doing it. I will make her steer in three days." Ericsson was indefatigable and he sent his chief draftsman, William MacCord, on a blistering winter morning to the Navy Yard and there they soon managed to correct the fault without having to dock her again.

MacCord gives the following description of what happened before:

> The result of this trial was anything but encouraging, as reported in the daily papers, one of which made it the text of a "crushing" article, wherein, under the heading of 'Ericsson's Folly,' the battery was pronounced an ignominious failure, which could neither be propelled nor steered. The captain was called an incapable schemer, and a stern reproof was given for the sin of thus wasting the country's resources. No words too harsh, no denunciations too severe, for the zeal of this fiery crusader.[11]

Finally the guns were mounted on March 4; on the final trial run, when they were tested, it was discovered that the 11-inch Dahlgrens bounced too far back against the wall of the tower and injured a seaman. The problem was inadequate setting of the recoil stopper. The recoil mechanism was another innovation that Ericsson had introduced as an improvement over the old rope lashings for taking up the rebound of the guns. It was found that somebody had forgotten to screw down the friction gear. Luckily the problem was easily amended and the *Monitor* was nearing completion.

At this time another spy from Norfolk managed to reach Washington and went to the Navy Department, reporting that the *Merrimack* was nearly finished. Now the race to complete the *Monitor* became urgent and Fox wired to Ericsson: "I congratulate you and trust she will be a success. Hurry her for the sea, as the *Merrimack* is nearly ready at Norfolk and we wish to send her there."[12]

The Crew

Commissioning of the *Monitor* started on the 25th of February. The young Samuel Dana Greene, just out of the naval academy in Annapolis, had been the first to sign up for duty and became executive officer. Lieutenant John Lorimer Worden was selected for the post as commander by Joseph Smith. Shortly before he had been released from an Alabama prison as the first official prisoner of war and was eagerly waiting for assignment. Worden had been first officer, but never commanded a ship himself, let alone a mysterious vessel like the *Monitor*. When he heard about the promising ironclad of the North he immediately became interested by the challenge to serve and was appointed to take command. He followed the final period of construction of his vessel at the Continental Ironworks and became impressed by what he saw, thinking that she would not offer a target at all. When nearly finished he wrote to Joseph Smith: "I am induced to believe she may prove a success. At all events, I am quite willing to be an agent in testing her capabilities."

Louis Stodder, who had been with the *Monitor* during her construction, was appointed master. Among the officers was also a landlubber, William Frederick Keeler, a successful forty-year-old businessman from Illinois who could have spent the war at home. Instead, at the first call he joined the Navy and was appointed acting paymaster. Stationed at Brooklyn, he volunteered for the *Monitor* as her supply officer and stayed on after she was commissioned.

Alban C. Stimers, the engineering inspector of the Navy who had followed the process of construction, also remained on board and since he had actively participated installing the engines at Ericsson's request, he became a volunteer chief engineer. This proved to be a definitive advantage; he was a practical man and nobody like him had the experience with all the new machinery and strange gadgets on board. Ironically, Stimers previously served on the old USS *Merrimack* before she was rebuilt as the CSS *Virginia*. As first assistant engineer during construction, Isaac Newton was selected as chief engineer. He certainly was a man whose name must have inspired confidence and he performed well during the time he served on board.

So hazardous, according to general opinion, was duty in this strange craft that the department did not attempt to furnish a complement by ordering officers and men, but allowed John Worden to call volunteers. The crew therefore was composed of volunteers selected from the stationary receiving ships *North Carolina* and *Sabine* at anchor in New York Harbor. As the newly chosen crew walked down the gangway onto the flat iron deck they saw a strange-looking craft which floated barely eighteen inches above the riverbed

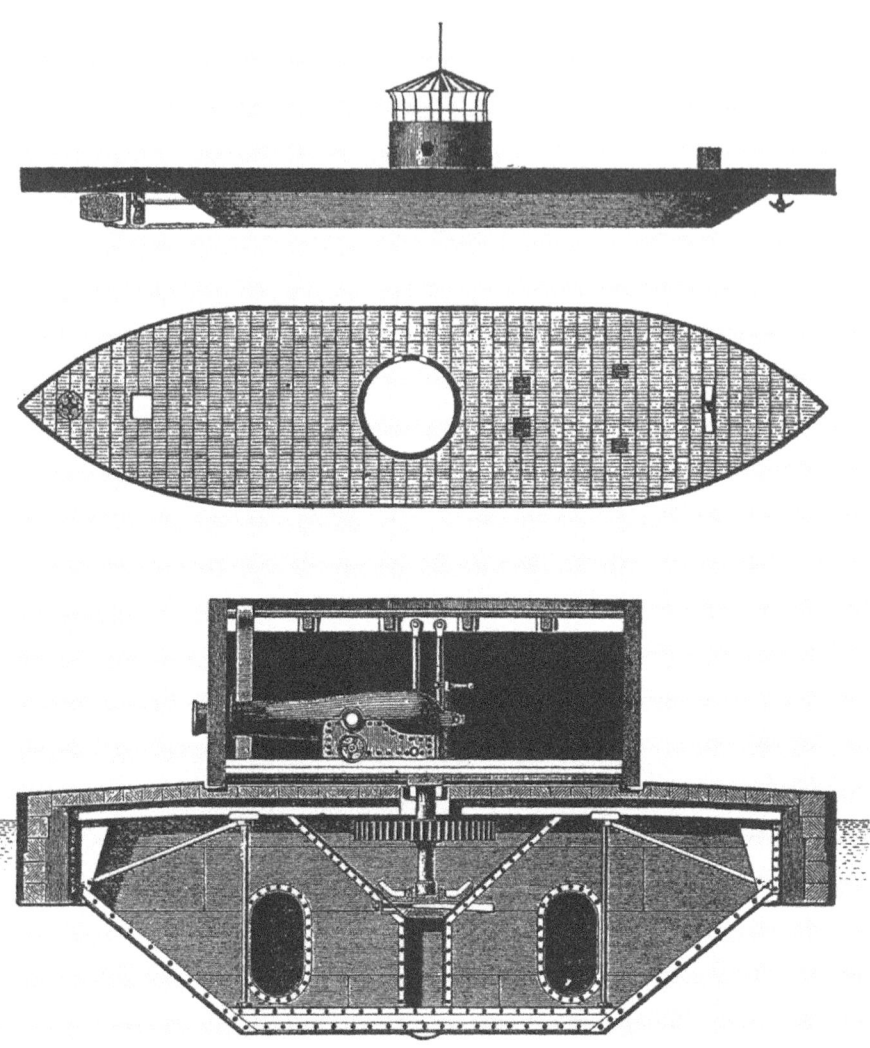

The *Monitor*, designed by John Ericsson and built 1861–1862 (*Contributions to the Centennial Exhibition*, New York, 1876).

and when leaning over board they easily put their hands into the water. All that they could see was a flat deck with a turret in the middle and a little wart of a pilothouse at the bow and a smokestack near the stern.[13]

Technical Marvel

When finally tested in the East River she attained 6½ knots. Commissioned at the Brooklyn Navy Yard, the *Monitor* at last became a ship of the United States Navy. She was a small, flat raft with a length of 179 feet, a beam of 42 feet and a tonnage of 776, only 18 inches of freeboard and 11 feet depth.

At first glance her modest appearance was not that of a warship and to the public she was not frightening. It was said that the *Monitor*, according to different sources, incorporated 40 to 250 potentially patentable innovations. Nothing was visible of all the latest technical marvels under the flat deck, but in reality the *Monitor* was nothing less than the most revolutionary warship of the nineteenth century. This vessel — with an ironplated upper hull, driven by a screw propeller, carrying a revolving turret with two huge guns, equipped with a new forced-air ventilation and blower system — set the standard for battle ships that dominated naval warfare for the next eighty years. Even compared to famous vessels still afloat such as the *Constitution,* today the *Monitor* undoubtedly is the most remarkable warship in American history.[14, 15]

These were some of the novelties: at the bow an enclosed anchor well, behind it the pilothouse, a squat rectangular structure of wrought iron-bars, rising nearly four feet above the deck and barred windows with 1-inch slits on all sides, just big enough to hold the wheel and three men who had access by a ladder from the berth deck. This was the command center from which the captain had to navigate, operate the engines and give orders to the gunners in the turret. Steering was done by a wheel connected by chains to the rudder. Communication with the engineers in charge of the steam engines and blowers was by way of signal bells, and through a speaking tube orders could be given to the gunners in the turret.

Amidships the gun-turret, twenty feet wide inside and rising nine feet above the deck, was built of eight layers of one-inch iron plates and the roof protected by railroad iron. It revolved around a big central spindle attached to a bulkhead below, dividing the living quarters up front from the kitchen and engine room abaft. On this spindle the turret could be turned in any direction and could make 2.5 revolutions a minute. It carried two 11-inch Dahlgren guns, throwing 168 pound shots. The guns were fired through portholes in the iron wall. They had to be loaded from the front end and while this was going on, the portholes could be closed by heavy iron shutters. Aft, behind the turret, was a smokestack and two ventilation shafts that could be collapsed in time of action.

In the rear below deck was the engine room. Here were two fire-tube boilers that supplied steam to the engine. The boilers were fed by forced air, sucked down by belt-driven fan-blowers from air intakes behind the turret. The main "vibrating lever" engines generated 320 horsepower, sufficient to produce nine knots under full steam, instead of the required eight. They had 3-foot double-pistons in one cylinder and were directly connected to the shaft which extended through the rear end of the hull to a four-bladed propeller.

These vital parts plus the rudder were protected by an overhanging upper deck so that even under gunfire or ramming, the ship's navigation would not be endangered.

The vessel was equipped with independent auxiliary donkey engines for blowers, pumps and rotation of the turret. Ericsson anticipated possible problems with water seeping in from deck-level vents and other openings. Therefore he added a channel in the keel sloping back to a container in the stern connected with bilge pumps. In order to make the ship livable for its crew Ericsson had spent much time designing special features such as a ventilation and heating system and underwater toilets. The enlisted men were accommodated in hammocks in a common room while the officers had their own eight-by-six-foot cabins built around a central wardroom and the captain's separate stateroom. These were all below the water line and without windows, but waterproof glass skylights in the roof could be opened and shut and provided illumination in the daytime; at night light came from oil-lamps hanging from the roof.

The rooms were luxuriously appointed with woodwork of polished black walnut and brass railings. Blowers that ventilated the berthing spaces brought 7,000 cubic feet of fresh air per minute into the lower hull, forcing out the old, heated foul air. Radiators for heating could be supplied with hot water from the boilers. In order to get rid of excrement and waste Ericsson had designed an ingenious rubbish gun operated by a force pump. It was a wide-bore tube with two locks, an upper, inside the vessel, and a lower in the sea. When in use the upper was opened, waste and excrement dropped into it, then it was shut and the lower outlet opened while the pump drove the contents out. This system to evacuate body waste was the same as that used in World War II–era submarines.[16]

Strange Sights

No warship in history had to face such a frenzy of criticism and ridicule as the *Monitor*. To eyes accustomed to towering square-riggers and formidable bulwarks with guns sticking out from the sides, this "flatiron" must have bordered on the ludicrous. She was nothing more than what President Lincoln called her: a *raft*. You couldn't tell the bow from the stern! Yes, she was a strange vessel, the design was eccentric, flat as a board barely above the waterline, on deck no masts, no sails, only a round tower. She appeared more like a huge Mississippi flat-boat with its raftlike deck. To a viewer of today, used to the utilitarian looks of the modern navy, the long, narrow body with a single tower-like superstructure looks like a submarine. But we have to realize that in mid-nineteenth century the concept of a man-of-war was totally different.

The executive officer of the *Patrick Henry*, Lieutenant James H. Rochelle, spoke for most of the Confederates when he wrote: "Such a craft as the eyes of a seaman never looked upon before ... an immense shingle floating in the water, with a gigantic cheese-box rising from its center; no sails, no wheels, no smokestack, no guns. What could it be?"[17]

The public both in the North and South made fun of the *Monitor* and many names were given to her such as *Cheesebox* or *Hatbox on a Raft*. Others had called her a *Tin Can on a Shingle*. Even the outspoken advocate for modern ironclads, the Union Admiral John Dahlgren, was shocked and disappointed when he first looked at her. He thought she was "a mere speck, like a hat on the surface." Today we probably would have called her a *Can-on-a-surfboard*.

Outwardly the *Monitor* appeared insignificant compared with the frightening sight of the Confederate ironclad *Virginia*. But also this new floating iron-plated gun platform did not escape ridicule. By some she was called a *submerged crocodile* or *a barn gone adrift*.

14

The Right Track

Time is everything; five minutes make the difference between victory and defeat.
— Horatio Nelson, (attributed), 1803

The early ironclads were unseaworthy monsters. The French armored steam batteries engaged in the Crimean War were slow, hard to steer, ill-ventilated and had to be towed to the Black Sea.[1] The much more advanced new American ironclad warships also still had their problems at sea either due to water leaks in the *Monitor* or engine trouble in the heavy *Virginia*.

Treacherous Passage

Because of threatening weather conditions it was decided to guide the precious *Monitor* in a convoy to Hampton Roads. On March 6, 1862, at eleven a.m. they left New York Harbor in tow by the tug-boat *Seth Low* and escorted by two gunboats, the *Currituck* and *Sachem*. Captain Worden's sailing orders were: "When the weather admits you will proceed to Hampton Roads and on your arrival report to the senior naval officer there. Wishing you a safe and successful passage."

As a secret mission for the *Monitor*, Gideon Welles, the secretary of the Navy, had in mind to send her to Virginia, up the Elizabeth River to Gosport and to place her opposite the dry dock with her guns destroying the *Merrimack*.[2] Just after the *Monitor* left New York, a tugboat was sent in chase of her with new orders to change her mission to protect Washington, but in vain. Similar orders were also telegraphed to the commander of the fleet in Virginia, Captain Marston at Hampton Roads.

The first day in the Atlantic was calm, the seas smooth and the *Monitor* moved undisturbed until the next day. When approaching the Capes of Delaware she was hit by a winter storm. The water swept white over her, breaking through the viewing slits of the pilothouse so that the helmsman was knocked from the wheel. The difficulties that followed had nothing to

14. The Right Track

do with the vessel's stability, as predicted by the Ironclad Board. The two gunboats convoying her rolled so violently that the muzzles of their guns dipped into the sea, whereas a glass inkstand on the table in the captain's quarters on board the *Monitor* was found to have remained stationary throughout the trip.

The deck hatches soon began leaking and water came down under the turret pouring "like a waterfall," so the sailors on berth deck had to leave their hammocks. Ericsson had intended that the turret resting on its bronze base-ring provided its own watertight seal. But someone in the shipyard had decided to jack up the turret and stuff oakum — bits of rope — under it in the groove in which it turns. As the seas swept the ship and battered the turret, the tarred hemp was washed away so that water leaked through the opening and at the bow through the hawse pipe.

At night a full scale storm blew and now water broke over the six-foot smoke stacks and also entered the blower pipes which were only four feet high, loosening the leather belts of the fans so that the furnaces could not get air for combustion. One crew member wrote: "The water poured into the engine room around the smokestacks and ventilator like a miniature Niagara and it was doubtful whether we would float during the night."[3]

Without forced air the fires below the boilers began to die and the engines stopped. It became an inferno: suffocating fumes filled the engine-room and threatened to poison the firemen and machinists. Engineer Stimers, who knew best of all the technical details and weak points of the *Monitor,* since he had helped to build her from the start, took over and tried his best with the help of Isaac Newton. Despite the smoke he went below clinging to the ladder and stepped down into water halfway to his knees. After his efforts he nearly suffocated and had to be dragged up to the tower, where he collapsed but fortunately recovered in the fresh air.

The *Monitor* was taking on water at a frightful rate and the pumps that were designed to get rid of it were no longer working, being dependent on a functioning boiler. Now the crew was ordered to rig hand pumps and a bucket line to bail out the water, an activity which according to coal-heaver Roberts "diverted the members of the crew from panic." Signals of distress were flown, but the accompanying vessels did not seem to respond until finally Lieutenant Dana Greene raced up the ladder and managed to get the tugboat *Seth Low* to pull them closer to shore, where the sea was calmer. When the winds calmed down at nightfall, Stimers with his men fortunately were able to repair the damage in the engine room. Here, in safer waters they were able to restart the engines and get the blowers to run again. But the disaster was not yet over, Greene writes: "At midnight passing over a shoal, rough water was again encountered, and our troubles were renewed."[4,5]

Finally in the morning, on March 8, they weathered the storm. The gale which had endangered the *Monitor* calmed and her towing steamer moved steadily southward to calmer seas and to smiling skies. At noon they sighted Cape Charles and soon rounded it past Old Point Comfort entering the broad bosom of Chesapeake Bay.

Devastation and Panic

At night the moon was just rising over the waters but her silvery light was paled by the glare of the fire reflected in the waters. Moving slowly toward Fort Monroe the crew heard the distant booming of heavy guns, an ominous sign of battle. Was it land engagement or possibly, maybe the *Merrimack* (*Virginia*) coming out for battle? The *Monitor*, which barely escaped foundering, arrived in the nick of time but her efficiency in action had yet to be proved.

When a pilot arrived on board he told the dreadful story of the most gruesome naval defeat ever suffered by the American Navy. At first it was difficult to believe what they had been told but soon all doubts vanished as they crept into the bay and saw a ship burning in the distance. It was the mighty frigate *Congress* hit by hot shots and incendiary shells, surrendered and in flames.

The *Virginia*, winning the battle of the shipbuilding race of seven and a half months by one day, had begun the battle of Hampton Roads with a devastating result. A defeat of the entire fleet at Hampton Roads seemed inevitable the next day. The remaining *Roanoke* and *Minnesota*, steam frigates of forty guns each, the pride of the fleet, lay hard and fast aground in their efforts to escape from the attack of the *Virginia*, which had rammed and sunk the sloop *Cumberland*.

Welles, in order to prevent the threat of the *Merrimack*, contrary to his original order now expected the precious ironclad at Washington, to anchor below Alexandria and protect the Union capital. Fortunately this order never reached Worden before he arrived with the *Monitor* at the place where he was needed the most for a decisive battle.

When news of the devastation of the first day of battle at Hampton Roads reached Washington it created a sensation. Later, on March 9, a delayed telegraphic message to Washington of the previous day arrived from the commanding officer at Hampton Roads, saying: "The ironclad Ericsson Battery has arrived, and will proceed to take care of the *Merrimack* in the morning."[6, 7]

These were hopeful words which came after the first day's devastation. At this point the *Monitor* became the hope of frightened politicians. Was she a David to fight Goliath, the terrible *Merrimack* with sling and pebble?

When in the morning the *Monitor* arrived in the bay she did not inspire great hope and was described as a "tin can on a shingle," but in reality she challenged the *Virginia* in a fight that lasted for almost five hours. There was

14. The Right Track

The crew of the USS *Monitor* after the battle of Hampton Roads, 1862 (*Century Magazine*, 1894).

a constant bombardment between the two ironclads and neither was seriously damaged, but in the end the *Virginia* withdrew without harming the *Monitor* or the wooden warships. Details about the famous battle have already been well told, such as by William Davis in his *Duel Between the First Ironclads*.[8]

Finally, on Sunday night, March 9, 1862, in Washington, the telegraph clicked out a message that changed despair into exultation, and vindicated the judgment of the secretary of the Navy who had predicted that the *Monitor* would protect the Federal fleet. Now it was clear: the little *Monitor* had forced the *Virginia* to retire to Norfolk. The battle was the first between iron-armored warships that ended in a tactical draw, but the *Monitor* preserved the Federal blockade of the Norfolk area. A new age of naval warfare had dawned.

15

Happy Experience

O Captain! my Captain! our fearful trip is done,
The ship has weather'd every rack, the prize we sought is won...
—Walt Whitman, *"O Captain! My Captain!"* 1865

The battle at Hampton Roads was an important chapter of the Civil War. At the eleventh hour a chain of purely fortuitous circumstances made it possible for John Ericsson against conflicting views of experts and the public opinion to construct his extraordinary vessel and bring it to the right place in the right time. Here she had been capable of coping with the larger Confederate ironclad. Now there were high expectations for a further victories.

New Outlook

The reaction in Europe was swift. Hjalmar August Edgren, a Swedish officer and volunteer in the Union Army who had witnessed the battle, reported his experience back to Sweden. Positive reactions from international observers at the battle gave England and France second thoughts before attempting intervention on behalf of the South.[1] In London both the Lords of the Admiralty and the press expressed the opinion that wooden ships were something of the past and it would be madness to trust them to engage the little *Monitor*. The battle had changed Naval history. For the first time two steam-powered ironclads had slugged it out. Sir Winston Churchill in 1939 said about it:

> The combat of the *Merrimac* and the *Monitor* made the greatest change in sea-fighting since cannon fired by gunpowder had been mounted on ships about four hundred years before. As soon as the news reached Europe it was realized that all the war-fleets of the world were obsolete. The British Admiralty, by an intense effort, in the course of a few years reconstructed the Royal Navy so as to meet the altered conditions.
>
> But even now there are fools who build large ships to fight at sea with hardly any armour.... The *Merrimac* had made naval revolution, but the *Monitor* was a whole lap ahead of her.[2]

In Paris Napoleon III stated: "it is now settled that there is no navy in the world that can make head against ironclad vessels." Italy and Austria sent naval experts to study the design of new warships and to look at gun turrets, and in Sweden it was realized that its navy was useless.[3]

After the success of the *Monitor* Ericsson finally was acknowledged as the great inventor and patriot he was. On March 28 Congress passed a resolution of public acknowledgement to be made to John Ericsson: "For his enterprise, skill, energy, and forecast, displayed by him in the construction of his ironclad boat the *Monitor*, which under gallant and able management, came so opportune to the rescue of our fleet in Hampton Roads, and arrested the work of destruction."

In New York, all of a sudden Ericsson became the hero of the nation. From the State Legislature he received an acknowledgement of thanks, bands serenaded and gifts from grateful citizens and societies were given, poets praised his fame in verse and even cigars were named after him. Castle Garden was temporarily called *Monitor Garden*. All this excessive praise made Ericsson happy but he did not show overjoy or astonishment at the tremendous achievement of the little *Monitor* because that was what he had expected of her.

Only One Monitor

After the battle, the injured commander of the *Monitor,* John Worden, was immediately brought to Washington to recuperate at a friend's house.

When President Lincoln at a cabinet meeting was told that the wounded Captain Worden was in the city he instantly rose and took his hat, saying, "Excuse me gentlemen, I must see this fellow." He went immediately to visit the hero and said: "I am honored in being able to thank you personally for what you did with the *Monitor* at such a cost to yourself."

During the conversation Worden told the president that while he found that the *Monitor* was an excellent shot-proof attack weapon, he had come to realize that she was vulnerable to another form of attack, namely boarding. The attackers could jump on board, wedge the turret and stop it from turning and create chaos by tossing a few hand-grenades into the air-intakes, smoke-stack and the turret.

After visiting Worden, President Lincoln gave the following order to Secretary Welles: "I have just seen Lieut. Worden, who says the *Monitor* could be boarded and captured very easily—first, after boarding, by wedging the turret, so that it would not turn, and then by pouring water in her & drowning her machinery. He is decidedly of the opinion she should not go skylarking up to Norfolk."[4]

Welles thereupon sent a telegram to the naval commander at Hampton

Roads about what possible dangers the *Monitor* could face and not to engage the *Virginia* in battle. However, the officers and crew soon became impatient and wrote a petition to the president to be allowed to find the *Virginia* and destroy her, but they received the reply: "We have only one *Monitor* and cannot risk her."[5]

During the next few weeks, in anticipation of new attacks the two ironclads were doing repairs. The *Virginia* was badly damaged and the day after the battle she was put into dry dock. Her captain, Franklin Buchanan, was also severely wounded and had to be replaced.

On the *Monitor*, engineer Alban Stimers remodeled the pilot-house. He altered the sides, instead of being perpendicular he made them slanting so that, greased with tallow, shots and shells would glance off. In order to prevent the danger of being boarded, a variety of small arms were brought aboard, including hand grenades, rifles, and bayonets. With these weapons it was hoped to fight off possible attackers.

In April the crewmembers of the *Monitor* again became very disappointed and restless when they were not allowed back into action. They expressed their feelings to Captain Worden, whom they admired: "We are waiting very patiently to engage our Antagonist if we could only get a chance to do so. The last time she came out we all thought we would have the Pleasure of sinking her, But we all got disappointed, for we did not fire one shot, and the Norfolk papers says we are cowards in the Monitor — and all we want is a change."[6]

John Ericsson was simply enraged by her inactivity after the battle. He himself represented activity and therefore passivity was absolutely incomprehensible to him. Like a hot and angry bee who never rests and wonders how others can, he always saw in the end of one task only the beginning of another. He had built his ship to fight and never liked excessive caution.[7]

Lincoln Visits the Monitor

After the historic battle the *Monitor* became a big attraction to military leaders, congressmen and the press, who streamed down to Virginia for a visit. A U.S. Navy Admiral who saw her there was impressed and exultantly wrote: "She exhibited in a singular manner the old Norse element of the American navy, Ericsson (Swedish: *son of Eric*) built her, Dahlgren (*branch of a valley*) armed her.... How the ancient skalds would have struck their wild harps in hearing such names in heroic runes!" Added to that was the name of the Swedish-blooded Yankee from Massachusetts, Gustavus Vasa Fox, whose insistence in the face of doubters gave Ericsson his chance to launch an idea that junked the wooden navies of the world."[8]

It was of course expected that John Ericsson would show up for a visit, particularly since G.V. Fox suggested that he come south to inspect and discuss some shortcomings of machinery with Stimers and Newton, the engineers who now had practical experience of his vessel. Ericsson refused, writing to Stimers: "What can I do, you all know your business so well that my presence is useless. Time will tell that nothing has been lost by me not visiting the *Monitor* as you suggested."

Ericsson stayed at his drawing board, thinking that new designs were more important than wasting time traveling. He argued that he already had ideas far in advance of the current design, underestimating the importance of practical experience.[9]

In reality Ericsson, however, never lost interest in his ship and he remained in contact with the Navy Department through Rear Admiral Francis H. Gregory, who had been selected to supervise the construction of monitors. There are several letters which confirm his active participation. In one of these Gregory wrote: "I have to acknowledge your letter of the 8" inst.— and thank you for your judicious suggestions — tending to the comfort of the crew and safety of the Monitor which I shall endeavor to have adopted."[10]

On May 6 when moored at Fort Monroe, the *Monitor* had a surprise visitor: President Lincoln, who the day before had arrived together with two members of his cabinet, Edwin Stanton and Salmon Chase, on board the U.S. revenue cutter *Miami*. The president was on a six day inspection to the Chesapeake Bay to speed up the slow pace of the Peninsula Campaign. He was disappointed with McClellan's progress and wanted to see some action.

The mood on board the *Monitor* was joyful and patriotic. The president, impressed by the little ship and its brave crew was visibly moved, as one account stated, "His lip was trembling and his gaunt form shaking."

Was not this the little vessel the navy brass had ridiculed against his advice? Then followed a much appreciated tour of the vessel by someone "well versed in its construction and mechanics." As the president left, the crew gave a rousing three cheers to their beloved Abe. After the presidential party left, a boatload of congressmen arrived for a tour but the visit had to be cut short because the *Virginia* reappeared at the mouth of the Elizabeth River.

The next days were characterized by a cat and mouse game. The *Virginia* without success tried to engage the *Monitor* near the Elizabeth River Channel and the Confederates were amazed by their opponent's timidity.

The president now ordered Federal ships, including the *Monitor*, to bombard the outpost of the Confederate forces, the batteries on Sewell's Point, in an effort to draw the *Virginia* out for a decisive battle. She emerged but hurried back before the *Monitor* could engage her and meet the Union fleet, now reinforced by the USS *Vanderbilt*, "that leviathan of ocean steamers," a million-dollar gift from her namesake. Despite all these operations the two ironclads never again met in battle.[11]

In July President Lincoln for the second time visited the *Monitor* when on an inspection trip to Hampton Roads.

Peninsula Campaign

The fight between the two ironclads coincided with the advance of Federal troops on Richmond, the capital of the Confederate states. The chief of military operations of the Union, General Winfield Scott, the designer of the "Anaconda Plan," had retired and was succeeded by "Little Napoleon," the young General George B. McClellan. His strategy, called the Peninsula Campaign was new. He wanted the Union forces to attack the Confederate capital of Richmond moving by sea and on land on the peninsula between the York and the James Rivers.

As McClellan wanted to move quickly something unexpected happened. He was told by the navy that as long as the Confederates' *Virginia* blocked Hampton Roads and the entry to the James River, his plan would not succeed and he therefore postponed his attack.[12]

On May 8 President Lincoln finally wanted progress and ordered a convoy of ships up the James River, disregarding the possible threat of the *Virginia*. Accordingly the new ironclad *Galena* and the gunboats *Aroostook* and *Port Royal* were sent with instructions to assist McClellan's advance on Richmond. The *Galena* was the armored ship that initially prompted Ericsson's own proposal for the *Monitor*. She had been built by Cornelius S. Bushnell and was of a special design with two-inch plates of armor on her sides, separated by an air space with iron bars. At the time some doubt was expressed that she could stand up to shore batteries, but since so much was expected of her, it was decided to give her a fair trial.

Tragic end came to the *Virginia* only a few days later. In order to defend Richmond the Confederates evacuated Norfolk, their stronghold near Hampton Roads, and the Gosport Navy Yard. The *Virginia* had been expected to steam up the James River to assist in the defense of Richmond, but now standing offshore she was a ship without a base. But even after the crew lightened her draft she could not move. Being extremely slow and not sea-worthy, an escape into the Atlantic Ocean was no realistic alternative because there she would have been exposed to the combined forces of the high seas and the Union Navy. In the end she was trapped and on May 11, when the famous ironclad could no longer be of service to the Confederacy and in order to keep her out of Yankee hands, she retreated down the Elizabeth River to Craney Island, ran aground, and was set on fire. She burned fiercely for an hour and then blew up with a huge explosion. Later, some remains of the wreck were salvaged and from the wood of her hull souvenirs were carved and sold. A couple of them were given to John Ericsson.

After the destruction of the *Virginia* the *Monitor* received orders to proceed in a convoy of ships up the Elizabeth River to Norfolk. One of these was the side-wheeler *Baltimore,* carrying President Lincoln and some of his cabinet members and officers. As they passed the *Monitor,* the president removed his stovepipe hat and bowed.[13]

Drewry's Bluff

After Confederate forces abandoned Norfolk and the *Virginia* was blown up, there was no longer any threat to advancing by water towards Richmond. Union optimism was great when the commanding officer of the Federal fleet suggested that the *Monitor* be sent up the James River to join the *Galena* and if possible, shell the city into surrender. At that time the secretary of the U.S. Navy, Gideon Welles, and other cabinet members were on a six-day trip with the *Baltimore* up the James River into Virginia, were they landed at City Point. Here white flags waived, and on shore in an optimistic spirit spectators cheered the convoy of the *Monitor,* the *Galena,* the *Port Royal,* the *Arostook* and the semi-armored gunboat *Naugatuck* when they set further up the James towards Richmond.

Threatened from both land and water, Richmond went into panic. General Robert E. Lee, however, was confident. He knew that there was one important obstacle that lay in the path of the Federal gunboats eight miles below the capital. It was Fort Darling at Drewry's (or Drury's) Bluff, also sometimes referred to as the "the Gibraltar of Virginia."[14] The bluff, rising 110 feet above the James, commanded a sharp bend in the river. It was the last outpost of defense before Richmond. Here, on the hill the Confederates, reinforced with sailors from the destroyed *Virginia,* had prepared a battery of guns that commanded a long stretch of the James River. Directly in front of the fort in the river they had effectively blocked the passage to Richmond by placing hulks of barges and crates of stones between rows of piling and finally the Rebels' scuttled the two-gun MSS *Jamestown*.

The Union convoy of five ships had been steaming slowly up the James, methodically pounding Confederate shore batteries when it finally at 6:30 on May 15 reached Drewry's Bluff. The *Galena* in the lead maneuvered so that a broadside of her guns could bear on the bluff. The *Monitor* steamed ahead but could not elevate her guns enough to fire at the high fort and retreated behind the *Galena*. Here, with the advantage of a lower angle, she continued to fire from a distance. Now from early in the morning a fierce battle started and for more than three hours the roar of shots rattled the windows in the Confederate capital.

Both sides took a beating. First the cannon of the battery fired non-damaging shots on the irresistible *Monitor* but soon changed focus and concentrated their fire on the thinly armored *Galena*, which was as vulnerable as a sitting duck. Plunging shots from the fort penetrated her armor through her deck and sides. She was badly battered, hit forty-six times with a loss of fourteen killed and ten wounded. The *Monitor* was also hit but without damage or casualties. The defenders also suffered fifteen casualties, among them seven killed and eight wounded. When the commander of the Federal squadron, John Rodgers, decided to retreat, the soldiers of Fort Darling cheered.[15]

While Welles and his party were still in Virginia he received notice that the naval attack on Richmond had been unsuccessful. Although further naval operations seemed possible, it was not supported by ground troops. An officer on the *Monitor*, Louis Stodder, who had participated in the attack on Drewry's Bluff, said, "If we had a regiment of men on shore we could have taken that fort."[16]

The second engagement of the *Monitor* in the Civil War was unsuccessful in terms of damaging the fortifications of Drewry's Bluff but at the same time, and in comparison to the other ironclad, the *Galena*, she proved to be invulnerable. When a Union nurse saw her, she remarked that she looked "like a great fish with iron scales."

The *Monitor* remained in the James River throughout McClellan's Peninsula Campaign and then returned to Hampton Roads because a new threat was looming: it was feared that the CSS *Richmond*, often called the *Merrimack II*, would soon come down the James River from Richmond, where she had been commissioned, for an attack. Paymaster William Keeler was sick of these constant rumors and said: "Some of us will die off one of these days with *Merrimac*-on-the-brain."[17] But the deep-draft *Richmond* never made it, got stuck on a sandbar and finally met the same fate as her sister, being set afire in 1865.

Up the Potomac

After participating in the unsuccessful Peninsula Campaign the *Monitor* withdrew down the James River to Hampton Roads, arriving at Newport News on August 30. Here the crew spent the rest of the summer.

When waiting for further action some deficiencies detected during the previous battles were to be taken care of. Also, marine fouling of the bottom had grown so thick that it reduced her speed to half. Now orders came to proceed to Washington for an overhaul, therefore the *Monitor* was towed up the Potomac and arrived at the Navy Yard on the 3rd of October 1862.

The Navy Department consulted Ericsson for advice on improvements and the mode of removal from the water in order to make repairs. She was successfully docked on October 13 and for nearly six weeks the *Monitor* was to remain at the capital, during which time much needed changes were made. Davits and cranes were added to hold boats, the old smokestacks were replaced with new telescoping ones, and the shot marks covered with iron patches and markings of their origin. The guns were engraved with the text "MONITOR & MERRIMAC WORDEN" on one and "MONITOR & MERRIMAC ERICSSON" on the other.[18]

Welles and Lincoln made frequent trips to the Navy Yard to see the *Monitor* prepared for further action and to inspect Dahlgren's new big 12-inch guns for Ericsson's latest improved monitors, now under construction in New York.

The first of these was the *Passaic*, which was rushed to be finished to go to Charleston in November 1862 but broke down during her voyage from New York and had to be towed to Washington for boiler repair. Ericsson was asked to send a special workforce of 30 boiler-makers to the Navy Yard. While in the Potomac at Washington, the *Passaic* was inspected by high government officials including President Lincoln.

As fast as one breakdown was patched up, another showed itself... Ericsson "boys" completed their work in three weeks and the *Passaic* and her elder sister, the original *Monitor*, which had undergone repairs, left Washington together, each in tow of a wooden steamer, bound for Hampton Roads. Here at the suggestion of paymaster Keeler, while at anchor, an iron "breastwork" to go around the top of the turret was added to protect those standing on it.

16

The Monitor Boys

Flaunt o sea your separate flags of nations!
A pennant universal, subtly waving all time, o'er all brave sailors.
—Walt Whitman, "Song for All Seas, All Ships," 1865

Already during her construction the new Union ironclad, originally called the *Ericsson Battery*, attracted much attention and there were many enterprising young men who responded enthusiastically and wanted to sign up for service on board. In the end there were many more volunteers than were required.

She Meant Business

When the *Monitor* left New York she had a crew of sixty-three, seven officers and fifty-six seamen. Crewmembers of the later famous *Monitor* developed a bond to each other during the ten months they stayed together and referred to themselves as Monitor Boys. The young sailors were three-year volunteers who wanted to serve their country. They came from the cramped quarters of receiving vessels in New York Harbor. These usually were old sailing warships stripped of their guns, masts and sails and located in navy yards and by many regarded as a "floating hell." When going to the *Monitor* they eagerly expected some excitement serving on the latest warship of the navy.

The crew of Union vessels were referred to as Blue Jackets because of their dress code. On assignment they were issued blue woolen frocks and trousers. One sailor recalled: "I was conducted to the [receiving ship's] outfitting room where I was supplied with a uniform — two blue flannel shirts, socks, etc. in a clothes bag, a hammock with hair mattress and a pair of blankets."

The men had a mixed background; many were born in northern Europe, including Ireland and Scandinavia. This recruitment was the result of the navy's efforts to expand its sphere since the number of native seamen was very limited. More and more inexperienced men, many of them immigrants, had to be commissioned and foreign-born seamen constituted at one time during the war one fourth of enlisted Union navy personnel.[1] The *Monitor* in particular attracted Swedes because of her designer.

One of the crew was a sailor who had just arrived from Bombay. With the far-east route on hold he was tired of being ashore and was looking for action. With a friend he decided to volunteer for Ericsson's *Monitor* "about which something had been whispered among the men." After having seen her, he gave the following description: "She was a little bit the strangest craft I had ever seen, nothing but a few inches of deck above the water line, her big round tower in the center, and the pilothouse at the end.... We had confidence in her though, from the start, for the little ship looked somehow like she meant business, and it didn't take us long to learn the ropes."[2]

In addition to enlisted crew the top officers also had the privilege to hire private servants, usually colored boys, called "contrabands" because they had been Confederate "property" and therefore were liable to confiscation as an act of war. Since September 1861 the secretary of the navy (not the army) ruled that escaped slaves could be enlisted, but at "no higher rating than 'boys.'" As such they were treated as second-class sailors. Most of the African Americans served as cooks or stewards. On board the *Monitor* there was a "first class boy" by the name of Thomas Carroll who became very popular.[3] When Paymaster Keeler was looking for a manservant to tend to his needs he wrote: "I have spent a portion of two or three days in hunting up a contraband & finally found a good looking young darky that came to me well recommended."[4]

On Wednesday, March 5, 1862, when the *Monitor* was supposed to leave Brooklyn, a severe storm prevented her departure. Waiting out the weather, the officer of the watch penned in the log: "John Aitkins deserted and took with him the ship's cat and left for parts unknown."[5]

The poor boy probably was frightened by the enclosed atmosphere below deck and never came back with the pet, but later another ship's cat again had become part of the crew when the *Monitor* foundered off Cape Hatteras.

Captain Worden was proud of his crew and declared: "A better one no naval commander ever had the honor to command." Before sailing, he fully explained the dangers of a sea passage, with the absolute certainty of a battle to follow.

In the Iron Pot

Accommodation on the *Monitor* was all below the water line on the berth deck. The living quarters were in front of the bulkhead that divided the vessel in two halves with engine and boiler rooms aft. As a relic from the age of sail, officers almost never associated with sailors, for they considered "the men" as belonging to a lower class. It was an insult to refer to an officer as a "sailor." As a result, officers accorded themselves better food, better uniforms and better quarters than they granted enlisted men.[6] The seven commissioned officers selected by the Ironclad Board were given private cabins and a handsomely fitted ward room near the bow while the crew had to hang their hammocks in a big common room behind the ward room with storage lockers on the side.

Life below decks was in a totally enclosed artificial environment. Ericsson had tried hard to make it as bearable as possible and designed the interior with skill. There were no windows on the nicely decorated iron walls, but skylights of thick glass in iron frames allowed light to enter during the day. In rough sea they were awash with water and during action had to be covered with iron plates from outside. The *Monitor* had a ventilation system that was powered by a donkey engine and supplied fresh air through openings in the floor to cabins and boilers. Despite Ericsson's intricate ventilation system one crew member certified: "Probably no ship was ever devised which was so uncomfortable for her crew" and "the worst craft for a man to live aboard that ever floated upon water."

Hot Ship and Rubbish Gun

During most of the summer of 1862 the *Monitor* was anchored at Harrison's Landing, the headquarters of the Army of the Potomac. There, she became a great public attraction. But everybody on board was very disappointed in the uncomfortable and hot ship.

The iron ship magnified surrounding temperature, making it hotter than outside during the day and cooler during the night. During the summer months there obviously was a problem with the heat inside and when a blower belt broke, the temperature rose to 150 in the galley and 132 Fahrenheit on the berth deck, therefore members of the crew slept on deck while in the James River, although even that was not always possible due to enemy fire. Paymaster William Keeler described the situation, "We lay broiling in our iron box, or cage as it has now become, out of humor with ourselves & the world generally."[7] In winter the air was chilled by the ocean, although steam heaters had been installed in the wardroom. The problem of a hot environment, however, was nothing specific to the *Monitor* and also men of the Confederate ironclads suffered enormously from heat, cold and sickness. Their accommodation was located on a berth deck and among guns and they did not have the Ericsson ventilation system.[8]

As we have seen, in addition to forced ventilation, Ericsson also had installed a "rubbish-gun," for dealing with waste and excrement. On the *Monitor's* first voyage, Dr. Daniel Logue, the ship's surgeon, tried to use it when he felt the urge to go to the toilet. He had a vague idea that it involved the activation of levers for its forced evacuation into the sea. Unfortunately he omitted an essential part of the procedure and "found himself suddenly at the end of a column of water rushing up from the depth of the ocean and pouring into the ship." When Dr. Logue was found lying in a big fountain of water and his own excrement, engineer Isaac Newton had to be called to close the lower port of the tube. Then he lectured the crew on how to operate the gun.[9]

The only recreation was to be found on deck, when the weather allowed. One photo of the *Monitor* shows members of the crew outside on deck covered in smoke near a stove with pots and pans. Here sailors were cooking their own food next to the turret. The crew was divided into messes, and the men in each were issued rations and were responsible for preparing their own meals. In the *Monitor* these rules also applied to the limited space and small kitchen below deck.[10]

Author Nathaniel Hawthorne, who visited the *Monitor* after the battle of Hampton Roads, was frightened by what he saw and called her "the strangest-looking craft I ever saw, a giant rat-trap.... There is no remoteness of life and thought, hermetically sealed seclusion, except, possibly, that of the grave, into which the disturbing influences of war do not penetrate." He had a romantic view of things and was disappointed with the modern fighting environment as it had developed: "How can an admiral condescend to go to sea in an iron pot? ... All the pomp and splendor of naval warfare are gone.... Henceforth there must come up a race of engine-men and smoke-blackened cannoneers who will hammer away at their enemies under the direction of a single pair of eyes."[11]

Problems

Following the struggle to survive the fearful seas and after the stressful engagement against the big *Virginia*, the crew initially was happy to settle down for a while to take it easy. After the battle the military leaders of the North decided that they did not want to expose their precious ironclad to dangerous engagement. The Monitor Boys, however, wanted to proceed to Norfolk for a final and decisive victory. Ericsson was very disappointed that the *Monitor* had not done her utmost during the engagement and by her subsequent inactivity he was simply enraged.[12]

But for some time there was no opportunity to show the *Monitor*'s superior ability to fight and soon life on board became monotonous and trying. Like a caged eagle the crew passed many a weary week of dull monotony without a chance for a decisive battle. Keeler expressed the frustration of the crew over the order not to engage the *Virginia* in Hampton Roads, "I believe the Department is going to build a big case to put us in for fear of harm coming to us."[13]

Another source of worry was the frequent change of command after the loss of their beloved captain, John Worden. During her short service of ten months the *Monitor* had no fewer than five different commanders. Immediately after the historical battle Lieutenant Samuel Dana Greene initially took command and hoped to continue in that position. In a letter to his mother he proudly wrote: "The fight was over, & we were victorious. My men & myself were black with smoke and powder. All my underclothes were perfectly black with smoke, and my person in the same condition. As we ran alongside the *Minnesota,* Secretary Fox hailed us, & told us we had fought the greatest naval battle on record, and behaved as gallant as men could. He saw the whole fight.

"I felt proud and happy then, Mother, and felt fully repaid for all I had suffered.... I was Captn. & first lieut. and had not a soul to help me."[14]

Despite the words of praise Fox replaced Greene, who was sad and disappointed, but he was only 22 years old and before coming to the *Monitor* he had never served in a higher position than as midshipman. After the battle he was criticized for not continuing the battle with the *Virginia* but he faithfully stayed on until the end when the *Monitor* foundered at Cape Hatteras.

The next man temporarily in command was first Lieutenant Tom Selfridge, a survivor of the *Cumberland*'s crew. Not much later Lieutenant William N. Jeffers, a short fat ordnance specialist, was selected as commander. Jeffers was not at all popular and according to William Keeler he lacked "that noble kindness of heart and quiet unassuming manner to both officers and men which endeared Captain Worden to all on board." He constantly criticized the ship's construction and was of the opinion that "for general purposes wooden ships ... have not yet been superseded."

On April 24, 1862, while near Fort Monroe the disappointed ship's crew sent a letter to their former commander, whom they wanted back: "To our Dear and Honored Captain. These few lines is from your own Crew of the *Monitor* with their Kindest Love to there Honored Captain, Hoping to God that they will have the pleasure of Welcoming you Back to us Soon, for we are all ready able and willing to meet Death or anything else, only give us back our captain again. Dear captain. we have your Pilot-house fixed and all ready for you when you get well again, and we all sincerely hope that soon we will have the pleasure of welcoming you back.... Since you left us we have had no pleasure on Board of the Monitor. We remain until Death your Affectionate Crew, The Monitor Boys."[15]

Fortunately in August, the *Monitor* got rid of the much disliked Jeffers, who was replaced by Commander Thomas Stevens, a capable and experienced officer who gained the approval of his men. Finally the command was turned over to Commander John P. Bankhead, a forty-one year old South Carolinian who had remained loyal to the Union.

Big Attraction

After the historic battle the *Monitor* and her crew became the center of attraction for visitors of all kinds, from the president, congressmen, and newspaper reporters to family members and friends. When moored in Hampton Roads, in the James River or at Fort Monroe people made every effort to see the little monster. As we have seen, President Lincoln came twice, in May and July of 1862, and had much praise for the ship and the Monitor Boys.

In July a photographer, James Gibson, arrived from New York to take a number of stereographic pictures of the ironclad and her crew. Gibson was part of a team employed by Matthew Brady, the pioneer of U.S. photography, who organized a series of famous photographs of the Civil War. Some pictures show officers lined up before the turret and others were taken to demonstrate dents of gun-shots from the battle. *Century* magazine and *Harper's Weekly* had a series of engraved pictures of the *Monitor* and her crew.

The summer months became very boring. The monotonous routine at sea started at 5:30 A.M., when petty officers rousted the crew from their hammocks. The ship was swept, bright metalwork polished and clothes scrubbed. Later during the day the sailors were kept busy standing watch, and drilling at the cannon and the firemen had to serve the engines.

Happy Repairs

The happiest day for the Monitor Boys came when on September 30, 1862, their ship was ordered up the Potomac to the Washington Navy Yard for extensive repairs. Now furloughs were granted to many men and those remaining enjoyed the change of routine, better food and the company of visitors, particularly women.

When out of the dry-dock and again floating in the waters, on November 5, a notice in the newspapers stated that the public was allowed to enter the navy yard to visit the ship. Now the *Monitor* and her boys became a big attraction for many visitors and on the day it was announced that the ship was open to visitors, carriages lined the wharves and her deck was jammed for hours. Keeler wrote: "They rushed in by thousands. Our decks were covered and our wardroom filled with ladies and on going into my stateroom I found a party of the 'dear delightful creatures' making their toilet before my glass, using combs and brushes." Understandably the boys were particularly interested in these visitors. "We couldn't go to any part of the vessel without coming in contact with petticoats. There appeared to be a general turn-out of the sex in the city, there were women with children and women without children and an extensive display of lower extremities was made going up and down our steep ladders."

As the day was over, the men discovered that the visitors had taken souvenirs. "When we came up to clean that night," wrote master Stodder, "there was not a key, doorknob, escutcheon — there wasn't a thing that hadn't been carried away."[16]

The recently published letters by the *Monitor*'s twenty-five year old first-class fireman, George Spencer Geer, to his wife Martha are moving documents of life on board the *Monitor*. Geer enlisted from New York City less with the ambition to save the Union than to earn money for his family, but he soon became proud of his choice and was an ambitious crewmember. On June 26, 1862 he wrote: "You should feel very proud to think your Husband is not a Coward at home, but is fighting for a country for his Wife and Children. And at the same time be thankful that I am not in some of these old Wooden tubs.

When at the Washington Navy Yard in November for repairs, he wrote, "They are fixing the Monitor up much bettor than she was before. They will make a perfect little Pallace of her. The workmen work nights and Sundays. I can hear them hammering away as I am writing. They have named her Guns Worden and Ericsson, and have the names engraved on them in very large lettors."[17]

17

Tragic End

Waves roll ashen gray.
"He's gone down,
you can't see him any more, captain!"
Is that so?
The sea roars, the storm whistles.
— Carl Sandburg, *"The Way of the World"*

After the enjoyable time in Washington and before departing from Fort Monroe on their final voyage south, the Monitor Boys tried to have a nice Christmas celebration. Those who could afford it, that is to say the officers, had a feast of turkey, fish, oysters, a selection of meats, apples, figs, plums, jellies and wines with much of it having been sent from the men's homes. Sailors and firemen like George Geer had a more frugal feast, but: "We hade every thing to make a splendid Dinner in your hands, but our Saylor Cook made very bad work cooking to suit me, but these poor devils that never had as good before thought every thing splendid."[1]

Apocalyptic Voyage

The crew was anxiously waiting for new orders where to go next. They had high hopes for new action and did not expect tragedy, but now the center of naval confrontation was farther south and that could be dangerous because it meant entering the open sea. Their ship was able to navigate safely on rivers and bays, but as experience had shown, in the ocean she was at the mercy of rough weather.

They had just started to celebrate a nice Christmas with letters from home when orders were received to proceed to Beaufort, North Carolina, to assist in blockade operations.

Since it was already known that their vessel had problems in high seas it was a surprising order at the worst time of the year down the most dangerous waters of North America. The coast of North Carolina at Cape Hatteras is the center of the Atlantic's worst weather. Since ancient times angry storms and currents had been driving ships to their doom and dotting the sandcoast with wrecks.

Captain John Worden with the new larger monitor, the *Passaic,* had just arrived from the Washington Navy Yard to join the convoy, barely catching the last opportunity he would ever have to see his old ship. Bad weather delayed the departure until December 29 at 2:30 P.M. when they finally shipped anchor and got under way. They sailed with a crew of sixty-five under the command of her fifth skipper, Captain John P. Bankhead. Now on a smooth sea a little convoy of four vessels left Fort Monroe: the *Monitor* and the *Passaic* in convoy with the steamers *Rhode Island* and the *State of Georgia* as towboats.[2]

At the time of departure the sea was calm and everything looked promising. The *Monitor* was attached by two hawsers to the *Rhode Island,* a powerful side-wheeler, in hopes that towing would guarantee a safe passage. Because the *Monitor* had no mast on which to hoist the regular naval code signals, Bankhead and the commander of the *Rhode Island* had agreed to communicate by writing messages on a chalkboard held up to view. At the onset of darkness such communications could no longer be used and therefore it was agreed that a red light would be hoisted as a signal if the *Monitor* was in danger.

At 6.00 P.M. they passed Cape Henry in pleasant weather and during the night the vessels proceeded southwards toward the coast of North Carolina. Captain Bankhead gave orders to the engine room: "Give me more steam, chief, full ahead! Too late to go back now." Surgeon Dr. Grenville Weeks, who was proud to know that the *Monitor* should be the first to round the cape, noted: "About seven p.m. we discovered the *Passaic* four or five miles *astern* of us, in tow of the steamer *State of Georgia.* A general hurrah went up — 'Hurrah for the first iron-clad that ever rounded Cape Hatteras! Hurrah for the little boat that is first in everything.'"

Iron Coffin?

The next day the sea started to rise and pitch in the peculiar manner only seen at Cape Hatteras. High waves broke over the bow and completely submerged the pilot house, spraying across the deck and splashing against the tower. The wheel had been temporarily rigged on top of the turret where assistant Helmsman Francis B. Butts was on duty. He saw what was happening: "The vessel was making very heavy weather, riding one huge wave, plunging through the next as if shooting straight for the bottom of the ocean, splashing down upon another with such force that her hull would tremble, while a fourth would leap upon us and break far above the turret, so that if we had not been protected by a rifle-armor that was securely fastened and rose to the height of a man's chest, we should have been washed away."[3]

17. Tragic End

Shortly before dark they encountered even stronger westerly winds and tumbling waves and the *Monitor* plunged wildly so that men on the *Rhode Island* lost sight of their charge. Now Captain Bankhead noticed that they had to face the same problem he had heard happened on the fearful journey from New York: water was gushing in at the juncture of the turret and hull where the caulking had loosened. Water also streamed down through the blower pipes and soon the bilge pumps could no longer handle floods entering the engine room. Sailors worked desperately to bail the incoming water. The engineers who handled her machinery found it impossible to keep up full steam.

Strange things happened as if to signal an ominous end, Francis Butts, who was in the bucket line, suddenly noticed: "A black cat was sitting on the breech of one of the guns, howling one of those hoarse and solemn tunes which no one can appreciate who is not filled with the superstitions which I had been taught by sailors, who are always afraid to kill a cat. I would almost as soon have touched a ghost, but I caught her, and placing her in another gun, replaced the wad and tampion; but I could still hear that distressing yowl."

Finally at 10.30 P.M. the situation was catastrophic. Now the red signal lamp was displayed from the top of the turret and the crew was ordered to abandon ship. The *Rhode Island* tried to come alongside but the towing line had become entangled in the side wheels of the vessel which made steering difficult. Two men who tried to cut the line were washed overboard and drowned in the icy waters.

The next man, Master Louis Stodder, finally succeeded, but was nearly also swept away by the waves before he could return to the turret. Captain Bankhead decided to try to steady his craft by releasing the anchor. As it struck bottom for a while she rode more easily, but at the anchor-well the packing had been torn away by the release, and more floods came gushing in and the water was drowning the heating fire. All pumps came to a standstill.

"Words cannot depict the agony of those moments as our little company gathered on top of the turret, and stood with a mass of sinking iron beneath them, gazing through the dim light, over the raging waters with an anxiety amounting almost to agony," wrote paymaster Keeler.

The *Rhode Island* came as close as possible and rescue operations were started in the moon-silvered waters with the launch of two lifeboats. The rescuers were able to make it to the stricken ironclad, which at the time did not carry boats of her own. Now crew members could be transferred and fortunately they were safely pulled aboard the steamer by means of some lines thrown to them.

Many tragic scenes developed when crew members tried to help each

Rescue operations by the *Rhode Island* off Cape Hatteras as the *Monitor* sinks on December 30, 1882 (*Harper's Weekly*, 1863).

other. Assistant Surgeon Grenville Weeks told: "We had on board a little messenger-boy, the special charge of one of the sailors, and the pet of all. He must have been lost but for the care of his adopted father, who holding him firmly in his arms, escaped by miracle." It was an old quartermaster who saved him by holding him like a cloth bag which he threw into the life boat. The sailor himself was swept from the deck by the next wave.

The last successfully transferred to lifeboats were Captain Bankhead and Lieutenant Greene, but later attempts failed because soon after they reached the *Rhode Island,* the red light in the *Monitor* disappeared. She had fought her final battle and succumbed not to the shot and shell of the Confederates, but to another enemy and friend, the sea. The *Monitor* sank about ten miles offshore near Cape Hatteras at 01.30 A.M. on New Year's Eve 1862. Sixteen crewmen and the ship's mascot, a black cat, were lost at sea. Many of them were swept overboard trying to get into the lifeboats. The forces of nature at the cape behaving as though they were in league with the South, had taken their toll. Paymaster F. Keeler lamented: "What the fire of the enemy failed to do, the elements have accomplished."[4]

More Than Cotton

Lieutenant Rodney Brown and the crew of eight in his cutter from the *Rhode Island* made a third trip to the sinking *Monitor* in an attempt to rescue the last survivors. Arriving at the scene he saw nothing more than an eddy from the sinking vessel and no survivors in the water. Brown also lost sight of his steamer and despite an extensive search from the *Rhode Island* no trace of the *Monitor* or a missing lifeboat was found.

The next morning highly distressed, the men in the boat sighted a full-rigger and signaled for help. Mr. Brown on board the little craft remembers: "She came nearer and I could plainly see the officer on her quarter-deck smoking a cigar. He leveled his spy-glass at us, looked aloft and went below, leaving us to our fate." The ship was a blockade runner with bales of cotton. "She *knew* that a boat in that place must be in distress but cotton was of more value than human lives."

Later the men in the cutter were lucky to be picked up by a passing vessel from Maine carrying bricks. Its captain told Brown: "I own the most of this vessel and it is all I have got in the world, but even in our present situation, I do not regret having picked you up, for human life is worth more than money." He was a different man than the Captain of the blockade runner — to him human life was the most precious.

They were safely taken to Beaufort where the crew was reunited with the men of the *Rhode Island*. Captain Trenchard, the commander of the side-wheeler, was so happy to see Brown, who had steered the lifeboat, that he was "throwing his arm around me and gave me a good hug. This was *the only time*, during the time I served under his command, that he ever forgot his dignity. They all thought that we were in 'Davy Jones' Locker'" (an old seaman's phrase for grave of those buried at sea).[5]

With the rescued crewmembers of the *Monitor* on board, the *Rhode Island* returned to Fort Monroe to the place where it started. The *Passaic* weathered the storm, passed Cape Lookout and reached Beaufort safely but had to be taken in for repairs. Captain Worden was assigned to the new monitor *Mantouk*.

The real reason the *Monitor* sank in a storm off Cape Hatteras will never be known. Some people speculated that it was due to separation of the upper and lower part of the hull. That however, is not supported by findings on the recovered wreck. The ultimate reason was bad judgment on the part of the officers of the navy who let her go during the storm season.

After the *Monitor* sank the forty-nine survivors returned to Fort Monroe on the tugboat *Rhode Island*. Now they were back where they started and all remembered their service on the famous little "cheesebox on a raft" that had so helped the Union cause. They were proud to have served her, and continued calling themselves the Monitor Boys.

After the loss of the *Monitor* Geer reported to his wife: "I am sorry to write you we have lost the Monitor, and what is worse we had 16 poor fellows drownded. I can tell you I thank God my life is spaired. You need not worry for me, as I am always looking out for No. 1 and I am not going to get killed or Drowned in this War [Jan 2, 1863]."[6]

Following the loss of the *Monitor* the crew spread in divergent directions. Captain John Worden after recovering from his injuries commanded the new monitors *Passaic* and *Mantouk* until 1863, when he was appointed to lead the naval academy at Annapolis for five years and rose to the rank of rear admiral before his death in 1897. After their rescue, Keeler, Greene and Bankhead all subsequently served on the USS *Florida,* a conventional side-wheeler. Stimers was assigned to develop more new monitors for the U.S. government but he fell out both with the Navy and Ericsson. Master Louis Stodder was the last surviving crew member of the *Monitor*; he lived well into the twentieth century.[7]

Surgeon Grenville Weeks wrote: "Our little vessel was lost, and we, in months gone by, had learned to love her, felt a strange pang go through us as we remembered that never more might we tread her deck, or gather in her little cabin at evening.... The little 'cheesebox,' or 'sodabottle on a raft' has made herself a name which will not soon be forgotten by the American people."[8]

18

Monitor Craze

A moving tower, an iron vesuvius
With flash and thunder.
— Carl Snoilsky, 1890

The battle of Hampton Roads started a wave of developments in new naval technology and logistics. In the North more and bigger monitors were ordered and the South continued building casemated rams of the *Virginia* type, introduced mines and built submarines such as the famous *Hunley*. Initially all these innovations were the product of imaginative engineers and looked promising but the final test was the battle.

Floating Revolution

The battles at Hampton Roads and the River War in the West with shallow draft ironclads radically changed naval policies. Assistant Secretary of the Navy Gustavus V. Fox, who had witnessed the first battle of the ironclads, became a devoted Ericsson disciple and the most ardent proponent of a clearcut "monitor program." Fox also observed that the *Virginia* had not been overtly damaged and therefore realized that the present guns were inadequate to destroy such vessels. Stepping ashore at Fort Monroe, he saw an impressive 15-inch cannon designed by the army ordnance expert Thomas J. Rodman and on the spot decided that this was the answer for combating armored warships. Therefore he ordered Commander John Dahlgren, the ordnance expert at the Washington Navy Yard, to design 15-inch guns for new monitors.

After the striking success of Ericsson's revolutionary ship, Washington suddenly was in "monitor-fever." Gideon Welles, secretary of the Navy, who in the beginning of the war had been skeptical of the "Ericsson's Battery," became convinced of her value and added an increasing number of these to his fleet, which the British initially termed "Upstart Yankee Navy." When new types of turreted ironclads were ordered, the name of the *Monitor* now became generic designation of a distinct type of low freeboard ironclads with one and up to three turrets per vessel.

Ericsson was in high favor and he and his associates obtained contracts for a new version incorporating improvements on the original vessel. They were twenty-eight feet longer with a displacement of nearly double that of the *Monitor* and more heavily armed. Of these there were to be ten with a monstrous fifteen-inch plus an eleven-inch gun. The first of these, the *Passaic*, was commissioned in December 1862 and the remaining would in the future be referred to as the passaic class. Soon even larger versions were launched, but the passaics became the most successful and the real workhorses that participated in many battles. The last of the class was the *Camanche*, which entered service in May 1865 at San Francisco.

The little *Monitor* really was an inventor's dream; costing only one-third as much as a frigate, it had revolutionized the construction of warships. The original vessel already incorporated many innovations and now more were added to the new vessels. With these Ericsson could have made a fortune during the boom time of the Civil War but he turned his patent rights over to the government and said it was his "contribution to the glorious Union cause."[1]

When designing his new ships Ericsson realized some of the *Monitor's* shortcomings, such as the forward location and vulnerability of the square iron pilothouse. He said that he from the very beginning had been aware of the problem and would liked to have shifted the navigational command-center on top of the turret, but was prevented from doing so because of lack of time.[2] Now, in the passaics, the pilothouse was on top of the turret for greater safety and better visibility, keeping it out of the way of the ship's own guns. He worked out a system so that it remained stationary while the turret rotated freely beneath it with an increased field of fire.

Being a perfectionist, Ericsson not only was responsible for the general design of his vessels but also wanted to oversee every minute detail to make sure that things were executed properly. Unlike wooden construction where workers used hand tools, which allowed on the spot reshaping of the material, iron shipbuilding relied on precise fitting of every piece before assembly. Each of the thousand metal parts were separate units for which patterns must be drawn and copies made for the contributing foundries. Day and night, blacksmiths brought Ericsson iron plates which had to be fitted in size and marked by letter and number to correspond with those drawn and numbered on a scale model of the vessel. Every plate had to have fitting pre-drilled or punched holes for the rivets. Ericsson's increasing workload with new designs at Franklin Street and the shipyards was enormous and he had to struggle with time. Fortunately he was able to solicit help from his chief draftsman, the competent and experienced William MacCord.

But soon it was not enough with the passaics; Washington wanted new

18. Monitor Craze

and bigger ships along similar lines. The next class designed by Ericsson were the nine *Canonicus* vessels, launched in 1863 and 1864. In these he again incorporated improvements of the passaic vessels. Displacement was slightly greater and they were also longer but with a narrower beam.

The biggest of Ericsson's monitors were the giant *Dictator* and *Puritan*, contracted for in the summer of 1862. These vessels had more than four times the tonnage of their mother, the *Monitor*. The Navy Department originally wanted these vessels to carry two turrets, but eventually Ericsson won his argument for only one, but thickly plated with 15 inches of iron. The *Dictator* became the largest iron vessel built in the U.S. She was launched in December 1863 and ready for action in November 1864. The even bigger *Puritan* was equipped with twin propellers. She was laid down in 1863 and launched on July 2, 1864. Ericsson originally wanted to install two 20-inch guns, but problems in the manufacture of these colossal weapons delayed construction and she was never completed and broken up in 1874.[3]

Some of the new vessels built by others eventually got double turrets such as the *Onondaga* and the *Miantonomoh*. Another attempt as the result of "monitor-fever" was the conversion of the frigate sister of the *Merrimack*, the *Roanoke*, to a triple turret monster, but the weight of the three turrets made her top-heavy and useless at sea.[4]

Monitors to Charleston!

One of the critical testing grounds of the new ironclads was Charleston, South Carolina, where the *Monitor* had been scheduled to participate. It was only eleven days after her historic battle at Hampton Roads that the War Department wanted to send her directly into Charleston harbor, but Gideon Welles and Congress decided first to build more monitors.

In 1863 despite the failure of the *Monitor* and the *Galena* in the battle at Drury's Bluff, the Navy now had high hopes that without the help of the Army their fleet could penetrate the forts of the harbor and force the city into surrender. This optimistic view was based on the fact that the fleet of ironclads had been expanded and now there was the positive experience from the battle of New Orleans the year before when Captain (later Admiral) David G. Farragut was able to steam past the forts upriver. The situation at Charleston, however, was totally different. Here the forts were much stronger and could not simply be bypassed because Charleston harbor was a *cul de sac* or blind alley and difficult to navigate.

On April 7, 1863, at noon seven of the new monitors and two more conventional ironclads, the huge *New Ironsides* and the *Keokuk*, built with the rail-plate system similar to the *Galena*, under the command of Admiral Samuel F. Du Pont steamed into Charleston harbor as far as they could. The procession was led by the monitor *Weehawken,* pushing a big raft ahead of her as guard against "torpedoes" (they would be called mines today since they were not self-propelled; the sailors called them "boot-jacks").

The raft was a "bottom scraper" designed by John Ericsson and intended to clear all obstructions including fixed or floating mines. Built of two layers of 18-inch pine, it was 50 feet long and 27 feet broad, shaped to fit the bow of a monitor, to which it was secured by chains and ropes. It also could carry an explosive charge under its leading edge, like a spar torpedo, later used by the *Hunley.*[5]

The Confederates had two hundred heavy land batteries firing on the attacking fleet. Fort Sumter was much damaged, but so were the ships. The *Keokuk,* like the *Galena* before her, had been shot right through the armor and sank that night. The monitor *Weehawken* was hit fifty-three times but had only one hole in her deck. The *Passaic*'s turret was jammed by a shot that struck just at its base. The *Nantucket* had a gun disabled. None of the monitors sank but they had to take turns going down to Hilton Head for repairs. The battle lasted four hours and failed and so did another attack three months later.

Alban Stimers, former acting chief engineer of the *Monitor* and later the Navy Department's inspector of ironclads, pointed out that Ericsson had never intended these vessels to take on forts — a great surprise to all who had spent the day under the most terrific fire from the fortifications. He knew that the capture of Charleston would not come easy and he warned Fox in a letter of April 10, 1863:

> I candidly confess that I cannot share in your confidence relative to the capture of Charleston. I am so much in the habit of estimating force and resistance that I cannot feel sanguine of success. If you do succeed, it will not be a mechanical consequence of your "marvelous" vessels, but because you are marvelously fortunate. The most I dare hope is, that the contest will end without the loss of the prestige which your iron clads have conferred on the Nation abroad. If armed with proper guns I believe that your seven turret vessels now before Charleston, would destroy the whole present fleet of England. A single shot will sink a ship while a hundred rounds cannot silence a fort, as you have proved on the Ogeechee. The immutable laws of force and resistance do not favor your enterprise. Chance therefore can only save you.— I feel sure you will not feel offended at my remarks.— I have only one object in view — the good of the country.[6]

World's Biggest Navy

After the initial success of the *Monitor* the U.S. Navy finally was convinced of the importance of having powerful modern warships. The change in the construction of the United States Navy was disclosed by President Lincoln in his annual message to Congress, on December 9, 1863. At the time the number of ironclad ships completed or being built was larger than that of any other nation. He said the Navy had 588 vessels, completed and underway; of these 75 were ironclad or armored steamers. Most of them were suitable for harbor defense and coastal service.[7]

Of the sixty monitor-type vessels begun during the war, thirty-seven were completed by the end of 1865. The low freeboard monitors were perfect vessels to ply on calm inland waters and for operations in the shallow sounds and inlets which penetrate the shore of every state from Virginia to Texas. To take them on sea and more especially the sinister Atlantic Ocean was altogether another kettle of fish. But later monitor-class vessels through technological development were made apt as a seagoing warships, still maintaining the basic elements of Ericsson's concept of few powerful guns in revolving turrets, speed and maneuverability instead of mammoth weight, but with higher freeboard.

Only the twin-propeller 258 foot long *Miantonomoh*, named after an Indian chief, made a successful transatlantic crossing. She had two Ericsson turrets and after the war in 1866 steamed on what was going to be a diplomatic mission to Europe. G.V. Fox was her commander and before he left, Ericsson wrote to him: "Your appearance in an English port with a monitor will create a profound sensation all over Europe and it will be recorded as one of the great events in naval history. I hope you have sent plenty of anthracite to England and to Russia so as to be able to run without smoke."[8]

In England, Fox was received by the commanding admiral of a coastal fort and after exchanging salutations, the admiral asked somewhat abruptly: "Did you cross the Atlantic in that thing?" When he replied that he did, the admiral said, with much emphasis: "I doubt if I would." The London *Times*, however, was very positive and reported that the British Navy was "henceforce useless."[9]

The trip also included Russia, partly to congratulate the czar on his escape from an attempted assassination, but chiefly to advertise the virtues of U.S. monitors and to show Europe the flag of a reunited America.

In general, the monitors performed well for what they were intended, to combat other warships in coastal defense, but not to fight in the ocean or to destroy fortifications. Only direct hits could disable the fort's guns, whereas most of the time all that the slow bombardment did was to plow up sand and dust.

Contrary to what one would expect, the monitors had high resisting qualities against bullets and were relatively secure to their crew. Of 35 monitors operated by the U.S. Navy during the Civil War and despite being hit many times, hardly any sailors were ever seriously and permanently disabled by gunfire. What was even better: only few crew-members were killed by gunfire during the entire war. Damage was often due to snapped bolts inside the turret and pilothouse. In combat, the most seriously damaged of the passaic monitors in the battle at Charleston was the *Nahant*; she was hit thirty-six times, her turret was jammed and she had seven injured. Only one man was killed, though many had been knocked down and wounded by flying boltheads.[10]

A new threat to all warships were torpedoes and mines. In August 1864 the *Tecumseh*, which belonged to the canonicus class of monitors, was struck by a mine in Mobile Bay and sank within two minutes, with the loss of ninety-three of her crew.[11]

International Reactions

French and British man-of-war squadrons present at the entrance to Hampton Roads witnessed at close range the whole battle and foreign ministers were eager to learn the details of the fight of armor-plated ships which they transmitted to their countries. The reaction in Europe was swift. In London both the Lords of the Admiralty and the press were of the opinion that wooden ships were something of the past and "it would be madness to trust [them] to an engagement with the little *Monitor.*" The London *Times* affirmed that England had before this day 149 first class warships, now there were only two, the ironclads HMS *Warrior* and the HMS *Black Prince.* Beyond these there was not one that could safely be pitted against the *Monitor*, and even these were not invulnerable, being only ironplated amidships.[12] In Paris Napoleon III stated: "It is now settled that there is no navy in the world that can make head against ironclad vessels." Italy and Austria sent naval engineers to America to study the design of new warships and to look at gun turrets. The Swedish minister in Washington, Count Piper, was bursting with pride about John Ericsson and the achievements of John Dahlgren, the son of a Swede who had designed the guns of the *Monitor.* At the same time the Swedish government in Stockholm had to admit that it no longer had "a single vessel that was fit for fight."

The monitors fought and served in every river and harbor of the South as the Union waged its war to victory. It is a truism to say that ships change but the sea does not. Types of warships, like children, show an inevitable tendency to grow up and the *Monitor* became the prototype of later warships such as the destroyer and the small cruiser. The new monitors were more seaworthy and faster shooting. The "subaquatic" construction became less evident but the turrets remained, but smaller in size because breech loading guns (introduced later) required less space. Development went further and from mere coast-defense, they eventually passed to sea-going warships. The British navy developed the monitor design further into large sea-going vessels such as the HMS *Dreadnought,* a low freeboard battleship. Britain also built a number of small monitors for coastal operations. These vessels were still actively deployed during World War I and II.

Ericsson tried hard to help his native Sweden build low-draft monitors for an effective coastal defense system. Between 1867 and 1873 Russia built ten monitors, several of which were the American-type, double-turreted vessels. Her largest, the huge *Peter the Great*, was 320 feet long and displaced 9,600 tons. Even France adopted the monitor principle and bought American ironclads.

Survivors

After the war, most monitors were laid up and rusted away at the various navy yards until 1874, when a number were sold. The double-turreted *Onondaga* was bought by the French Navy, served in Europe until 1903 and was scrapped in 1904. For some time the U.S. was in the humiliating position of having no armored ships afloat except some of the old passaic monitors. The majority of these had long careers, the last being until 1904, forty-two years after completion. They had been repaired and the old obsolete 15-inch smoothbores were substituted with 10- and 12-inch breech-loading rifles. During the Spanish-American War two monitors took part in the bombardment of San Juan. Monitors for coastal defense were still employed in active duty in the 20th century, like the *Canonicus*, which was sold in 1908. The last surviving monitor in the U.S. Navy was the *Cheyenne* which was employed for several years in training naval reserves, and for some time was at the Naval Academy.[12] She was stricken from the Navy List in January 1937, and sold 20 April 1939!

Some monitors lived a long and useful life in civilian service such as the double-turreted USS *Chickasaw*, having served with Admiral Farragut in the battle of Mobile Bay. She was sold to the Texas and Pacific Railroad in 1882, converted to a train ferry, and was still in use near New Orleans when World War II began. The *Amphritrite* became the only American hotel with a war record. She took part in the Spanish-American War operations at San Juan, and later was sold and converted to a floating hotel at Fort Lauderdale, Florida, until 1941.[13]

The last and only monitor designed by John Ericsson and still "alive" is the gunboat *Sölve* launched for the Swedish Navy in 1874 and now on display in Gothenburg Harbor.

19

The *Destroyer*

I am one of the most fortunate individuals that ever lived. A great naval power asks my assistance to help it out of the defenseless condition.

— John Ericsson, April 1874

After the Civil War interest in naval armament faded and there was no interest in building new warships or incentive to introduce technical improvements of ordnance. Monitors were sold abroad or broken up, but Ericsson continued to be worried about the U.S. navy and came up with new ideas on how to defend the country with torpedoes.

Forerunners

Originally stationary submarine mines used for defense purposes were called torpedoes but later the term was applied only to movable submarine weapons for offense. The forerunner of these was Robert Fulton's underwater gun, developed in 1813. He simply had used guns on a warship shooting cannon balls below the water line. On their exit from the firing ship a sliding piece of leather would descend and stop water leakage from the barrel. However, Fulton's experiments on Governor's Island in Upper New York Bay were not encouraging because of the limited range and force of cannon balls shot under water.[1] In 1842 Samuel Colt, the inventor of the revolver, also made experiments with torpedoes, but his plans were abandoned.

During the Civil War "spar-torpedoes" with explosives were used on the CSS *Hunley*, although they remained primitive particularly in the way they were launched, usually being placed at the end of a long pole attached to the outside of ships or submarines, as outrigger bombs.

Torpedo-food

In the post-war period Ericsson again was eager to create something revolutionary for maritime warfare. After the development of increasingly larger ironclad warships, he realized that heavy armor *per se* was no guarantee for safety if such a vessel was hit by a powerful underwater explosive. This time he wanted to realize his concept to create a "moveable self-propelled torpedo" that could reach the enemy under water. It was by no means a new idea because the first design of a pneumatic gun firing under water goes back to 1854 when it was part of Ericsson's cupola vessel warship he had offered to Napoleon III. The principal design is evident on rough drawings found by William C. Church after Ericsson's death.[2] In the final design and the model sent to Paris this innovation, however, was omitted. Here the vessel was armed only with a high-caliber smooth-bore gun.

In 1866 Ericsson finally started practical experiments with his self-propelled underwater projectiles. They were cigar-shaped barrels of steel with screw propellers at the end, carrying an explosive at the tip. The torpedoes were 25½ feet long, weighing 1,500 pounds, capable of carrying an explosive charge of 320 pounds of powder. In later models Ericsson even used Alfred Nobel's dynamite as an explosive. The torpedoes were discharged with compressed air or by a small quantity of explosive powder. Underwater control was by a tubular cable.

Ericsson became convinced that the time of large ironclads had passed and that his torpedo could destroy these behemoths. In a letter of April 10, 1875, to his brother Nils he wrote: "I am so concerned in the welfare of my native country that I cannot refrain from asking you to do all you can to correct the mistake of the Government in building large iron-clads. We now call such vessels 'torpedo food.' The larger, the better targets they will be for the torpedo."[3]

He had high hopes that his torpedo would be accepted by the U.S. Navy. In 1878 he was encouraged by G. Vasa Fox, the former assistant secretary of the Navy, who said that he was impressed by the idea Ericsson had adopted "to attack the present system of iron-clads.... I am sure that your invention will become as national as the monitor."[4] Unfortunately things did not work out the way he had hoped. The government refused to pay for the expensive projectiles and in targeting experiments considered their range inadequate.

Ericsson was not alone in producing movable torpedoes but he hoped to outstrip his rivals when he in 1878 added a specially designed fast gunboat to fire his projectiles. It was the *Destroyer*, a "semi-undersea fighting craft," powered by a 1000 horsepower engine which gave it a speed of 18 knots. The vessel was 130 feet long with a draft of 11 feet. At the bow, below the waterline was an opening from which the torpedo could be fired. After approaching the enemy a powder charge was electrically ignited to eject the torpedo. After that the *Destroyer*, reversing her engines, could quickly escape.

Two years later he seemed to have succeeded, proclaiming: "Ironclads are doomed. We can sink an enemy without ram steam-launch or spar torpedo of our navy. All these devices are now gone to the dogs." In December 1881 trials for the Ordnance Bureau showed that Ericsson's torpedo was capable of reaching a distance of 300 feet in 3 seconds.[5]

The new system seemed promising and on February 10, 1885, Ericsson wrote to his son: "The question of the necessity of the Destroyer-system for the defense of harbors is presently with great interest debated in Congress."[6]

Even the British Admiralty became interested in Ericsson's new warship and approached him with the request for a demonstration. They were offered Ericsson's torpedo-gun after Lieutenant Charles E. Gladstone had become impressed by its performance on a visit to the U.S. A positive report induced the admiralty to purchase a submarine gun and four projectiles and agreed to give it a try. The tests were performed in shallow water on the coast of Wales at the Pembroke Naval Dockyard of the Royal Navy. To Ericsson's great surprise, it was a failure when at the 13th trial a shot exploded inside the tube and broke the arm of a sailor so badly that it had to be amputated below the elbow. The reason was considered to be the fact that the detonator used

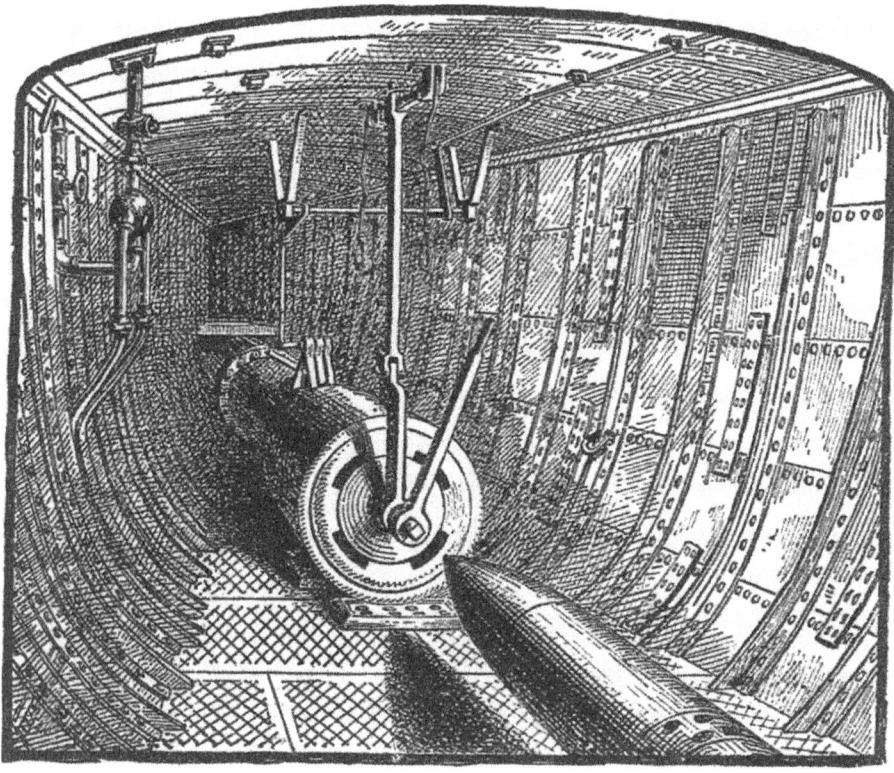

Interior of the *Destroyer* looking toward the bow.

was not of Ericsson's design but "a thing from Woolwich, most radically different."[7]

Washington was not satisfied with Ericsson's system and when the promoter of the project, Commander William Jeffers, a former captain of the *Monitor*, left the Navy, work on the *Destroyer* was suspended. The government had already spent too much money on warships and weaponry during the Civil War and now became reluctant to support further development. Even Ericsson's friend Harry Delamater was hesitant, he too was running out of funds for speculation.

In the end despite much work and investment in the project all attempts to promote his torpedo and the *Destroyer* failed. After Ericsson's death the "Ericsson Coast Defense Company was established with an office on 35 Broadway. Cornelius S. Bushnell became its vice president with the Swede Emil Hesse as consulting engineer.[8] Bushnell was able to obtain a grant of $30,000 to continue the development of torpedoes and finally in 1894 the *Destroyer* made good its promise during a brief civil war in Brazil when the rusty, reconditioned *Destroyer* was finally sold for $100 000 and renamed *Pirating*. On a perilous journey south she was leaking and had to be kept afloat by the bailing crew. At Cape Hatteras the vessel nearly met the same fate as the *Monitor* and in the Caribbean Sea she had to face a hurricane, but finally when arriving in Rio de Janeiro she was greeted as the savior of the Republic without having shot a single torpedo. The fame of her constructor was enough to frighten the aggressor.[9]

In the end a modern version of Ericsson's self-propelled torpedo became one of his most enduring contributions to naval warfare. Until today the torpedo is a crucially important piece of ordnance that made the devastating underwater war of modern submarines a forceful reality. Even today fast torpedo boats roam the coasts of Sweden and many other countries.

Monitors to Sweden

After the Civil War one of Ericsson's priorities was to help his native Sweden to improve her defense against Russia. In response to his offer, the government sent Lieutenant J. C. August d'Ailly, an able member of the mechanical corps of the navy, to New York to obtain plans for a Swedish monitor. Ericsson happily agreed to supply detailed drawings of his passaic-class vessels and in 1864 after a long period of political wrangling in Stockholm it was finally decided to build four monitors after Ericsson's design. These were to be the *John Ericsson*, the *Thordön*, the *Tirfing* and *Loke*.

Meanwhile an ironic event took place in Sweden. On August 9, 1865, a fleet of 11 Russian warships, with 10 monitors made a grandiose entry into Stockholm harbor on a "friendly mission" to the king of Sweden. In Russia

The first Swedish monitor, *John Ericsson* (1866 engraving).

the dictatorial czar, impressed by the U.S. *Monitor*'s success, had already acted to build Imperial monitors. This was possible because no international patent right prevented Russia from copying the latest military hardware and marine innovations.[10]

The first Swedish monitor was completed only three months later, when on November 15 the *John Ericsson* was launched. The stingy Swedish government only agreed to arm her with two 9-inch guns, but thanks to the generosity of her designer, who paid $15,000, the vessel was to carry the most effective ordnance then available, two huge 15-inch American Dahlgren guns. Today they are all that is left of the first Swedish monitor and can still be seen near Ericsson's mausoleum in Filipstad. After the launch of the *John Ericsson*, in the end three more of its kind were delivered to the Royal Swedish Navy.

20

Solar Energy

We owe to the heat and the light of the sun the incalculable store of potential energy upon which the human race is dependent.
— George Stephenson, 1835

For most of his life John Ericsson belonged to the age of coal and steam and did not live to see the revolutionary impact made by the introduction of internal combustion engines powered by products of mineral oil, and he only witnessed the early development of electricity. But being a visionary who jumped far ahead to our present time, he addressed the vital question of solar energy, aware of the coming scarcity of fossil fuels. In 1868 he wrote: "A couple of thousand years — drops in the ocean of time — will completely exhaust the coal fields of Europe, unless, in the meantime, the heat of the *sun* be employed."[1]

Today with a constantly increasing demand for fuel this statement can equally well be applied to the oil fields of the world. According to Paul Roberts' recent study, the picture is grim and if our oil-dependence does not lessen drastically, the global economy is likely to slip into a recession so severe that the Great Depression will look like a dress rehearsal.[2]

Hot Monitor?

What made Ericsson choose to devote tireless work to the development of solar energy? A popular story expressed the view that his idea of working with solar heat came in 1862 from the experience of excruciating heat suffered by crewmembers of his *Monitor* while stationed in the James River.[3] Simply walking on the iron deck exposed to the sun was a striking experience: one had to run not to burn his feet or to seek shade at the tower. It was equally bad to be confined in the windowless quarters below deck. During the summer months when moored at Hampton Roads the temperature inside the *Monitor* could rise to 128 degrees. Although equipped with an ingenious ventilation system, when run by steam-driven blowers it was often unbearably hot and humid beneath the iron sheeting on deck and inside the turret. "Hot, hotter, hottest," wrote a man on board the *Monitor* in August 1862. "Could stand it no longer, so last night I wrapped my blanket 'round me and took to our iron deck — if the bed was not soft it was not so insufferably hot as my pen."[4]

It is true that in the summer months heat was a problem on board the *Monitor* and although he never visited his ship after it left New York, Ericsson certainly was aware of it and worked on improving the ventilation system. The story of the hot *Monitor* as being the reason for Ericsson's research on solar heat only is a legend because his research on solar power started much earlier and had to do with the ideas of hot air engines and his efforts to explain the mysterious concept of "calorics." Nevertheless, the situation to 1862 may have contributed in stimulating his inquisitive mind.

During Ericsson's time very few solar thermal utilities were known, such as small water heating devices for cooking rice out in the countryside of India or large mirror collectors to run water pumps in Algeria. Most people consider the French scientist Auguste Mouchot as the first pioneer of solar energy because in 1861 he was granted a patent for a motor running on solar power, but Ericsson's research with the celestial body which energizes, governs and illuminates the earth started in the 1840s. In 1850 he had perfected an instrument for measuring high temperatures where ordinary mercury-glass thermometers would melt. Ericsson found that if a bladder, partly filled with air and tightly closed at the neck, was heated, the contained air expanded, and the bladder was distended. As it cooled it again became flaccid. Realizing this, Ericsson was able to construct his first "pyroheliometer" or simply "pyrometer" for measurement of high temperature that was based on the expansion of air by measuring the volume of confined gasses exposed to heat. He used this instrument for the determination of radiant heat of the sun and his measurements constituted the basis for calculating solar energy. In 1851 he presented the pyrometer together with seven other inventions to His Royal Highness Prince Albert for display at the International Industrial Exhibition held at the Crystal Palace in London.

In 1864 after moving to Beach Street Ericsson started exploring the practical applications of solar energy using the roof of his house for undisturbed experiments. At this time he was fortunate to have gained some capital and during the following years he freely spent money on costly solar experimentation. During the summer months the rising sun was a spectacle he newer wanted to miss, not even for one day. He climbed onto the roof where he had built an observatory for testing heat sensing instruments and sun motors, using an array of pyrometers and solar panels. In the evening, he had to stop experimenting when he saw the sun melting away over the New Jersey coastline. No wonder Ericsson did not want to leave his celestial world of the Manhattan sky to go back to the cold North in Sweden!

Methodically he started by estimating the quantity of solar radiant energy per square foot that reached the earth and which could be utilized for driving engines. For this purpose he further developed his "pyroheliometers" and came up with fifty different measuring devices such as actinometers, calorimeters, and finally thermo-electric devices similar to those developed by Siemens which measure the change in the electrical resistance of platinum wire exposed to heat. Ericsson was the first to make a correct determination of the solar constant, that is the amount of heat the sun delivers per unit surface area. His measurement only differed by one percent from the generally accepted value, determined forty years later.[5]

When he recorded the heat of sun rays it soon became apparent that there was a great potential for developing an efficient technique that could capture some of the immense amount of useful energy from the sun that strikes the surface of the earth every day. The next step was to build solar panels of silvered glass to collect radiant heat. These were like mirrors and his first ones were similar to Mouchot's devices but later he greatly improved the design. Ericsson managed effectively to focus solar rays on the cylinder of a caloric engine or the boiler of a steam engine or applied them to heat water in homes.

To Lund?

The first description of Ericsson's theories about the immense source of untapped energy offered by the sun appeared in the 1868 proceedings of Lund University, Sweden. This happened when Ericsson had been chosen to receive an honorary doctorate for his work on caloric engines and solar energy by the Philosophical Faculty at the occasion of the bicentennial festival of the opening of the university in 1668.

He decided that he could not just go and receive the award, but he climbed the roof of his Beach Street house and there, surrounded by his solar instruments, wrote an article entitled "On the Sun's Utilization as a Mechanical Power." In the introduction he mentioned that not only construction of machines had occupied his time during the long absence from his native country. He continued giving an account of his latest achievements in solar research with such topics as the origin and magnitude of solar power and details about three different solar motors.

He had the ambition to show that his reputation rested not just on the development of war-machines. Although not required, the honored and ambitious inventor quickly decided to send his contribution to be included in the jubilee collection of the university. He wrote:

> I have devoted much time and money towards experiments to find out if the sun's radiation can be concentrated in such a way that it can be utilized as motive power. I thus have constructed three machines I call *Sun-Engines*. One of

these is powered by steam, generated by concentrated radiant heat and the others by the power of expanding hot-air.

Calculations I recently completed to estimate how much power could be obtained from the roofs of Philadelphia, if solar heat was to be utilized, show that 5000 steam engines of 20 horsepower each could be set in motion. The solar engine now is a practical reality, which in the days to come is going to be appreciated as one of humankind's greatest necessities.

I write this with a solar engine in front of me, making 150 revolutions per minute.[6]

Ericsson received a cordial invitation to attend the ceremonies in Lund but he felt that he had to decline. We do not know the reason but apart from being too busy to travel he probably wanted to avoid a confrontation with Dr. Carl J. Schlyter, a professor of law at Lund University who was one of the speakers at the bi-centennial celebrations. Schlyter was the lucky man who in 1835 had managed to marry John's former sweetheart, Carolina Lilljeskold, and mother of their son, Hjalmar. Perhaps he was thinking that surely there would be dinner parties with ladies and meeting his sweetheart with another man would have been hard to bear.

The Original Fountain

By 1869 Ericsson had developed a conical, dish-shaped reflector that concentrated solar radiation in such a way that it resembled a modern day satellite television dish. Solar radiation was concentrated onto a boiler and a tracking mechanism which kept the reflector directed toward the sun. One of his instruments he intended to send as a present to the French Academy of Sciences.

Van Nostrand's Engineering Magazine in 1868 reported on John Ericsson's "Working the Solar Rays": "The probability of utilizing the direct heat of the sun, as proposed by Capt. Ericsson, is the grandest scheme that science has presented to man. It should almost appear that the Creator has laid up a little condensed heat in the coal mines for our use during our schooltime; a little condensed milk for our babyhood in science; that we are now grown and learned, we shall draw power from its original fountain."[7]

On the roof of his house he had erected an observatory, turning on a pivot by mechanisms resembling a monitor turret. The tables supporting the instruments had been provided with a mechanism by which they automatically were kept perpendicular to the central ray of the sun.

Ericsson was keen to make calculations of the sun's temperature and solar energy. Based on his "pyrometric" measurements and previous data presented by Sir Isaac Newton he calculated the temperature on the surface of the sun to be 2,986.000 degrees.[8] This number later proved to be incorrect

20. Solar Energy

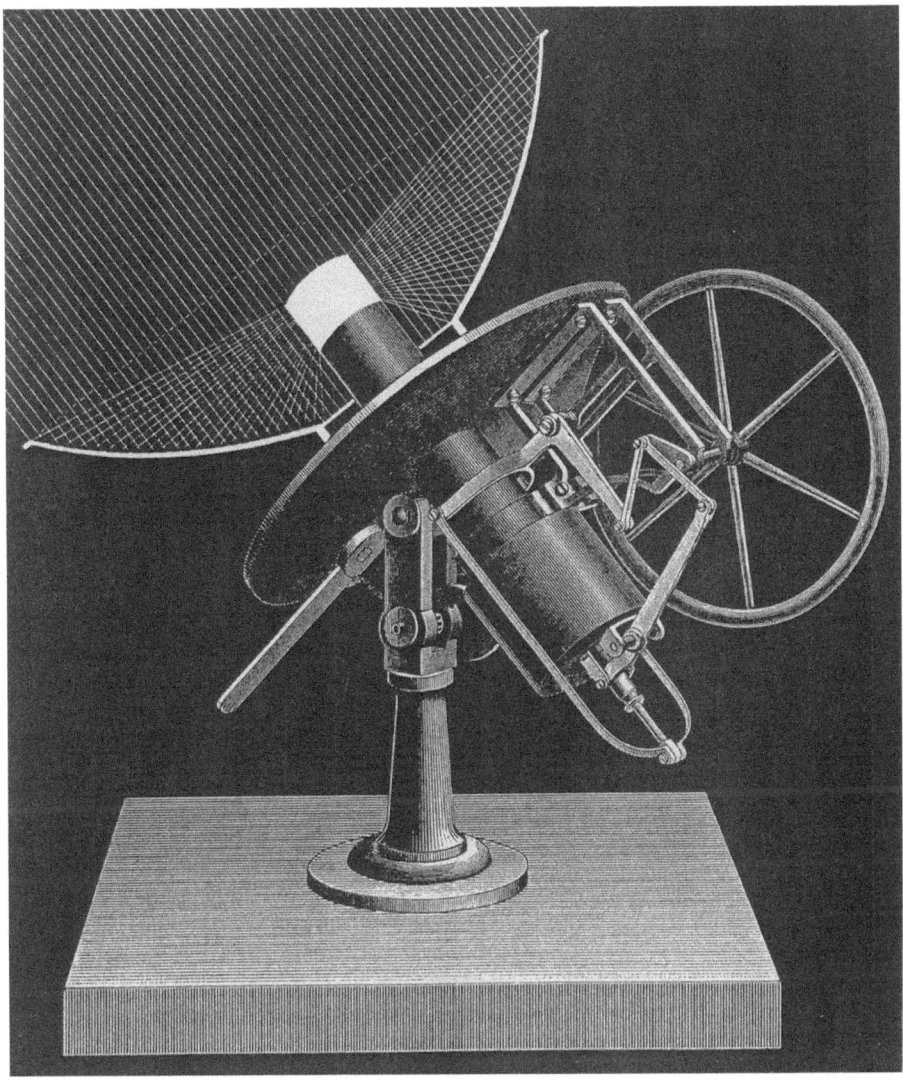

Solar hot-air engine built 1872 (*Contributions to the Centennial Exhibition*, New York, 1876).

and was much too high and now is estimated to be 9,900 degrees. Here Ericsson did not succeed because he did not have the theoretical background as the Austrian physicist Ludwig Boltzmann, who some years later came with the correct estimate. Furthermore he assumed that "an area of 10 feet square on the sun's surface develops heat enough to drive a steam engine of 45,984-horse power, demanding a consumption of more those 200,000 pounds of coal every hour," taking into account a 50 percent loss during its passage through the atmosphere.⁹

In later years totally obsessed not only with the theory of solar emission, he also developed theories about distal planets and the moon, which he called "that shining lump of ice." He assumed that volcanic "ring mountains" on the lunar surface were simply inert glaciers. Ericsson did not shy away from taking issue with the highest authorities of solar dynamics such as the astronomers Sir John Herschel and Angelo Secchi. In 1837 Herschel had made his observations on the sun's heating power with a small water container in Cape Town. Ericsson in his own experiments thirty years later was able to challenge these findings by experiments made on the rooftop of his Manhattan house and he reported his results in the proceedings of the University of Lund.¹⁰

Instead of using a steam engine as a sun motor he also attached his own energy-efficient caloric engines, simply based on heated air. These soon worked in Manhattan sunlight when using the small, simplified version of his heat engine. The more he worked with his project the more he got absorbed and already beginning in the spring of 1873 he was constantly on the roof of his house. On October 22 there had been a shower earlier in the morning and Ericsson became impatient, but soon a moist breeze from the South was driving the puffy clouds across a pale blue heaven and the Manhattan sky was glistening in the warm sun. He immediately rushed onto the roof, opened the cover to his sun machines and was so excited with his experiments that he burned his fingers, but he shouted: "Eureka!" Finally Ericsson's new collector worked perfectly and powered his engine. In the afternoon he rushed down to his office and quickly wrote a note to his friend Harry Delamater:

> The world moves — I have this day seen a machine actuated by solar heat applied directly to atmospheric air. In less than two minutes after turning the reflector toward the sun the engine was in operation, no adjustment whatever being called for. In five minutes maximum speed was attained, the number of turns being by far too great to admit of being counted.... The solar engine is operated without valves, and therefore absolutely reliable. As a working model, I claim it has never been equaled ... it marks an era in the world's mechanical history.¹¹

The Parabolic Trough

Over time Ericsson designed a variety of solar panels and finally ended up with a new method of collecting sunshine, by the "parabolic trough," a conical, dish-shaped reflector that concentrated solar radiation onto a boiler or air container. This type of reflector offered many advantages, it was comparatively simple and less expensive to construct. Ericsson continued to refine his invention, trying lighter materials for the reflector and simplifying its construction which had the advantage of being simple, and, unlike a circular reflector, only had to track the sun in a single direction.

Until the final years of his life Ericsson continued to improve his system with new materials for the reflector and simplifying its construction. In 1888, the year before his death, he was so confident of his design's practical performance that he planned to mass-produce and supply the apparatus to the "owners of sunburnt lands on the Pacific coast" in California and Mexico for agricultural irrigation pumps.

Today a great variety of collectors on roofs and pediments are used to capture solar radiation for heating water and producing steam to generate electricity and even now Ericsson's parabolic trough is the most commonly used equipment for solar energy. Dr. Charles Smith, an expert in the history of energy in 1995, states: "The new collector became popular and eventually became a standard for modern plants. In fact the largest solar systems in the last decade have used Ericsson's parabolic trough reflector because it strikes a good engineering compromise between efficiency and ease of operation."[12]

Altogether Ericsson developed seven different sun-motors that were activated by radiation. One of them he showed to his neighbor, Harris, and said proudly that he called it his solar "furnace," and that "the fact it requires no fuel but sunlight, free to all, is its great advantage. "Why not use solar energy and save the exhaustible sources of fuel on earth to apply it for the process of heating in winter and driving all sorts of machines? Ericsson now made a historic statement when he considered his achievement "of greater importance than any other physical truth practically established.... Who can foresee what influence an inexhaustible motive power will exercise on civilization, and the capability of the earth to supply the wants of our race?"[13]

Brave New World

When it came to solar energy Ericsson refused to apply for patent rights; on the contrary, he expressed hope that solar engines should be made freely available to developing countries with sunshine, such as "Upper Egypt and Peru." He therefore frankly disclosed details about his inventions since he was of the opinion that promotion of new energy-saving methods should be a gift to mankind and its future generations.[14] Unfortunately therefore the honor of being the father of solar energy in the United States goes to Clarence Kemp, who patented and marketed a solar water heater in 1891, two years after Ericsson's death. His machine became popular and was marketed in California.

Working with solar energy expanded the sphere of Ericsson's imagination and led to a number of interesting results and speculations. Obviously heat comes from the sun, the life-sustaining source of all energy on earth, but how is it generated? This had been a central issue of all his work since he started with hot-air or "caloric" engines and now occupied him when working with solar energy. The "burning" question became, what is heat? When working with solar engines Ericsson began to question the idea of "imponderable calorics" and appreciated that the driving force was a form of energy that could be transmitted through the radiation of the sun. Much later with the development of modern thermodynamics and quantum physics it was realized that solar thermal energy may be directly converted into electricity using photovoltaic cells.

One major reason why Ericsson did not want to return to Sweden was the fact that he would have missed the long period of good weather with sunshine on the roof of his Beach Street house. In 1886 in his last letter to his Swedish friend, Adolf von Rosen, he wrote: "Without doubt you share the general opinion that I should have returned to my homeland immediately after the Civil War. I would probably have done so if I had been able to separate myself from my great plan to call down solar power for the benefit of mankind."[15]

A contemporary text about New York from 1870 says about the weather: "The climate is delightful. It is not savage and rasping. The winter is short, and seldom severe. The spring and autumn are long and delicious. New York, unlike London is blessed with a clear atmosphere, so that despite the smoke of a hundred thousand chimneys, its inhabitants can nearly every day in the year look upon a sky as blue and fair as the Italian." The pleasant climate of New York is a fact and it should be realized that not for nothing is New York State the second most important place for U.S. vineyards.

Although most historians say John Ericsson's greatest contribution was the cannon in the revolving turret, Ericsson felt differently. He had devoted his later life to solar heat as the ultimate form of energy. War, unfortunately, had temporarily altered his goal. He wrote to a friend: "Satisfaction with which I lay my head on the pillow at night, conscious of having through my small caloric engine conferred a boon on mankind ... is far greater than the satisfaction the production of an engine of war can give."

With the use of solar power and his engines he envisaged a bright future for the tropics, so that the desert might "blossom abundantly, and rejoice even with joy and singing." One final problem that troubled him to the end was how he could solve the problem of storing energy. What could be done on cloudy days with the abundant energy of previous sunny days? How can you store solar energy? The task of utilizing solar power for practical purposes was one of the last projects that occupied his mind and fading energy at the end of his life. In February 1889 he received the latest solar engine from the workshop of Delamater. When it was mounted on the roof and Ericsson managed to make it run, Taylor advised him to take it easy. To this the reply was: "Being able to make this maskin run at 400 revolutions per minute with the power from a heat source 150 million kilometers away must mean that I am still able to work."

Like many great inventors, John Ericsson conceived imaginative yet important practical ideas that were never carried out during his lifetime — solar energy, for everybody the power of the future. Ericsson predicted that "the time will come when lumps of coal will be as scarce as diamonds." And in a letter to his son, Hjalmar, he confessed that taming the energy of the sun with solar engines was "my life's most important work!"[16]

The scientific and business communities were far from ready to accept John Ericsson's practical work on solar physics and in the end "two heavily laden wagons carried to a dumping ground in New Jersey, what appeared to be the debris of a canning factory. These were the shattered remains of Ericsson's elaborate equipment of solar apparatus, some of the instruments having passed through several transformations before assuming final shape."[17]

Now only models of his solar engines and pyrometers survive and are on display at the American Swedish Historical Museum in Philadelphia.

21

Centennial Exhibition

*To fame a nation's hundred years
A camp of palaces appears!*
— Anonymous poet, 1876

The latter part of the nineteenth century was the "Gilded Age" of great international exhibitions. The 1876 Centennial Exhibition at Philadelphia stood at the mid-point of ten world fairs. Nothing else so gloriously captured the American Spirit of '76 as the year 1876. Americans were a proud people as they celebrated their nation's anniversary if the *Declaration of Independence* with an international show of human progress.

Crystal Palace

When Ericsson in 1851 was reached by an invitation to participate in the "Great Exhibition of the Works of Industry of All Nations" in London he immediately realized the importance of such an event. The theme of the exhibition was "Progress." The concept came largely from Queen Victoria's Prince Consort, Albert, who optimistically saw in displaying new machinery and works of art evidence of human history's inevitable advance toward "the realization of the unity of mankind." He added: "The exhibition shall give a vivid picture of the stage at which industry has arrived in the solution of that great task."

The exhibition was housed in what the *Punch* called the "Crystal Palace," an immense outsized version of a greenhouse, a soaring, glittering wonder of cast iron and glass. Ericsson here exhibited seven of his inventions, among them the pyrometer for measuring high temperatures, the "Sea Lead" for measuring depth, and an "Alarm Barometer."

As a sign of wealth and importance in 1853 the city of New York decided to build a rival Crystal Palace on Manhattan to hold another "Exhibition of the Industry of All Nations." When it was finished it was an imposing build-

21. Centennial Exhibition

Solar calorimeter, 1874 (*Contributions to the Centennial Exhibition*, New York, 1876).

ing in the shape of a Greek cross peaked by a 123-foot glass dome, the highest in the country. Again Ericsson participated in this exhibition, this time with a caloric engine. Unfortunately, the "mighty Exhibition" was not the expected success everybody had hoped for. The enterprise went bankrupt and in 1858 the palace building, reputed to be fireproof, went up in flames.

The Centennial

A great international exhibition to commemorate the Declaration of Independence, proclaimed on July 4th in 1776 in Philadelphia, had been planned for a long time. In March 1871 Congress endorsed the plan to host an exhibition of "Arts, Manufactures, and Products of Soil and Mine." When Ericsson got to know about it he immediately decided that now it was time there to exhibit all inventions of his lifetime, the fruit of years of his inventive activities.

Staged in Philadelphia, and opened on May 10, 1876, this exhibition quickly acquired the nickname "The Centennial." Unfortunately Ericsson did not participate personally. There were differences of opinion between the inventor and the organizers. According to Samuel Taylor, Ericsson once had referred to a "Swedish schoolmaster" at the Philadelphia Exhibition and a "garrulous old fool."[1] This must mean that Ericsson had some personal quarrel with a member of the organizational committee of the Centennial. They only wanted him to exhibit drawings and a mockup model of his *Monitor* tower but Ericsson had so much more in mind. He was very disappointed that the leading men of the exhibition did not realize the importance of his contributions to the future of mankind. In particular he was thinking of his latest constructions of solar engines and successful research on solar energy. To him this was a vital issue because he was looking ahead of his time and anticipated a shortage of fossil fuel that would eventually cripple the world economy and future technical development.

Another bone of contention had been George Corliss, the steam engine builder from Rhode Island and one of the commissioners of the exhibition. Corliss submitted to the organizers plans for a huge 1,400-horsepower steam engine capable of moving all the machinery of the exhibition. Originally it was expected that more than one steam engine, among them one of John Ericsson's latest models, should be used to run the large number of machines on display. When Corliss insisted on his plan and offered to spend $100,000 on his construction the organizers agreed to his proposition.

"The Centennial" became a tremendous success and an amazing preview of things to come. The exhibition was opened to the tune of a specially composed "Centennial Inauguration March" by Richard Wagner. The whole world participated on a huge scale. There were six colossal buildings plus an avenue of houses built by each state and various other displays such an Arab tent erected by Tunisia. The main building covered 20 acres and contained pavilions of the different nations, such as Germany, Britain and Sweden.

Everything from the latest achievements in industrial design to remarkable farm implements, Italian statuary, and exotic foreign exhibits to corsets and a fountain of French Cologne were on display. Queen Victoria's personal contributions comprised a number of etchings by her own hand, also table napkins spun by herself, and drawings and embroideries from her princess daughters.[2] Italy and France had sent a large number of life-size female nudes, an unaccustomed sight in Victorian America. Some critics denounced these frivolities, with the inevitable result — the Italian and French galleries were always crowded.

A Dying Breed

One of the most spectacular attractions was the Machinery Hall. Here, in its central transept, the visitor was met by the world's biggest steam engine, the towering eight hundred ton, 10-foot stroke "Corliss Centennial Engine" with two tremendous walking beams and a gigantic flywheel. It supplied the driving power through eight miles of shafting to thousands of different machines of the whole exhibition. The Corliss engine with its huge dimensions became the marvel of the exhibition. At the opening ceremony the steam engine was officially started jointly by President Ulysses S. Grant and the little Emperor Dom Pedro II of Brazil by taking hold of a lever and opening a valve. Then Corliss waved his hand as a signal to admit steam into the cylinders from the boilers outside the building. "It was a scene to be remembered," wrote a reporter, almost overcome with excitement. "Perhaps for the first time in history of mankind, two of the greatest rulers in the world obeyed the order of an inventor citizen." (In 1889 the emperor was deposed and Brazil became a republic.) All of the important U.S. engineering achievements were on display, such as Washington Roebling's cables for the Brooklyn Bridge, the first typewriter and a telephone by Alexander Graham Bell.[3]

The Alsatian sculptor and designer of the *Statue of Liberty*, Frederic Auguste Bartholdi was lyrical about the huge steam engine and considered her a piece of art when he said: "The lines are so grand and beautiful, the play of movement so skillfully arranged, and the whole machine was so harmoniously constructed, that it had the beauty and almost the grace of the human form." Bartholdi, who with his statue wished to express "liberty enlightening the world," had not been able to finish his statue, but he was at least able to bring part of his creation made of sheets of metal and welded over an iron framework engineered by Gustave Eiffel. It was the extended arm with the torch which was on display in the open air; it became a leading attraction. From a little stand below, visitors were invited to ascend to the freedom torch. The finished statue was not dedicated until ten years later.

Although admired by everybody, the world's largest steam engine was a dinosaur of an already dying breed because internal combustion engines now stood on the threshold of an incredible expansion. Few present at the exhibition would have guessed at the changes that took place by the end of the century when Henry Ford developed his gasoline automobile in 1892 and Thomas A. Edison produced more practical electric motors. At the Centennial already viable alternatives to steam where shown by the German Nikolaus A. Otto, who presented his compact gasoline internal combustion engine which would replace boilers, pumps, blowers, furnaces, coal bunkers and ash pans.

Ericsson's small but practical "caloric" would have totally faded in comparison with the gigantic Corliss contraption. But what he could not manage, bringing to Philadelphia his compact steam and hot-air engines, was cleverly achieved by an attractive young Canadian woman named Emma Allison, who in the Women's Pavilion operated a small six horsepower Baxter steam engine running six looms and a press that printed a journal, *The New Century for Women*. The Women's Pavilion was an innovation that disregarded the monopoly of the Machinery Hall and its dominating masculine Corliss steam engine.[4] The pavilion was devoted entirely to the results of woman's skill and was filled with the *dulce et utile* from all lands.

Ericsson's Contributions

When Ericsson was not invited to participate in the Centennial, he was furious and had other plans: he decided to publish a book presenting all his works and ideas and send it to the organizers of the exhibition. The book was entitled *Contributions to the Centennial Exhibition*. In the preface he wrote: "The Commissioners of the Centennial Exhibition having omitted to invite me to exhibit the results of my labors connected with mechanics and physics, a gap in their record of material progress exceeding one-third of a century has been occasioned. I have therefore deemed it proper to publish a statement of my principal labors during the last third of the century, the achievements of which the promoters of the Centennial Exhibition have called upon the civilized world to recognize."[5]

Ericsson's book is a mammoth, leather-bound, gold embossed, quarto volume of 45 chapters with 664 pages, printed on heavy plate paper, and illustrated by 67 engravings. To make his point about the importance of solar energy thirty-seven of the forty-five chapters of Ericsson's huge book were devoted to radiant heat, solar dynamics, and sun-motors. Some three hundred copies of this book were printed, at an expense of over thirty thousand dollars, and these were distributed to public libraries, to "men of scientific reputation," and to few personal friends. One was sent to the judges of the international exhibition, Group XXI, and with a polite acknowledgement it was returned signed by all of the members.

Although Ericsson did not officially participate at the exhibition, he had some spies who told him about the event, such as his own son, Hjalmar

Elworth, who as an official guest sent by the Swedish government as a commissioner to the centennial was more privileged than his celebrated father. Hjalmar was accompanied by Ericsson's secretary, Samuel Taylor. At the time John was very depressed and contrary to his pervious beliefs he wrote to Hjalmar when he had returned to Sweden: "My fatherland and all concerning its interests mean tenfold more than what is going on in America."

Despite his refusal to come, some of his works had to be shown. In the Gallery of the U.S. Patent Office the ambitious Edward H. Knight, outstanding expert on American inventions, showed a model of the 1864 U.S. patent number 103, one of Ericsson's marine engines. Then there was an improved version of his hot-air engine patented by Ericsson's collaborator, Alexander Rider. Also the U.S. Navy Department in its own exhibition had a model of one of Ericsson's monitors, his pioneering design of the 1862 *Passaic,* which fought at the battle of Charleston and in the park a model of the gun-tower was on display.[6]

Unfortunately Ericsson did not live to see the World's Columbian Exposition held 1893 in Chicago, where some of his latest achievements would have had to appear, such as his latest equipment for the use of solar energy. But who knows, obviously the world was not yet ready for that.

22

Alfred Nobel

...I left in early youth
My home for distant lands beyond the sea,
But, strange to say, even when the Ocean spread
Its grandeur round, it struck me not as new.
— Alfred Nobel, "A Riddle," 1851

Alfred Bernhard Nobel, the inventor of dynamite but best known for his Nobel Prize, was born in Stockholm in 1833. At age nine he moved with his mother and brothers to St. Petersburg to join their father, Immanuel, who had emigrated from Sweden to Russia and established a factory producing ordnance and munitions. Immanuel was an inventor and ambitious industrialist who wanted to expand his sphere of production to include marine propulsion.

Visit to Ericsson

In 1850 father Immanuel Nobel sent his seventeen year old son, Alfred, on a two-year educational world-tour to study modern technology instead of writing poetry and mixing chemicals. After a stay of some months in Paris at the laboratory of professor Théophile Pelouze, where Nobel shared workspace with an Italian chemist, Ascanio Sobrero, who had first prepared nitroglycerin in 1846, he apprenticed in New York with John Ericsson. Here he was encouraged to seek information about new marine steam engines and above all about his revolutionary hot-air motor or "caloric."

Immanuel Nobel currently was involved not only in the development of explosives and mines but also ships. He had heard about Ericsson's work with the promising new caloric engines and "his favorite idea was that hot air might be substituted for steam and might completely supersede it. He therefore thought it would be a good plan for one of his sons to undergo a thorough education in order to be able to carry out his idea in practice."[1]

When young Alfred in 1850 arrived in New York he was amazed by what he saw. Coming from the monumental cities of Stockholm, St. Petersburg and Paris, he was struck by the lack of public buildings and chateaux in the freewheeling boomtown. Unfortunately there are no detailed records of Alfred's first American visit, but he surely had an interesting time in Manhattan. He received practical experience in engineering and learned the language so that he, after a year, was able to write poems in English.[2, 3] He made frequent visits to Ericsson's residence on Franklin Street and above all spent much time at the Phoenix Foundry with Delamater's team to observe the production of "calorics" and steam engines.

During the year that Nobel stayed in New York he witnessed intense activities connected with starting the construction of the *Ericsson*, his master's ambitious project to introduce caloric power to propel a big ocean liner. Nobel was busy copying some of Ericsson's engines and after he left he wrote to his uncle, Ludwig Ahlsell, in Stockholm: "When I was in America, I arranged with a certain Captain Ericsson that he should send me certain drawings and designs that I required, which he could not finish during the time that I was in America. He is sending them to Herr Arfvedson in Stockholm."[4] (Arfvedson was John Ericsson's agent in Stockholm who handled his financial affairs).

This passing notice seems to indicate that the rapport between the busy Ericsson and young Alfred during his first visit probably was mostly businesslike and not very intimate. The reason for this probably was twofold. We know that Ericsson, although delighted to have a young intelligent Swedish visitor, always had serious reservations about Russia, arch-enemy to Sweden and its allies. Did he think that Immanuel Nobel and his sons were traitors because they were helping to build weapons for the czar? We also can assume that another bone of contention was that Alfred Nobel at the time on his part did not care too much for mechanical engineering; he preferred to busy himself with new developments in chemistry rather than caloric engines, but he had been forced by his domineering father to pursue a different course. Alfred therefore probably during his time in America also took the opportunity to follow his own interests. He must have told Ericsson about his own ambitions to develop new explosives and there is a distinct possibility that he was advised to seek instruction by his good friend James Mapes, professor of chemistry and president of the Mechanics' Institute of New York. He could also visit the well established department of chemistry at Columbia College (later called Columbia University). Then there were plenty of other interesting sites for him such as the nearby New York Chemical Manufacturing Company in Greenwich Village.

When Alfred returned to his father's establishment in St. Petersburg he was full of new ideas and a story of the Swedish wizard of inventions in America. He came back just in time to take part in his family's boom in munitions work. Russia had become involved in a conflict with Turkey which was raising war tensions in Britain and France, and the czar wanted to be independent of European war supplies. Now was the time when Immanuel Nobel's efforts were very much in demand and his factories kept enlarging until they were gigantic by nineteenth century Russian standards, employing a thousand workers. When the Crimean War broke out in 1853, Immanuel's underwater mines helped keep the British fleet away from the naval fortress at Kronstadt in the Baltic Sea, and his shells, mortars and other machinery fed the Russian army. At the Nobel Foundries and mechanical workshops Alfred's father had received orders for 500-horsepower engines to be mounted on three warships for the Baltic and Mediterranean. He also had civilian orders to construct twenty marine engines for vessels working on the Volga and Caspian routes.[5, 6]

Despite initial silence on the matter, Alfred Nobel was much impressed by what he had learned during his Manhattan visit and although for the next forty years he had other priorities, much later when in Stockholm, he again started working with the machine he was sent to study in New York: the hot-air engine. It happened when he met the mechanical engineer Oscar Ljungström. In order to improve the efficiency of the engines he made extensive mathematical calculations on the thermodynamics of the hot-air motors. This resulted in a completely new construction, which at test runs promised excellent performance. Nobel made some additional suggestions for improvement, asking Ljungström to proceed with a new construction. Developmental work was made at the Nobel laboratories in Bofors which became too small and therefore it was planned to build a new mechanical workshop. When in 1896 Nobel died the new machine was nearly ready, but now further development was discontinued.[7]

Dynamite

Back in Europe, Alfred Nobel started his own inventive work on nitroglycerine, the explosive liquid which had been synthesized by the Italian chemist Ascabio Sobrero, whom he met in Paris and who had given it up as too unstable and dangerous. It is made by treating glycerol with a mixture of nitric and sulphuric acid. Nitroglycerine is extremely sensitive to shock and in the early days, when impure nitroglycerine was used, it was very difficult to predict under which conditions nitroglycerine would explode. Alfred Nobel studied these problems in detail, and was the first to produce nitroglycerine on an industrial scale. He realized the true value of this fearsome product that could move mountains. The problem that needed to be solved was that liquid nitroglycerine was difficult to ignite safely for practical purposes. Nobel had a solution: the new principle he realized was that a small amount of an explosive ignited by a fuse through a long wire can safely trigger a bigger one holding a batch of nitroglycerine. In 1862 he succeeded in developing a blasting cap detonator made of gunpowder next to a nitro charge. When ready, his newly developed product was much in demand in peaceful blasting operations the world over, such as in the construction of tunnels and canals. For this successful invention Nobel took out patents in five countries.

In 1864, an explosion at the Nobel's Stockholm factory killed his younger brother Emil and four others. Saddened but undeterred, Alfred continued to work on a safer way to handle nitroglycerine. In 1866 he succeeded. It became his greatest invention: dynamite, liquid nitroglycerine absorbed by a porous silicate called kieselguhr, turning it into a solid that was somewhat less potent but infinitely safer. It could be shaped into sticks that were secure to handle.

The 18-year old Alfred Nobel after he returned from America (© The Nobel Foundation).

At the time little was known about the properties of the new explosive, and a wrong impression had been current regarding its harmlessness. After some unfortunate explosions in New York and at the initial blasting operations of the Panama Canal, the U.S. government had plans to ban nitroglycerine.[8]

In 1866 Nobel again traveled to America in order to plead for his U.S. patent claim and to establish the U.S Blasting Oil Company. He arrived in New York with 12 cases of nitroglycerine and met with his former mentor, John Ericsson, in Manhattan. This time Ericsson looked at him with other eyes, admiring his achievements in explosives that were of great interest for his own new designs in marine ordnance of torpedoes and his new warship, the *Destroyer*. In 1875 Ericsson collaborated with commodore William N. Jeffers, a former captain of the *Monitor* and now chief of the Bureau of Ordnance. The two went out to Sandy Hook to test fire torpedoes which had a charge of Nobel's dynamite.[9]

Nobel also patented his first smokeless gunpowder and blasting gelatin, an explosive as safe as dynamite but more powerful than pure nitroglycerine.

Eventually he would hold 335 patents, which included methods to produce synthetic rubber and leather. In 1873 the Nobel brothers were attracted by the enormous unexplored deposits of mineral oil at Baku in Azerbaidzhan, at the time a province of southern Russia. There they developed Europe's biggest oil industry. When Alfred Nobel died he controlled more than 90 factories on five continents, a global business empire that anticipated the era of multinationals by a century.

In November of 1895, Nobel wrote his final will at the Swedish-Norwegian Club in Paris. In it he decreed that the bulk of his estate, "shall be dealt with in safe securities and shall constitute a fund, the interest on which shall be annually distributed in the form of prizes to those who, in the preceding year, shall have conferred the greatest benefit on mankind."

He instructed that those monies, equally divided, should be given as prizes in physics, chemistry, physiology or medicine and literature. Nobel intended for the award to allow creative dreamers to do their work uninhibited by financial concerns, but it was soon realized that the bestowal usually comes too late in the career of winners to have the intended impact.

When Nobel faced political opposition in France he moved to Italy and there he died alone in his villa at San Remo, on December 10, 1896, only ten years after Ericsson. Ironically, he was suffering from coronary artery disease that today is treated with nitroglycerin.

Alfred Nobel was a man who, like Ericsson, shunned publicity yet he managed to create an outsized, pharaonic memorial to himself. The paradox is apt because Nobel made his name and his fortune by solving a paradox: he figured out how to tame nitroglycerine, how to take a volatile explosive, stabilize it, package it, and make it available for use in peaceful construction, mining, and the military.[10]

War and Peace

The nineteenth century credo was mostly optimistic and thinking was that humankind through its own effort could achieve not only technological but also moral progress. This concept equally was applied to the technology of warfare and had been a widespread ambition among engineers of ships and weaponry, such as Robert Fulton. At the beginning of the Civil War, *Scientific American* praised progress in war technology and proclaimed: "There is much to cheer and awaken faith and hope for the future. Many philosophers believe that wars are tribulations which exert similar influences among the nations that thunderstorms do upon the atmosphere. They are evils while they exist, but when the clouds are dispersed, men breathe a purer and more serene atmosphere. May this be the happy consummation of our national troubles!... The war has stimulated the genius of our people and directed it to the service of our country. Sixty new inventions, relating to engines, implements, and articles of warfare have been illustrated in our columns."[11]

Alfred Nobel and John Ericsson had much in common in terms of ideology and determination. They were intensely private and elusive: shy, lonely, moody, never allowing anyone else close to them. According to a biographer of Nobel they followed the popular stereotype of Swedes, disinterested in human beings, sitting in isolation with their thoughts, which was the popular reason "why every second Swede is an engineer." Both men had difficulties in their relationship with women; Alfred Nobel never married and John Ericsson had his own problems.[12]

Despite diverging opinions on certain things the two also had the same interests and motivations. During most of their lives both men devoted their energy to creating lethal weapons in hopes of wiping out the threat of war. Alfred Nobel finally realized the unfortunate course of events of political conflicts such as the Franco-German War of 1870–71 and Ericsson was appalled by the carnage in the great battles of the Civil War. The problem of war and peace had occupied Alfred Nobel a long time and he was a good friend of the peace activist Bertha von Suttner, whose pacifist movement he supported.

After having introduced his irresistible ironclads of the monitor-type, Ericsson now faced the challenge of how to sink them. He designed a "moveable torpedo" with a destructible warhead, to be launched from a fast, low freeboard ship. It was part of his *Destroyer* project on which he worked for ten years. At one stage in the construction his revolutionary self-propelled underwater missile he used Nobel's dynamite as explosive and torpedo propellant.[13]

The design of lethal weapons which sprang from Ericsson's imagination did not come because he loved the butchery of war but his ultimate objective was that of making war so terrible that it must eventually be wiped from the face of the earth. After 1865 Ericsson thought that a further development of his monitors like the frightening *Dictator* would deter war. He expressed his optimistic credo: "I have always maintained that the art of war is in its infancy, but when it is perfected, man will be forced to live in peace with each other." Another time he said: "My object is that of seeing the sea declared by all nations as a sacred neutral ground. The torpedo shall serve humankind by making the oceans free. That has been the dream of my life."[14]

Was John really convinced that developing more and more sophisticated warships and pieces of ordnance would end wars? Deep down for him, building weapons was not really a satisfying undertaking and after the Civil War he again enjoyed much more working with hot-air engines that could be used for peaceful purposes to make life easier at home and in small business and farms. In the end he had an even more peaceful ambition: to tame solar power. He was never so happy as when he climbed to the roof of his house on Manhattan and tested his promising solar panels driving rotating engines.

The optimistic view of eliminating the threat of war by further developing sophisticated armament was not new. When in 1783 Benjamin Franklin as ambassador to France witnessed the public demonstration of the brothers Montgolfier's hot-air balloon, he made the following prediction about aerial warfare: "It appears to be a discovery of great importance, and what may possibly give a new turn to human affairs. Convincing sovereigns of the folly of wars may perhaps be one effect of it, since it will be impracticable for the most potent of them to guard his dominions. Five thousand balloons, capable of raising two men each, could not cost more than five ships of the line ... ten thousand men descending from the clouds might in many places do an infinite deal of mischief before a force could be brought together to repel them?"[15]

Nobel initially had a similar opinion but when finally his powerful explosives changed warfare he realized that there were enough destructive weapons, but war still existed. In 1888 at the passing of his brother, Ludwig, a French newspaper mistook him for Alfred and published a cynical obituary, calling him the "merchant of death." Feeling the sting of that epithet, Nobel became obsessed with his legacy and wanted to clear the family name. Therefore he decided to do more for the sake of peace and dedicated money to aid a battled mankind. After his death in 1896 his testament which bestowed a prize for "the greatest benefits on mankind," it was revealed that he had made provisions not only to promote science but also give money for a peace prize. It should be awarded "to the person who had worked most effectively in the interest of brotherhood of nations, the elimination or reduction of standing armies, and the institution and popularization of peace congresses." This came as a big surprise for many people because he was best known for his work on explosives and weapons.[16]

During the life time of Ericsson and Nobel there also existed another view about warfare. After the battle of the *Monitor* and the *Merrimack* (*Virginia*) at Hampton Roads historian Henry Brooks Adams in April of 1862 wrote this pessimistic note: "Man has mounted science, and is now run away with. I firmly believe that science is the master of man. The engines he has invented will be beyond his strength to control. Some day science may have the existence of mankind in its power, and the human race commit suicide, by blowing up the world."[17]

World War I finally concluded the view about the celebratory progress of the Western world which had believed that advances in science and technology promised the eventual perfection of human society because it was realized that death could be the fruit of progress.[18] Today we know that an advance in technology is always accompanied by new risks not only in warfare but also with other threats, such as environmental pollution and global warming.

In America Alfred Nobel is honored by a monument in Theodore Roosevelt Park, New York.

23

Manhattan

Lo, body and soul—this land,
My own Manhattan with spires, and the sparkling and hurrying
tides, and the ships...
—Walt Whitman, "When Lilacs Last in
the Dooryard Bloomed," 1865

Over the years John Ericsson realized that the great city of New York was for him the ideal place to be and he did not want to leave. Manhattan was something out of the ordinary, there was nothing like it, the center of technical development and equal opportunities for everybody, no matter if Yankee, Swede or Irish, black or white. Matthew H. Smith in his 1868 *Sunshine and Shadow* writes: "A man in New York can live as he pleases—dwell in a palace or in an attic, dine at night or not at all, live in style or be old fashioned. No one will meddle with or trouble him unless he undertakes to make a great display."[1]

Ericsson Place

Despite having accumulated some wealth, the aging Ericsson was a man of very simple habits without great demands for luxury. During the first twenty-five years since moving to New York he did not have a place of his own but in 1864 his friends and companions in the *Monitor* project, John Griswold and Harry Delamater, urged him to buy a house on lower Manhattan at St. John's Park, just a few streets up from his old rented residence on Franklin Street. It was a district with a row of comfortable houses, at one time the place for the ultra fashionable. It had the added attraction of a variety of beautiful greenery in a park next to the imposing St. John's Chapel.

In April 1864 Ericsson moved to his new house on 36 Beach Street in an area now called "Ericsson Place" in Tribeca. The home was on the south side of the beautiful St. John's Park, with its large number of American and foreign trees, such as Chinese mulberries, horse chestnuts, silver birches and catalpas. According to the records of Trinity Church, "It had a greater variety of trees and shrubs than any other plot of ground of its size in the world. In short it was the pride of the city."[2]

Here he was happy, made some renovations to fit his needs and bought furniture. The house was a respectable 3-floor brownstone with a magnificent marble entrance and gleaming door knockers, and in the back a little garden with a lawn and bushes. Here Ericsson planted his favorite flowers, red roses.

The area had started out as a fashionable district on lower Manhattan, also known as Hudson Square, originally developed by members of Trinity Church. Ericsson had moved to a place planned by the artist and inventor of steamships, Robert Fulton, and it was also nearby where an even earlier pioneer of steam navigation, John Fitch, had been testing his little steamship on waters in the middle of Manhattan. At the time the area had been a wetland of the Lispenard's Meadows with its adjacent "Collect Pond." In the beginning Fulton wanted to construct a navigable canal, draining the pond and meadows (the only reminder now is Canal Street). But reason and Fulton's artistic ambitions prevailed and it was decided to convert the place into a peaceful residential area with comfortable houses and the green oasis of a park near the busy Hudson River.[3] Here in 1807 Trinity Church members started their development by building St. John's Chapel, a refined church in neoclassical style with a 214-foot clock tower, and in front of it created the green meadow of St. John's Park.

At the time any city dweller who wanted to lie down on a bit of grass and look at the sky through the branches of a tree or to stroll on something other than a city street had to go to the Battery or the Washington Parade Ground (today Washington Square), or a cemetery. Now St. John's Park offered this relaxation to residents nearby. It became one of the first city parks in America, long before the huge Central Park was started in 1857–61. Central Park later was considered to be the major playground and when laying out new residential areas on Manhattan the idea of adding new parks was more or less abandoned.

In 1827 lots had been sold here and the well to do moved in. The neighborhood soon was filled with prominent families "whose elegant brick town houses afforded refuge from the sweaty commotion of the city below. Nothing else in New York so closely approximated the beauty and exclusiveness of the great squares of London's West End."[4]

Commerce had made New York, and after the Civil War, it seemed to be strangling it. The slogan was "New York is always new" and construction meant abandoning old buildings and to build again, in a different way for a different purpose. Ceaselessly shifting, changing, growing, always provisional, there was no other city like this. When the city was expanding northward, the old residential areas were transformed into high-rise business complexes. Expansion meant segregation. Nowhere in the world was there so much lavish wealth and such hideous displays of poverty. This is what James McCabe in his 1872 *Lights and Shadows* said about New York: "It presents a wonderful series of contrasts of individual and national characteristics. It is always fresh, always new. It is constantly changing, growing greater and more wonderful. Its magnificence is remarkable, its squalor appalling."[5]

From Oasis to Destruction

In 1868 Cornelius Vanderbilt wanted to build a new combined freight and passenger terminal for his Hudson Railway. He looked for a site on lower Manhattan near the Hudson River and selected St. John's Park. For one million dollars he bought it from the trustees of Trinity Church, including Ericsson.

On this place, he erected a large railroad terminal just in front of John's house. It became a massive three story granite structure, topped with a bronze pediment and a giant statue of himself set in a niche. A contemporary voice said: "As a work of art it is bestial." The peaceful park was transformed into a noisy railroad terminal with an enormous complex of grain depots, stockyards and stables along the waterfront. Here cattle, sheep and hogs — fifteen thousand head each week — were slaughtered in new assembly line abattoirs and dressed for shipment to foreign markets.

When Ericsson moved to Beach Street a slow decline had already begun which now ended in a sudden and irrevocable plunge, and crushed the region utterly as far as its suitability for polite society was concerned. Destruction of beautiful St. John's Park was regretted by many and the *New York Times* ironically commented that it fell "to the omnivorous appetite of improvement."[6]

In the spoiled neighborhood not only carts and trains disturbed Ericsson but also dogs, noisy cocks and piano playing girls. To be able to work undisturbed he did everything possible, he bought all chickens and paid his neighbors for not keeping barking dogs. To the clinking girls he gave expensive gold watches to keep them quiet in the morning. In order to exclude noise from neighbors, walls were padded. Felt put under his bed-posts softened the rattle from passing trains and days.

Only one man of position stayed by the wreck, and may be said to have gone down with it. Sometimes he was talking about moving but was horrified by the prospect of change. Besides, he began to realize that he had found a good hiding-place, and as he grimly remarked, "the ladies ceased to visit him in that unpromising locality." Ericsson continued in his house, holding up in that untidy and bustling region with traditional respectability, until his death. In the end not even St. John's Chapel survived, it was finally demolished in 1918–19.

Entering Ericsson's house one immediately had the feeling that this was the residence of a bohemian in the best sense of the word. Over the years everything was adapted to Ericsson's work, with writing desks, bookshelves and engine models. The interior of this 1830 home must have been captivating. Downstairs the parlor, and dining room with heavy chandeliers and mantle mirrors had a certain air of old-fashioned dignity. In later years this no longer served entertainment but every corner was occupied by a handsomely finished and polished solar apparatus, which gave it the appearance of an alcove in the patent office. The second floor housed Ericsson's bedroom and design space, on the third floor secretary Taylor's office. Above it resounding from the fourth floor attic sometimes rumbling and hammering noise could be heard because here was a workshop and storage area which became the center of assembling solar and caloric engines in a moveable tower. In the dark cellar were food stores — and rats.[7]

Scientific Rat Trap

Millions of beasts were being butchered annually in the abattoirs of New York and near Hudson Square the air reeked from boiling bones and rendering fat. Instead of flocks of singing birds, Beach Street now was assaulted by hordes of rats and stray pigs that freely wandered the streets in search of waste.

The rats became such a problem that Ericsson seriously devoted some time and money on the construction of a "scientific rat-trap." Ericsson's serious friend William C. Church devoted a lengthy and very funny description to the efforts of designing such a scientifically perfect trap: "Regarding the situation as a problem to be solved by mechanical means, with his own hands he drew the plans for a vast and mighty trap. To the leading idea (of a water-tank beneath the trap-door) he laid no claim, but the details were wholly new, and upon an unheard-of scale. The tracings were made by an assistant draughtsman, and went the rounds of shops, the pattern-maker, the brass-founder, the finisher, the carpenter, the tinsmith, each had a share in this novel work."

When ready Church described the working of the trap:

> At last it was completed and erected. It filled up half the basement, and was baited with half a cheese. He had originally intended to use a whole one, but thought that cost had been disregarded in making the trap, he suddenly became gravely economical in the matter of bait, and at last decided that one moiety would suffice, the other being placed in an adjoining room, to guide the noble army of martyrs in the road to ruin. But he had underestimated the cunning of the rodents, as a place for keeping cheese in safety, the ponderous engine answered admirably, but it did not even frighten away the obnoxious animals, and he was forced to admit that 'these little beats have brains altogether too big for their heads.'"

23. Manhattan

Ericsson's house on Beach Street and his office on the second floor (contemporary illustration, *Scientific American*).

Unfortunately the fate of Ericsson's rat trap became a hilarious paradigm of failure: "Before this time, when some over-ambitious and unsuccessful piece of mechanism came to his notice, he used to say ... 'the man who contrived that couldn't plan a rat-trap. And the force of habit sometimes impelled him even afterwards to use the same familiar ejaculation, but the memory of this failure was ever present with him, and with a merry twinkle in his clear blue eyes he invariably added: 'and I couldn't do that either.'"[8]

Daily Life

In his house he made arrangements to care for his simple convenience and everything about him gave proof of his independent spirit. Utility and not taste and female sentiment controlled the appearance and running of the house. Cozy domestic life was not for him. No wife, no children must intrude to soften the atmosphere and interfere for one moment with his work. Each day John followed a strict routine and did not like to be disturbed. In later years he always had the same simple meals at regular hours of the day and, when working overtime late at night or on shipyards he carried food stored in a specially self-designed thermo-flask container now is at the Skansen museum in Stockholm.

Details of domestic matters were for many years under the care of Ann Cassidy, the tidy little Irish woman who was his cook and housekeeper. She had learned to accommodate herself to her master's simple tastes and eccentric ways.[9]

His most trusted personal secretary and butler was Samuel Taylor, who had started working with Ericsson in 1862. He took care of most official duties of his office and household. Among other things he had to re-write his master's rapidly hand-written letters, not only in English but also in Swedish. Once on a nicely written letter addressed to an officer in Sweden Ericsson added in his own handwriting: "In order to facilitate reading I keep the original and send the legible copy, written in the Chinese manner by my secretary who does not understand a word of Swedish."[10]

Pleasure Trips?

Ericsson preferred to be at home and truthfully said of himself that "I have been a steady New Yorker." The only pleasurable excursions he made were to Washington Irving's Knickerbocker territory, along the Hudson River. In later years he limited his excursions to Sunday trips with his secretary and devoted friend, Sam Taylor, to the Jersey shore. On warm summer days they took the ferry to wander in the what he called the "Elysian Fields" of Hoboken Heights. Here they watched the moving panorama of life along the water with the ships on the North River. What he thought about vacations is evident from his reply for a 4th of July trip to Bay Ridge on Brooklyn. On July 2, 1859, he answered:

> The intended, or rather the kindly proposed trip to Bay Ridge is quite knocked on the head by the model sent to me today, not to mention the fact that I have not yet got a summer coat, my friend Sherry, the fashionable tailor of Church Street having been on a spree with *both* his men during the week and now sends word I cannot have my coat until "after the fourth." My present coat — a winter coat — weighs 9 pounds 3 ounces, and measures including padding, wadding, lining, cloth and grease just 7/16 inch average thickness. — No friend would advise my venturing out whilst the thermometer stands at 90.[11]

Another time his associate and best friend, Harry Delamater, invited him: "John hear me. You must expend some small effort on your own behalf. Take a vacation — you will be well served by a holiday. I have got it!" Delamater paused to heighten the effect of sudden inspiration. "Have a look at Niagara falls!" Ericsson looked up. "Niagara Falls?" he repeated; then with suddenly aroused attention he replied "What's wrong with them?" As if he there was need for some construction. The intended trip north probably was to include a visit of Rhinebeck, N.Y., the birthplace of Harry with a stop at his cousin's place, the "Delamater House" which now is a famous inn.[12]

At night he regularly went walking alone. This was part of his health plan because Ericsson believed in exercise of mind and body. His mind had been active the whole day but at night time was devoted to the body. One would assume that in later years he strolled to Central Park, called the "supreme American work of art" which was supposed to have "everything charming, nature on parade in her gayest and sweetest attire." It was laid out in 1857 but completed first in 1876 by Frederick Law Olmsted. Ericsson admired Olmsted and his ideas about abolition of slavery, but he did not care for the park and preferred to walk the streets of Manhattan. This had become easier since by 1869 streets and squares in Manhattan were paved and at night illuminated by nineteen thousand gas lamps.

His exercise trips also included a visit to a secret lady friend, Miss Sarah Thorn, with whom he satisfied his emotional and other desires. Ericsson did not want to remarry and have another lady in his house to direct his life, but he cared very much for her in every aspect. He bought her a house, paid expenses and left her provisions in his testament. We do not know if they had children, but that is very unlikely during a period when Madame Restell's services were readily available. Her real name was Ann Trow Lohman. She was the notorious abortionist who lived in luxury on Fifth Avenue, attended church and in the city directory and in newspapers advertised herself as "female physician and professor of midwifery."[13]

Swedish Nightingales

On an autumn morning in 1850, there was a big commotion outside Ericsson's house while he was still living on Franklin Street. A huge crowd streamed from the harbor towards nearby Canal Street. The reason was the arrival of the S.S. *Atlantic* bringing the famous Swedish singer Jenny Lind from Europe. Her arrival was preceded by an intense press campaign which incited public curiosity. One editor wrote: "The visit of Jenny Lind to America is the first step in a new epoch."

Jenny Lind was brought to New York by Pineas T. Barnum, America's greatest showman who exploited her at every turn, and her golden voice reaped rich rewards. She was not only the world's most famous singer with an angelic voice but also noted for piety and devotion to good works and therefore a more amazing prodigy than any could see in Barnum's Museum. Her appearance was on September 11 at Castle Garden. The "Swedish Nightingale" enthralled a New York audience which paid up to $225 to buy a single ticket. So great was the desire to hear her that some people who failed to get tickets formed parties in rented rowboats and, resting on their oars, listened from the river outside the garden hoping to catch the echo of her voice. Her popularity brought a rash of Jenny Lind bonnets, robes, hats, cigars and even oysters — in fact everything was "Jenny Lind."[14]

John Ericsson always had been fond of music and in his younger years he liked to go to the opera, but later in America he was more reclusive and hated to leave home. He therefore did not attend Jenny Lind's concerts but she on her part was eager to meet her countryman and insisted on visiting him at 95 Franklin Street. There she sang for him only simple Swedish songs which he much enjoyed.

The other famous Swedish singer who enthralled Ericsson was Kristina Nilsson, by the New York press hailed as "The Matchless prima donna of the age. Spirit of beauty, eloquence and song!" During her first American tour in 1870 Ericsson was invited to one of her concerts but declined. In 1873, however, he could not resist meeting the prima donna when the Swedish-American Society, *Svea*, arranged a meeting at their clubhouse in Brooklyn. At the time Brooklyn Heights was a center of Swedish settlement and therefore attracted important visitors. Ericsson himself was often on business across the East River, at the Continental Ironworks at Greenpoint and the Navy Yard in Brooklyn, and therefore he did not resist the invitation.[15]

24

The Man

A tender-hearted and affectionate man, his intellect dominated his affections; he was to an unusual extent independent of them.
— William Conant Church, 1890

When characterizing John Ericsson, the person, one has to consider not only his roots, mental characteristics, environment and upbringing, but also the period of his life — because his personality changed. He began as an outgoing and happy youth in Sweden; after a brief story of success and disappointing experience in England he arrived in America, the right place at the right time. It was a nation moving across the continent into a future of the industrial revolution and the Civil War when technological innovations were in high demand. Full of new ideas, he had the ability to materialize them and here in America he became a paradigm of "Yankee ingenuity" in an optimistic but mostly seclusive period.

John Ericsson came from a mining area full of enterprising and clever people. For many generations his ancestors had all the solid bourgeois virtues of that industrious part of Sweden. The citizens of that cold region tended to be a serious lot and laughter was not one of their outstanding gifts. He always had good solid self-confidence and the ambition to prove himself.

What Was He Like?

A powerfully built man of medium size, John was five feet nine inches tall. When young he had long curly red-brown hair; somewhat vainly he never permitted his hair and whiskers to grow gray. Samuel Risley, his first assistant, described the way he appeared when he came to New York: "Captain Ericsson all his life was careful of his personal appearance; exceptional in his dress, not dandified, but more in keeping with the present morning call attire than an ordinary day habit. A close fitting black frock surtout coat, well open at the front, with rolling collar, showing velvet vest and a good display of shirt front. Usually light-colored kid gloves, and a beaver hat completed the dress. To this add a well-built military figure."[1]

But beneath a quiet and well-dressed exterior was a shrewdness of no ordinary kind, "with a zeal and energy glowing like a volcano." As we have seen, when in England his friends called him "Arnliot Gelina," alluding to his origin and characterizing his short Viking temper.[2]

Over the years we get a totally different picture, starting from the exuberant and optimistic youth to the isolated days at a forgotten place on Manhattan. In Sweden and England he was most of the time an extroverted enthusiastic person with an optimistic outlook on life and a flair for establishing relations to others. When he first arrived in America this attitude had not changed. He had great expectations but soon when confronted with growing problems, became more and more reclusive and the inner side of his character manifested itself. Problems that John Ericsson met during his life were not limited to the sphere of work but had to do with broken ties in relationships and unfulfilled expectations from sponsors.

We can judge John Ericsson's character by comparing him with his son, Hjalmar, who was supposed to be "mild in words and strong in deeds." John said of himself that "the hammer is my weapon." His personal friend and biographer, William C. Church, wrote: "He was not a man of varied knowledge, or culture but what he did know he knew thoroughly.... Accustomed to great intensity of expression, he had exceedingly clear and positive conceptions concerning matters he understood, and was indifferent to everything else."[3]

The key to his life was his drive to tireless endeavor. Acquaintances were of the opinion that he was "an intense, high-pressure steam engine," and when in front of the Ironclad Board in Washington he had to defend the design of his impregnable battery, he became "a full electric battery in himself."[4] He never gave up even though he often encountered opposition and open hostility to his ideas or, when in London, suffered in debtor's prison. Hardly anyone except a man like Ericsson would have persisted through these situations. Work always had priority over everything else, like time and money; for him there were not enough hours of the day to be at the drafting table or in foundries and shipyards to check ongoing construction.

John was single-minded in pursuit of what he saw as "the light" before him; he was impatient and had high demands of his sponsors and workers. He wanted things to be done immediately and loved not only intense mental but also physical activities. Once in a foundry, when not satisfied with the execution of his design, in the heat of the moment he lifted a heavy iron casting of 592 pounds and broke it into two with a sledge hammer; this in the end proved to be too much and he hurt his back. Another time, in 1854 when supervising a job at a cutting machine, he saw a worker sticking his hand too close to the blade. Trying to protect him, he himself got in trouble and lost part of the fourth finger of his right hand. Quickly he grabbed the lost joint, put it in his pocket and was driven home. When the doctor came to operate on him he refused anesthesia and watched the procedure with interest. Despite the painful accident Ericsson on the same day went back to the drawing board. When healed he made a drawing of his right hand, outlining the remaining digits, and send it to his sister in Sweden.

He disliked hypocrisy and pretense and had the boldness to say so, therefore he often was judged as a curmudgeon, a difficult bad-tempered person. Ericsson's friends had to get used to what they said was his rapidly enraged "Viking temper" because he sometimes exceeded the limits of polite friendship, but they also knew that he soon would apologize and try to make up with a friendly handshake. His friend and collaborator, Professor Charles W. MacCord, said of him: "John Ericsson was by nature sanguine and enthusiastic; impetuous, and impatient of contradiction, nor did he always in the heat of the moment consider whether his wishes could be executed by those not endowed with his own tireless energy.... He loved to do his own work in his own way. To quote his own words, 'If I ever do get into a scrape, I know exactly how to get out of it.'"[5]

Many inventors were stimulated by their passion for fame and fortune, not so Ericsson; taciturn and proud, he did not seek fame in the sense of promotions and medals, but he had a childlike vanity. He demanded recognition for his achievements and was quick to defend his reputation when assailed. Particularly in England he was never good at getting the credit he deserved because he had to depend on those who could finance his inventions and in whose names the patents of his inventions were registered.

Never motivated by hopes of accumulating wealth, although within easy reach, he did not have "the nose for money" but was described as "one born to own a million and to spend two."[6] Like his parents, he simply had no sense of economy. His father went bankrupt in the mining business and his mother was too generous to make a living when offering paid board to engineers and officers at the canal building project of her husband. Ericsson always was ready to invest freely in the development of his ideas, like solar engines, and was generous to family and friends but not for his personal use.

His Belief

God for him was not somebody who could do wonders but he was the ultimate rational creator, comparable to the best scientist and engineer. God is "supreme wisdom and infinite benevolence," making it possible for men to live in a cold Nordic environment by preserving body heat in the airways, described as: "the beneficial property the Great Mechanician gives to it as a fit medium for animated warm beings." In this context he referred to the principle of "regeneration" of heat in his caloric engine by the transfer of heat from the outgoing to the incoming air by passing it through a box filled with wire meshes.

The same prudent situation was created in the human body in which preservation of heat is achieved with a mesh of blood vessels inside the airways of the lung, a counter-current heat exchange system, present also in the extremities.

He was convinced that in his work he served God "because He is the great constructor — the chief mathematician and mechanic." He was smug, being of the opinion that people like himself were better fitted to understand the purpose of life than many preachers, "who occupy themselves in constructing artificial systems of philosophy and religion."

He was confident he had the wisdom of recognizing the world's problems and was able to solve them by working for a higher cause to "further liberty, freedom and the advancement of mankind." Progress in technology and industrial development was expected to offer nearly everything and a better life on earth with no need for an unfathomable heaven. He therefore did not miss a religious creed to fill in the unknown, the mysterious. Not given to speculation, he also had a materialistic outlook and considered the human body as a machine that has a defined life span and when its working parts decayed beyond repair there came a process of disintegration followed by a "cycle of change." He could not accept a doctrine of immortality and ascension to heaven but was on a similar path as Thomas A. Edison who believed in "re-cycling" of the elementary particles of the human body that he called "Life units."[7, 8]

Particularly in later years working with solar energy he was fully convinced that this was a gift for the good of mankind. To him his work was equivalent to religious service. This becomes very evident from a letter in 1887, when sensitive to religious hypocrisy, he became annoyed when a lady tried to convince him to be more pious, honoring Sunday. He was very upset and replied through his secretary: "Captain Ericsson directs to inform you that he has worked three hundred and sixty-five days in the year for upward of forty years. During that period he has devoted more time to the study of benevolent attributes and wonderful works of the Creator and Ruler of the Universe, than you have spent within the walls of religious houses. Captain Ericsson accepts your imperfect knowledge of the subject as an apology for your impertinence in writing to him as you have done."[9]

In America Ericsson never went to church although he belonged to the Lutheran Swedish Church of Gustavus Adolphus, established in New York in 1865. He supported the congregation economically and in 1865 donated $1000 but did not participate in its service. The following year Ericsson said: "I have not been in church since March, 1826, except once in London, when I married Amelia." Despite his viewpoints Ericsson was very liberal towards other religious beliefs. In his house he set up an altar at which his Catholic housekeeper, Ann Cassidy, could worship without molestation.

After Ericsson's death, Sam Taylor sent a small Bible to a friend with the note: "I have seen it on his working table hundreds of times. It shows little indication of being often opened but that he knew its teachings, every act of his life was evidence when he once said: 'Taylor! *Here* is all my religion!'" His belief also was "to improve the condition, and increase the happiness, of his fellow men."[10]

During the industrial revolution some used to say: "Ora et labora" (pray and work), but Ericsson's version would be: "Labora est ora" (to work is to pray).

Benefactor

He did not follow the usual path of self-seekers but was generous, tender-hearted, with compassion for the poor and needy, being terrible in wrath, but gentle in his kindness and unostentatious in his many charities. There are countless examples showing his generosity. When his former collaborator, Alban Stimers, died, Ericsson, despite serious controversies during the *Monitor* program, he took care of his daughter and paid for her education. Another time a young officer was responsible for the sinking of a cannon on a boat in New York Harbor. The man faced dismissal until Ericsson paid for an expensive rescue operation and saved his career. In 1867 he found out there was a great famine in northern Sweden. John immediately sent $10,000 and on other occasions he send money to poor families in his native Långban, near Filipstad, and also to people in the province of Dalarna and to Finland when there was famine.

All these charitable actions did not pass unnoticed by the press and therefore the generous engineer received many requests for donations. One of these came in 1886 from Dr. G. E. Klemming, the director of the Royal Library in Stockholm, who urgently asked for support to purchase a rare Swedish collection of 5000 antique books from Baron N.G. Djurklou for the new big library in order to prevent dissipation at public auction. Ericsson immediately responded with a telegraphic transfer of 15,000 francs.[11]

Among the many poor, sick and needy working families in his neighborhood Ericsson was known as a generous benefactor and he had a long list of people he regularly helped with food and coal. And although the door on Beach Street was shut for most visitors he had given instructions that no one hungry should be prevented from entering. One day, as he sat at his desk, just under the front window (he never had curtains or blinds), on a cold autumn day outside his window on the street he saw a "bare-legged boy, whose appearance attracted his attention on a cold day." He called the little chap to come inside and after "a pleasant chat" asked his housekeeper, Ann Cassidy to give "Willie" food and go with him to a shop to buy stockings and shoes. "Still," he remarked, "when I was that boy's age I enjoyed running around in the cold, barefooted." Therefore, there was more than his bare feet that excited his compassion. This had become obvious to him after a chat with the badly dressed youngster, who came back again.

Once during an excursion to New Jersey Shores with his secretary, he entered into conversation with an old beggar woman and offered her the contents of his pocketbook, reserving at the prudent suggestion of Taylor just enough to pay for the return ferry trip. Now Ericsson was satisfied; he said: "I have made one old woman happy for a day at least."[12]

Twelve years before his death and in the possession of assets, he prepared his last will in which he generously bequested gifts and lifelong pensions to relatives and friends. Unfortunately, at his passing there was not much left to honor his wishes.

Tight Schedules

Extremely focused on his work Ericsson, only left home when absolutely necessary. During the fifty years he lived in New York City he made only short business trips, such as in 1842 when he went to Richmond, Virginia, for trial runs on the James River of one of his first iron screw steamers, the *McDowell*, together with Sam Taylor and Governor James McDowell. Later he had to make frequent visits to supervise construction of the USS *Princeton* at a shipyard in Philadelphia, out visiting his successful *Monitor* after the battle at Hampton Roads he considered to be a "waste of time." He never went back to his wife in London nor to relatives in his native Sweden, although he had promised to come when eighty. In the end he was too busy to leave his dear sun motors and related gadgets on the roof of his house on Manhattan.

In 1866 Ericsson received the honorable offer by the Department of State to be

Boy tramp Willie in the street, seeking help from John Ericsson (*Darkness and Daylight*, A.D. Worthington & Co. New York, 1891).

a commissioner to the "Universal Exhibition" at Paris. He declined, thinking it was not worth crossing the Atlantic, because at the time he was too busy designing new warships for the defense of his native Sweden.

When in May of 1883 Brooklyn Bridge after a long and perilous building period was opened with a great publicity campaign, he refused to see it because he was too busy. Secretary Taylor thought that this was somewhat embarrassing because most people admired the great engineering achievement, why not show it to his master? Therefore he designed one of his tricks and took his boss out on a little tour in a covered coach and promised to show him something nice. He ordered the driver to stop in the middle of the bridge and said: "Now we have arrived at our destination." When the door was opened and Ericsson descended he could only laugh and now in admiration he saw the thrilling, impressive vaulting span over the river.[13] We must assume that he could not help to be impressed seeing the magnificent edifice.

Shy but Tough

John Ericsson was a very private man. He disliked ceremonial events such as when he in 1866 by the American Academy of Arts and Sciences was invited to receive the Rumford Medal for his discoveries that led to his caloric engine of 1858. To everybody's surprise he declined. Although John liked to see his work acknowledged, he shunned being seen in public. The only time it happened was when he and his friend James Mapes on board his "caloric" ship, the *Ericsson*, explained technical details to invited guests. The other time we know of was when he reluctantly decided to go to Washington to make an impassioned exposition of the merits of his ironclad steam battery which was to become the *Monitor*.

He actually was not shy to speak for the things he believed in but he preferred to express himself in writing with carefully drafted letters, frequently corrected before they were finally executed by his secretaries, Samuel Risley or later, Samuel Taylor and Valdemar Lassoe. In these he was often quite blunt and did not shy away from using offensive words.

Ericsson had problems with some people who he thought did not understand him: these he hated and despised. He did not want to argue with them in person, but in letters and articles in newspapers and magazines he was persistent in seeking his right and could use strong language. He also consulted numerous lawyers to represent his case or that of his associates, such as Hogg and Delamater. By temperament and instinct Ericsson was a man of testy moods and short temper and in discussions he could be cruelly sarcastic and scornfully logical. Most of all he hated chuckle-headed bureaucrats who delayed realizations of his plans. He would bluster against them and call them names. This happened when castigated, but never against the federal government, an institution he venerated.

John certainly was emotional but did not like to openly show sentimental feelings. Even when visitors and singers came to Franklin and later Beach Street to offer their congratulations and songs for his birthday, he did not go out to receive them but stayed inside, sending his secretary to convey his thanks.

Bias and Priorities

John was a patriot, proud of his native Sweden and loyal to his land of choice, the United States. Once he said: "I love this country. I love its people and its laws; and I would give my life for it just as soon as not." He also was a staunch supporter of President Lincoln and his policies.[16]

Dedication to his homelands, Sweden and the United States but hatred of Russia were motivating factors in his life. When asked why he in 1854 sent a model of the predecessor of the *Monitor* to the French Emperor Napoleon III, he said: "Because perhaps France is more ready for some new thing than England or this country, and because France is the enemy of Russia." Furthermore he wrote: "My object was the destruction of the fleets of the hereditary enemy of my native land."[14]

In September 1863, totally unexpected, the czar of Russia's Atlantic fleet of ten warships dropped anchor in New York Harbor and later also visited Hampton Roads. Ericsson was upset. Why had they come? The general opinion in the United States assumed it was a friendship visit indicating support for the Northern cause. Some forty-five hundred men of the Imperial Russian Navy were welcomed in an enthusiastic parade from Pier One along Twenty-Third Street, down Broadway, past a huge Russian flag displayed at Tiffany's, and on to City Hall, not far from Ericsson's residence. Later the city staged the greatest ball and most elaborate banquet for the officers the nation had ever witnessed.[16]

Ericsson and many citizens with him were angry because they thought it was hardly appropriate for unrestrained festivity at a time when hospital beds were filled with wounded soldiers. John was suspicious of the visit and did not believe that they had come to support the Union. From the start he was biased against the czar and Russia, the country he considered to be the arch-enemy of his native Sweden. He hated Russia because as a young boy he had witnessed the War of 1809 when the czar invaded and seized Finland, which had been an integral part of Sweden.

On the other hand many people hoped that this visit could be a positive strategic move against France and England, countries which secretly supported the Rebel states. Later, however, it was revealed that in reality the

Russian fleet was not at all on a mission of friendship but came to escape the threat of the combined opposition of Britain and France against Russian occupation of Poland, a country which rebelled against its aggressor. In case of war the fleet would have been bottled up in its home ports of the Baltic Sea by the enemy. It was unrealistic to assume that this was a "purely domestic affair" like the Southern Rebellion because Poland was a country with its own culture and language seeking independence from its suppresser.

Equal Rights

Ericsson believed in equal opportunity, and all his life he respected hardworking, ambitious people. Through his job he was much in contact with them and he himself sometimes participated in manual labor, making suggestions and checking the quality of half finished products. In Sweden he had been elected member of "Göteborgs Arbetarförening," a worker's association which he supported. He maintained a friendly, paternalistic relationship with construction workers at shipyards and foundries where he went in and out. His relationship to these people, who were devoted to their jobs, was better than to engineers who might have a difference of opinion about details of his constructions. For their part most workers respected him and liked to talk to him. He was particularly popular and had a sense of solidarity with Irish immigrants who, like him, had come to the United States to escape British dominance and conservatism.

One example illustrating his attitude happened in 1863. On the morning of Monday, July 13, there was a terrible noise outside 95 Franklin Street. Men were running and shouting down the road. John hated to be disturbed but was worried when he heard shots fired and saw smoke above the rooftops. He asked his secretary, Taylor, what was happening and was told that the day before the names of drafted men had been published and now armed mobs had gathered in the city opposing the newly enforced federal conscription.

In New York most drafted men were low-salaried workers such as mechanics and longshoremen of Irish and German origin, who were expected to serve three years. Another serious matter was the racial bias because the law pertained to "able-bodied male citizens of the United States" and therefore only applied to whites (blacks were not yet citizens). Now the fury was at once directed against innocent African Americans who were considered the reason for the whole conflict.[17]

Enforcement of the draft immediately ignited a tinderbox and angry crowds gathered in the streets. During the week of riots men were without work and pay and when Ericsson, as usual, tried to go to the Novelty Iron Works to present his drawings, he was stopped from entering because the plant was closed by a hostile crowd who carried placards with signs of "No

Draft." He went back home but soon a messenger appeared from the factory, knocked at his door and said: "If the old man has any use of the boys, to protect him, they are at his service."[18] Ericsson, politely refused. He must have been torn inside, at first he felt sorry for the Irish workers but later, when he heard that blacks had been lynched, he hated the riots and their instigators.

Slavery

Another cause John Ericsson religiously believed in and worked for during the Civil War was to save the nation and to free slaves. He despised countries that helped to perpetuate slavery and later recalled: "It was the cannon in the rotary turret at Hampton Roads that tore the fetters from millions of slaves."[19]

He always considered freedom of people a basic right. The institution of slavery or serfdom never existed in Sweden and as a boy it had been an upsetting experience to witness the enforced labor of Russian soldiers working on the canal project in his homeland. He also strongly objected to serfdom in Russia and while in England, Parliament in 1833 banned slavery within the British Empire. So, when Ericsson came to America he was surprised that in a country based on democracy and equal rights, slavery still existed. As late as 1856 the Supreme Court stated that "the negroe is not a citizen in the eyes of the Constitution."[20]

He strongly sympathized with the abolitionists. One of them was the famous English actress Fanny Kemble. They had already met in 1829 in England, at the Rainhill Locomotive Trials where Kemble had been an invited honorary guest watching with great interest the contest of "the iron horses" of Ericsson's *Novelty* and Stephenson's *Rocket*. She later came to America and married Pierce Butler, who inherited a big Georgia plantation with a large number of slaves. Fanny soon was aghast at the fate of colored workers on her husband's property and passionately wrote about the evils of human bondage. In protest she left husband and plantation and in 1848–49 when the divorce tangle and scandal was at its worst she renewed her popular appearances.[21] In 1858 she again met Ericsson in New York, when she read Shakespeare's plays at the Stuyvesand Institute on Broadway. Now she asked for his help to build her a reading desk.[22]

For the majority of Northerners the war was about preserving the Union, but after President Lincoln issued the Emancipation Proclamation, abolition of slavery had become a major issue. Many Northerners objected to the idea of fighting to free the slaves. Not so for John Ericsson, who by building his monitors always repeated that he was proud to "fight for the freedom of four million slaves!"

Health

To maintain good health Ericsson relied on both physical and mental activity. In his youth he liked to drink wine and other spirits but when reaching fifty he changed his habits, abstained from alcohol and gourmet meals and stuck to a simple diet.

Since his military service in Sweden he believed in hearty exercise, swimming in cold water and practicing the "Ling system" of gymnastics. Ericsson always tried to keep fit until the end. He impressed visitors with his muscular strength and at the age of eighty surprised his friends by standing on his head.

In later years he subscribed to a new craze, using cold water to improve health. In the 1840s the "Watercure" movement introduced these ideas into the United States. More scientifically it was also called *hydropathy*, or simply *hydro* and advocated the curative powers of pure and cold water. The quick spread of hydropathy to a large number resorts and the issue of special journals devoted to this fad is an example of the readiness of the Americans to accept anything new. Basically treatment consisted of some glasses of cold water, a plunge bath, wet bandages and rubbings. Water was believed to be a potent cleansing agent not only for bodily health. It was also considered as a metaphoric purifier of souls, leading to a prosperous and peaceful society. American hydropathy was not limited to the mere application of water but rules that included a healthy lifestyle. It prescribed simple food and non-stimulating drinks and elimination of excessive or deficient action of all organs of the body (including genitals). More exposure to daylight, loose-fitting clothing (for women: bloomers) and regular physical exercise was recommended. Warm water, strong alcoholic liquors, spices and sour tasting foods were blamed for all kinds of ills. Another invigorating fad was the "Swedish Movement Cure," a kind of urban variant of the water cure. The treatment advocated active movement instead of the passive procedures of massage, showers and baths.[23]

Ericsson was quick to follow the new fad and obviously with excellent results. Hydropathy in its moderate form certainly was a better option than contemporary medicine with questionable remedies and procedures such as blood-letting and purging. When sixty-four in a letter to his brother, Nils, he proudly confessed: "I am able to work harder now than when I first came to this country. I sleep better, have better digestion, a stronger arm, and do not suffer from the least indisposition. I ascribe all this to my way of living. I take three miles' walk every evening before going to bed, a cold bath and calisthenics every morning before breakfast, and very seldom take wine or any kind of spirits. That I never use tobacco in any form I think is unnecessary to mention."[24]

When John's good friend Axel Adlersparre in Stockholm heard about his health-promoting schemes he became curious and wanted to know details in order to follow his advice. To this Ericsson answered:

> It usually consists in gymnastics, with naked body, after the cold-water rubbing operation in the morning. My own experience in this matter is that a carpet, table, chairs and bedposts is all the equipment I need. Your assumption that I don't go out is a mistake. I never go to bed from the drawing-board, writing desk or books. At 10 to 10.30 I always put down the pen, close books and with a speedy march go to the northern part of town, irrespective of bad weather and frost. The distance I thus since 1854 have covered is slightly longer than the earth's circumference at the height of Stockholm since my nightwalk exceeds 1000 miles per year. Maybe 13 years is a long time, but on the other hand a promenade around the globe gives you sufficient knee-movement to prevent calcification of joints. It is 360 times a year of exercise and breathing of fresh air.[25]

His habits during the last thirty years of his life were regular and his diet was said to be "temperate as though he were an athlete in training, and his day always began with a cold bath, followed by dum-bell exercise."

Ericsson shared the opinion of people who considered disease to be the penalty of bad living and ignorance. John Roebling, the well-known contemporary engineer and constructor of Brooklyn Bridge, also was believer in hydropathy. Every night he applied wet bandages around his neck, and to his family he preached that "a full cold bath every day is indispensable." He regarded illness a moral offense and fought it with the same severe intensity he applied to everything else he did in his life.[26]

An Obstinate Fool?

John Ericsson always had waking dreams about new concepts and ideas and was eager to test them in reality. Most often the results were ahead of their time and therefore invariably met with violent resistance. Later, when it had become profitable to do so, less gifted inventors built on his pioneer efforts.

It is easy to heap praise on the work of Ericsson, but he also had his faults. His proud, optimistic attitude often led to failures, but that is the coin the inventor has to pay as the price for ceaseless ingenuity. The Ericsson success story was based on his amazing ability never to give up, but always to continue improving concepts and perfecting their execution. His legacy demonstrates the value of perseverance. But a stubborn conviction about his superiority was also his weakness since he seldom bowed to criticism and advice of others, because "he always knew best."

One succinct example was his refusal to inspect the *Monitor* after the battle at Hampton Roads. There and then he could have learned from mechanical defects how to improve future models that were already on order. He said: "Time will tell, that nothing has been lost by not visiting the *Monitor*."[27] He never went aboard his *Destroyer* but once, and then it was in search of his assistant. This example clearly shows that Ericsson at the time was out of touch with the real world around him. When he built a fleet of thirty Spanish gun boats he did not see the finished craft.

The opinion about Ericsson's creative engineering mind is unanimously positive. His biographer, William Church, said: "His one consuming passion was to bring forth some new thing, or to transform the old in the alembic of his creative imagination." Charles W. MacCord in 1890 testified, "Ericsson had no rival, past or present, and the outlines of new devices grew upon the paper as if by magic."[28] John Ericsson saw things not as they were, but as they should be, having a unique vision and imagination for physical concepts and machines. When he had an idea for a new important project he initially isolated himself, as if idle, to sort out his thoughts and develop the concept. After that he went to the drawing board and started working without interruption — he was never so happy as when engaged in his drawing.

John Rodgers, commander of the *Galena* and later the monitor *Weehawken*, made a very succinct comment about Ericsson: "He is a genius, and an obstinate fool — He sees what other men do not, and cannot see plain things — he is a genius to be used, not a man of sense to be followed — and yet so cranky and opinionated that doubt at his conclusions is an insult, or a proof of enmity, a gross stupidity unworthy of a thought."[29]

Gustaf Lindwall, a Swedish biographer of John Ericsson, admired his technological achievements but was of the opinion that he had an ill founded ambition to be remembered for scientific and philosophical achievements. "His intuition led him further than his mathematical ability and it is rather significant that he once was opposed to [being] called a mathematician." He was criticized for making incorrect calculations about the influence of the earth's movements on the flow of water in big rivers like the Mississippi and his calculation of the amount of water on the moon.[30] We all make our mistakes and fortunately, these speculations were of no consequence, but in the end Ericsson's perseverance and mechanical achievements in the practical sphere on earth will be remembered.

Ericsson had much in common with other great American inventors with creative minds, such as Robert Fulton and Thomas A. Edison. Fulton, the pioneer of steamships, a man with a proud, compulsive personality, was an artist turned engineer who like Ericsson always was fond of making wonderful drawings of his constructions. As Ericsson, he started his inventive career working on new canal projects and made wonderful drawings. When in 1807 his steamboat, the *North River* (later called the *Clermont*) was launched, initially people laughed and called her "Fulton's Folly"—just like "Ericsson's Folly" for the *Monitor*. Fulton also designed threatening warships, including the submarine *Nautilus* and a steam battery, the *Fulton,* and expressed the same optimistic hope as later voiced by Ericsson that "The liberty of the Seas will be the Happiness of the Earth." But there end the similarities; Fulton also was a clever businessman, he possessed entrepreneurial skills of marketing and successfully sold the unthinkable and at the time impractical ideas of submarine warfare first to France and then to Britain.[31]

When it came to work Ericsson can be compared to Thomas Alva Edison. Both were self-made men, suspicious of "egg-heads," university educated individuals who believed in authorities. Without question Ericsson was one of the most outstanding mechanical engineers of his time, a great innovator, a "wizard of mechanics," whereas Edison in his fold was a "wizard of electricity."[32] Both were one hundred percent dedicated to their work and did not want to leave the laboratory bench or drawing table, and when exhausted sometimes took cat-naps, Ericsson on the table next to his drawing board and Edison on a bench in his laboratory. Some people called inventions "discoveries" but Ericsson disliked this connotation because to him it meant that anybody who was awarded a patent for a "pepper-box" could be called an inventor. To Ericsson invention meant hard work and scientific research. Edison had a similar opinion and believed that the two words "invention" and "discovery" were confounded. He felt that "a discovery is more or less in the nature of an accident" and inventions were not strokes of luck by minds exploring at random, but the product of purposeful and tireless work, just as they had been for John Ericsson.[33] The two men had a very pragmatic attitude toward their creative work and they both succeeded not because they were trained in the art of higher mathematics, but their success was the result of incessant toil and the intuitive feeling for the right solution. Both are remembered for a few things. Ericsson for his ship's propeller and the *Monitor* and Edison for the electric lightbulb and the phonograph. But if we learn more about them we can detect many more milestones of progress. Only by intense efforts, constantly being focused and willing to solve new problems were they able to achieve great things.

Was John Ericsson really a genius? That depends on the definition of the Latin word which usually includes a natural ability for innovative work. In Roman mythology the *genii* of a man had two sides, one good and one evil, and the evil can show itself in a degree of craziness. Ericsson had both. Ivan Musicant in his 1995 *Naval History* said: "John Ericsson was a true genius of the nineteenth-century industrial revolution. Prickly, difficult, and extremely egotistical, the Swedish engineer was convinced there was absolutely nothing beyond his capacity to invent or improve upon."[34] Finally, according to Arthur Koestler, "The principle work of genius is not perfection but originality, the opening of new frontiers." In other words, genius is to develop the ability to go an unusual way and I think we can agree that's what John Ericsson did.

The Pulitzer Prize winning author James McPherson called Ericsson an "irascible genius of marine engineering,"[35] but the most significant testimonies come from experts who knew Ericsson's work, like Dr. Robert Sheridan, who recently said: "The *Monitor* display will honor John Ericsson, the genius inventor of this extraordinary vessel."[36]

25

Family and Friends

A man's growth is seen in the successive choirs of his friends. For every friend whom he loses for truth, he gains a better.
— Ralph Waldo Emerson, *Essays: First Series*, 1841

In order to get to know the person and character of John Ericsson it is worthwhile to take a closer look at his family, loved ones, acquaintances and friends. During his long life he came in contact with many people and through their correspondence and reports by others it is possible to get a better picture of him.

The Ericssons

As we have seen, John grew up in a loving, tight-knit family and all his life he maintained loyalty to his clan. Father Olof did everything in his power to give his children a good education and managed to have both his teenage sons enrolled as cadets in the Navy's Mechanical Corps. During his short life he had reason to be proud of their achievements while working at Göta Canal. John lost his father when he was fifteen but Olof had become a role model and John emulated his practical ideas and attempts at inventions.

In family relations John always was most close to his caring mother, Britta, who also was an important factor in his upbringing and shaping of his character. She inspired interest in reading books and learning languages. John also remained attached to his sister, Carolina Odhner, in whose house Britta later lived. Quickly answering their letters was a priority in the rigid scheme of work even if he had other pressing matters to deal with. During all his time in America he generously supported members of his family economically and awarded his sister the revenues of the sale of his caloric engines in Sweden. Carolina said of him: "In the whole world there is no such good brother as you."

Brother Nils made a successful career building canals and finally became director general of the Swedish Railways. He was a conservative man and had the ability to make the most of his chances in society and in 1854 was made a nobleman and ten years later was elevated to the rank of hereditary baron by King Karl XV. During his lifetime Nils supervised the education of John's son, Hjalmar Elworth. Initially John loved and respected his brother, who had visited him in debtor's prison in London. Later bonds were broken because John did not like his brother's snobbery as a nobleman and despised his decision to change the spelling of his name when he dropped an "s," now becoming "Baron Ericson." John thought it was done in order to distance himself from a man he considered to be an "impractical and debt ridden father and an equally impractical brother."

Nils had a propensity for condescension and after the success with the *Monitor* he wrote some insulting lines, inquiring into John's finances: "Your work has not only given you honor, fame and respect, but now a fortune. I congratulate you most heartily on this, for it is none too soon at sixty years of age." Further interrogations about his wealth became unbearable to the previously long struggling brother and now he explosively shut him up by responding:

"When you are questioning regarding my financial condition, you can say that your brother is rich. His income last year, consisting almost entirely of interest, amounted to 75,000 crowns ($20,000) according to the present rate of exchange. In a word, when I some day decide to go home, my baggage will consist, in addition to other things, of fifty or sixty tons of gold."[1]

Carolina and Amelia

Ericsson's relationship with the opposite sex is a long and complicated story. It can be traced back to the shattered engagement with his sweetheart Carolina Christina Lilljeskold in Sweden, whom he was determined and confident to marry when he as a young aspiring officer had an intimate relationship that resulted in fathering a son. As we have seen, despite all positive odds, he was coldly rejected by Carolina's proud father because John Ericsson, the ambitious ensign, was not considered good enough for his daughter to be a husband and father of their child. In 1824 Carolina without John's knowledge suddenly disappeared from her home and was sent to Stockholm.

It was probably the most traumatic experience of his emotional life because it affected his innermost feelings of love and pride. After their forced separation, letters to each other, written by both Carolina and John, were intercepted and burned. When John left for England she was still very much on his mind and therefore when his friend Adolf von Rosen returned to Sweden he asked him to find out what happened. Finally he got to know the details of Carolina's and their child's fate. This episode had an unforgettable impact on John Ericsson's character and not only destroyed confidence in marriage but also made fatherhood questionable.

In London John met his future wife, Amelia Jane Byam, for the first time when she was ten years old at his friend Charles Seidler's house. Amelia was the half-sister of Mrs. Seidler. At the time she must have been a cute little girl and over the years the two were attracted to each other. In 1836 when Amelia was nineteen, despite other suitors, she agreed to marry the young, ambitious engineer. The marriage can be understood as an act of compassion towards an attractive teenage girl who already had a baby from an extramarital relationship. Amelia herself was also an illegitimate child, a situation much despised in Victorian society but John liked her and wanted to give her a secure foundation in life. He also felt obliged to her foster parents, the Seidlers, who for a long time had helped him when he came to London.

Amelia did not immediately follow her husband to America but in May 1840 she arrived in New York for the first time. John now was very happy and had high hopes for a good future. Unfortunately when the two were reunited it came at a time when John became increasingly busy with his shipbuilding projects. Amelia was a person who required much attention and was not to be neglected. She therefore soon became "jealous of a steam engine" and was very unhappy. She had come alone without her daughter Ady and in the end decided that she did not like America and wanted to return to England. On September 1, 1840, Ericsson wrote to his friend, Adolf von Rosen: "Amelia will return with the *British Queen* but don't think we are unhappy with each other, on the contrary, our relationship has been an uninterrupted link of happiness and friendship. I will do everything in my power to go back to England during the winter in order to present my plans to the British government and therefore it is best that Amelia leaves now, during the pleasant season. She also *hates* this country and longs to see Ady and I cannot blame her for that."[2]

Therefore, in October the same year she departed in despair. Two years later, in July 1842, Amelia with new hope came back to New York. Initially everything seemed to be a promising new start. This time they moved to the big house in a fashionable district of Manhattan, at 54 Franklin Street. But gossip conveyed to John's mother by a certain Baron von Düben who met the Ericssons at a party painted a dubious picture of a wasteful couple living in an expensive house and of an extravagant Amelia, wearing lavish dresses. This gossip, however, was strongly refuted by John, who wrote to his mother:

> Last night we were at a party and as usual she attracted much attention and made people stare — but she wore a black dress I bought her in 1837! Baron Düben does not seem to understand that people can live in a comfortable house, wear nice clothes but be starving. It being my own experience does not matter but that my wife should suffer this for weeks and months mortifies me. Poor girl, during six months she spent no more than you, mother say you use in *one*.
>
> Hearing such wrong accusations makes me as usual consider the world's judgement with contempt."[3]

This letter reveals a situation when John Ericsson struggled to survive and, as always, he went his own way trying to be successful in the new competitive environment. It also reveals his strong determination to fight against all odds. Unfortunately this attempt at unification also failed when Amelia again left, never to return. Back in London Amelia was devastated by their renewed separation.

When alone in America Ericsson also was sad and angry because he thought that Amelia had "failed her duties as a spouse" but later he confessed that the marriage from the beginning had been a mistake when he, "on a certain morning committed the indiscretion of ... appearing before the altar and there giving a promise difficult to keep."[4] The couple never officially divorced but Ericsson lived up to his responsibilities and through the years continuously provided her with financial support. On the failure of his marriage Ericsson commented: "Fate by this misalliance, made it possible for me to devote twenty-five years of undivided, undisturbed attention to work, which would not have been so if I had lived in what is called a happy marriage."[5]

On July 20, 1867, Amelia, at the age of fifty, died at 2 Wellington Terrace in Marylebone, London. When she passed away her last words were: "I have always been a trouble to you all. Forgive me." Now John was finally on his own and not bound to any marital relationship.

Father John

As we have seen, John Ericsson's unfulfilled relationship to Carolina Lilljeskold in Sweden resulted not, as expected, in marriage but the birth of a son. When the Lilljeskolds realized that their daughter was pregnant, she was silently whisked far away from her home in northern Sweden to Stockholm to work as a maid in a family. There, on November 16, 1824, she delivered her baby, a son christened Hjalmar. The child was immediately supposed to be sent away to be taken care of by a family in the province of Dalarna. However, when John's mother, Britta, got to know about the situation she immediately volunteered to take care of the child in the household first of her oldest son, Nils. In order to hide his origin the boy got the English sounding last name of "Elworth," composed of the letters "E" derived from Ericsson and "L" from Lilljeskold; the last part "worth" grandma Britta picked up from the character, "Kenilworth" in a book by her favorite author, Walter Scott.

Later mother Britta and her grandson moved to be with her daughter Carolina, who was married to a minister in southern Sweden. In the new home Hjalmar was well taken care of and he grew up as part of the family. He received a good education and followed in his father's footsteps, first working with the continued construction of Göta Canal. Thereupon he joined the army and later was employed by the rapidly expanding Swedish railroad system and eventually became director of its lines and technical department.

John Ericsson kept in touch with his son's life and development by correspondence with his mother. When Hjalmar was eighteen Ericsson wrote in response to a letter: "Mother's picture of my son's critical situation is exaggerated. To meet trouble (the young lad has not yet experienced misfortunes) will only do good for the development of a man's character. Mother can be assured that expenses for the boy will be reimbursed before Nils needs them. Please convey many greetings to Hjalmar — the future will show him that I have not forgotten a father's duties."[6]

This was written at a time when Ericsson still struggled to make ends meet, but was confident he would repay his debts. He kept his promise and supported his son by sending money to pay for all expenses and gave advice about his education to brother Nils, who acted as surrogate father. Initially he only sent greetings but no personal letters to Hjalmar.

Over the years Hjalmar missed his father whom he had never seen and after his marriage, his wife, Sophie, very much wanted to bridge the gap. After Christmas in 1868 she wrote without her husband's knowledge a heartbreaking letter to her father-in-law:

> Dear Sir:
> Some years ago I wrote to you begging that you would write a few kind words to Hjalmar. You have certainly proved that you have not forgotten him, and he owes his education, which has enabled him to reach an independent position, to you. But all you have given him is through others and never yet has a kind word from you gladdened his heart. He cannot but believe that he is an indifferent person to you. I was confirmed in this belief when no answer to my former letter ever came, but I have also been thinking that it might never have reached you. I have heard so much about your benevolence and kindness to even the meanest of your countrymen. Why then this indifference towards us? I beg you again to let me, your son's wife, know if you wish the relation between us to remain for the future as it has been. Your wish in this case will be law to me, but I beg to assure you that a kind word would make us happy beyond description."[7]

Surprisingly, no response to this letter can be found. Nearly four years later, father Ericsson sent Hjalmar an un-autographed paper from a magazine about solar radiation, without a personal message. Hjalmar was very pleased and immediately on November 22, 1872, responded:

> My good Father:
> When I now, at the age of forty-eight, for the first time call you my father, it is with a moved and grateful heart for all you, Father have done for me and enabled me to reach the respected position I now have without being in debt. A long time ago I wanted to express my gratefulness directly to you and asked uncle Nils during his life-time if I should not write to you, but he did not think

it appropriate as long as you did not write to me first. The reason why I now think I may write is that I received a printed essay containing, according to my assessment, a killing disproof towards Pater Secchi's doubts about the accuracy of the instrument for measuring the sun's heat, which assay was sent from New York on October 26, and arrived here on my birthday, the 16th of this month. I do not think that anybody but you Father, could have sent it, and I look upon this dear message as a letter, though a few written lines from you would naturally have made me happier.

I should like to know if there is a good construction of snow-ploughs for locomotives in America. We often, especially in January and February, have heavy snow storms, and I have introduced ploughs for removing the snow after a model I saw during my visit to Austria in 1866. These are very well for drifts of 5-6 feet, but when the snow masses become larger, shoveling is needed, which causes a loss of time. It would be of even greater interest to me to get some more details of the sun-motor. From the general information I obtained about it I have not been able to figure out details about its cost and the ability to store heat.

If you, dear father would answer this letter and let me know something about you, it would make me very happy."[8]

Hjalmar Elworth, John Ericsson's son (Church, *Life of John Ericsson*, 1890).

As we can see from this letter, lack of communication between father and son was not only Ericsson's fault but had to do with the strange attitude of his brother Nils, who prevented Hjalmar from writing. Now after Nils Ericsson's death in 1870 the situation changed, although copies of father John's first letters to his son probably were lost or destroyed. But later a lively correspondence between the two lasted until Hjalmar's death in 1886.[9] (John Ericsson kept the thinly scribbled originals of his own letters and usually only copies made by his secretaries were dispatched.)

Meets His Son

Finally it happened, in 1876 father and son met for the first time. The occasion was the Centennial Exhibition in Philadelphia, to which Hjalmar had been selected as a commissioner of the Swedish government. At the same time he also was asked to inspect the railway system of the United States and

Canada to learn more about their technical innovations such as "locomotive snow-ploughs." As an official guest of the Centennial Hjalmar was more privileged than his own celebrated father, who had gotten into some obscure wrangle with the organizing committee and had not been asked to exhibit his own inventions.

On Hjalmar's arrival in New York, John Taylor, Ericsson's faithful secretary, arranged suitable accommodation in Everett's Hotel near Union Square, an imposing classical building with elegant rooms, because there was absolutely no chance of Hjalmar being put up in his father's big house. Every room was occupied. Even the third floor, which used to be available for guests, was filled with models of hot-air engines, gun locks, steam turbines and spare parts. Furthermore, the attic and roof had been transformed into a solar laboratory.

He assigned Taylor to accompany Hjalmar to the Centennial and the subsequent railroad inspection trip and he wrote a number of introductory letters to open doors for him in Philadelphia and on his travel across the country. After completion of his tour in the United States, Hjalmar visited Canada. Before his return to New York he announced his arrival, asking his father for a quick farewell: "If you would grant me half an hour's interview before my departure in the evening, I would be very thankful."[10] This certainly sounds very strange as an announcement of the last call of his only son before leaving, not expecting good-bye hugs and kisses.

When Hjalmar has back in Sweden a lively correspondence connected father and son. Although the subject matter of their letters mostly deals with Ericsson's writings and inventions, close personal feelings are expressed in initial address and closing lines and little notes about health and well-being. Sophie Elworth shared her husband's affection for his father and in a July 1880 letter Hjalmar writes: "Midsummer day, my father's names-day, every year she decorates father's portrait, an engraving we had for many years with fresh oak-leaves."[11]

Why was John Ericsson's relationship to his son initially so superficial? He certainly did not run away from the financial obligations of fatherhood but emotionally he obviously considered the birth of his son the result of a great personal failure and humiliation he wanted to wipe out from his memory. This type of reaction we can see in many other instances. Ericsson had a tendency to disregard the many failures of his life, the *Novelty*, the *Princeton*, the *Ericsson*, the time served in debtor's prison. In a way it was lucky for him and his work that he did not dwell on his misfortunes, but the question is why he wanted to equalize the birth of a child with a project gone awry. Here we have a parallel situation in the life of another great inventor, Thomas A. Edison, who always focused on his work and neglected the children from his first marriage.[12]

Significant Others?

Throughout his life John continued to be very fond of pretty young ladies and there is every reason to believe that the virile and handsome man who always tried his best to keep in good physical condition followed his inclinations when he came to America. During the first years as a solitary young man with an intense social life and many places of entertainment in New York City, he certainly would not long have to suffer any want of feminine companionship. Therefore scholars unsuccessfully have searched for Ericsson's romantic associations during his fifty years on Manhattan and I also looked for traces of a "mystery woman."

There was at least one female companion in John's life on Manhattan and some evidence for another one. With only few clues and Ericsson's confession in a letter to a friend there are the names of two women: Miss Sarah Thorn and Miss Mary Austin, both of Manhattan. They figured in Ericsson's 1878 will and appear in this document among the names of relatives, assistants and well known friends in Sweden and America. Both of them were designated to receive a cash sum of money and a life-time monthly pension. Therefore, these beneficiaries must have had a special personal relationship to the author of his last will. We can assume this because they are only mentioned by name and not designated as "housekeeper" or "assistant" like others of his staff; moreover, their addresses are clearly spelled out. For Sarah it said: "Living at 5 Abingdon Square." When Ericsson made his will Sarah was also remembered with the generous gift of the house which he had purchased for her before and she now was living in. The address of Mary Austin was "414-East 32 Street."[13]

With these clues it was possible to figure out some more details. Sarah, was born in 1824 and John probably started having an intimate relationship with her when Amelia finally refused to return to New York in 1843 or later. Details of her relationship with Ericsson remain a mystery, except that she was a cherished personal friend whom, he helped support financially and whom he most probably loved. Unlike his late wife, this woman must have been able to cope with the oddities of an inventor who lived entirely for his work. Ericsson apparently met Sarah at Harry Delamater's house. The aim of his regular nightly excursions were not, as one would have expected, directed to Central Park, which he for some reason always tried to avoid, but to his sweetheart.

Ericsson had very regular habits. In a letter, written 1867 to his good friend Axel Adlersparre in Stockholm, he described his daily routine:

"I *never* go to bed from my drawing-board.... At 12.00 or 12.30 my ear is resting on the pillow." Moreover, he confessed: "Evening calls of the most pleasant nature are made frequently, since Eve's kinsfolk has prerogatives and can make claims before which even the constructor of caloric-engines and Monitors has to yield."[14]

William C. Church, Ericsson's biographer and personal friend, in his extensive two volume biography was very secretive about the issue, but we have to remember that the book was published in 1890, during the "Gilded Age of Innocence" which was characterized by the view that what you do not talk about does not exist. Church, who for years had been a close friend, certainly was aware what was going on but he decided that nothing should be disclosed about these ladies. All revealing personal letters and documents such as stubs for Ericsson's checks had been destroyed except for the copy of his will, otherwise he discreetly prefers to ignore the existence of lady friends, although an oil portrait of Sarah hanging opposite his chair at the dining-room table had caught the attention of friends and visitors. We only get to know that it was a portrait of a lady, "not his wife or any relative to Captain Ericsson."[15]

Sarah's residence at Abingdon Square, in present day Greenwich Village, was located at a comfortable walking distance from Ericsson's house on Beach Street, twenty-one blocks up Hudson Street. During his lonely nightly strolls it was not easy to walk alone without being approached by hookers. Only a few blocks above Canal Street were many simple brothels and farther north the more fashionable "parlor houses" which offered light entertainment.[16] Ericsson, however, was a strict person who disliked such noisy and superficial environment and instead preferred to create his own pleasant and secure refuge.

We know even less about Mary Austin, but she probably was a younger lady he may have visited in later years when he walked the streets at night. Her residence was farther up Manhattan, not far from the location of the present day Empire State Building.

Social Life

During the early days in England and when he arrived in New York, John Ericsson actively sought the company of many influential people. In England he enjoyed parties with friends and dressed according to the latest fashion from an expensive wardrobe provided by a Bond Street tailor.

During the fifty years in America Ericsson's life changed significantly from being a dandy to a reclusive hermit. When he first arrived he was still full of youthful appetite; he dressed fashionably and mixed with the New York elite and members of the Union Club. At the time he also attended concerts and theatre performances and dined at Delmonico's restaurant, known for the elegant presentation of fresh foods, or he had oysters at Florencia.

His first assistant in New York, Mr. Samuel Risley, described Ericsson's way of communicating with others as follows: "Ericsson's manner with strangers was courteous and extremely taking. He invariably made friends of high and low alike. With those in immediate contact in carrying out his work he was very popular. He had few intimates of his own social level. Mr. John Osborne Sargent, brother of Epes Sargent, was one of them. With such I think he would be very hearty, and frank, and he was a good talker."[17]

Friends

John Osborne Sargent, lawyer, journalist and author, was one of his early American friends. They had already met in England when he came to Europe as a journalist and later he became Ericsson's lawyer, defending Delamater and him for many years during a patent battle over the ship's propeller with J.B. Emerson. The two were closely attached and Sargent, inspired by Ericsson in 1844, wrote "A Lecture on the Late Improvements in Steam Navigation." Ericsson and Sargent stayed in contact by a lively correspondence and in one of his letters Ericsson wrote: "There is no man in the world for whom I have deeper feelings of friendship. There is no one to whom I am more indebted than you, John Sargent."[18]

Peter Cooper (1791–1883) shared his interest in machines and so long as he lived was one of the few welcome visitors on Franklin and later Beach Street. Cooper, like Ericsson, was an inventor and industrial pioneer. He built the first U.S. steam locomotive, the *Tom Thumb,* carrying passengers on the Baltimore & Ohio Railroad. It happened in 1830, a year after Ericsson's trial of his *Novelty* at Rainhill. At the time Baltimore stagecoach owners were determined to squash the new competitor and challenged him in a race with a powerful gray horse hitched to a car on a parallel track. Though the horse won that day, it was the locomotive that became the ultimate winner. Cooper appreciated Ericsson and was, like him, a self-made man who believed in the principle of improvement of all human beings through education. Cooper is best known as the founder of the Cooper Union, an educational institute, established in 1859 on Manhattan. It became the first uniquely American place of education, intended for the underprivileged, the first coeducational and racially open school offering free classes in the mechanical arts and sciences, with emphasis on practical education. Peter Cooper was of the opinion that "the production of wealth is not the work of any one man and not possible without the co-operation of multitude of men." He contributed much to the cultural development of New York City when he founded his school.

Another innovation lasting to the age of the Big Apple was made by Cooper's wife through her culinary skills — the quivering, translucent gelatin desert now called Jell-O. Her achievement is understandable, taking into consideration that her husband had a glue factory where he developed popular home products such as gelatin and icing glass.[19]

With the author Washington Irving, Ericsson had a close personal relationship. He was one of Ericsson's most notable house guests. They already met when John lived in the Astor House. Strangely enough the two had a common interest in steamships. Irving had followed their early development when in France he bought stock in the pioneer Seine Steamboat Company operating side-wheelers from Le Havre to Paris. In 1853 John invited him to an official demonstration of his revolutionary caloric ship in Washington. After the inspection tour Irving wrote to a friend: "I went down yesterday ... to visit the caloric ship. In our party were two Presidents, Fillmore and Pierce, all the cabinet, and many other official characters. The *Ericsson* appeared to justify all that has been said in her praise, and promises to produce a great change in navigation."

After the successful demonstration on the Potomac they dined together in Washington, where Irving was busy doing research for his biography of his namesake, George Washington.[20]

Another early American friend was scientist and professor James Mapes, president of the Mechanics' Institute of New York. Ericsson became his champion and supported him in every way. After the launch of the *Princeton* and the caloric ship, the *Ericsson,* Mapes once in a speech said: "I consider there were but two epochs of science—the one marked by Newton, the other by Ericsson." When Mapes passed away in 1866 Ericsson wrote to his widow: "I now regarded that friendship as one of the warmest I ever had the pleasure to form. Never did it flag. James J. Mapes was always to me the same—true as steel—I shall ever cherish his memory with affection and esteem."[21]

Edwin Wallace Stoughton was not only one of Ericsson's competent legal advisers and a financial supporter of his caloric ship project, but he and his wife also became intimate friends. William Church had this to say: "Mr. Stoughton was fond of his joke, and though Ericsson was less given to jesting himself, he enjoyed humor in others, and when they were together a jolly laugh would upon occasion well up from the depth of the capacious lungs that filled his expansive chest."[22]

The Stoughtons remained among close friends an at their house on Brooklyn Heights Ericsson enjoyed Thanksgiving dinners until Edwin died in 1882. Later somehow Mrs. Stoughton maneuvered her way into John's household, often bringing flowers, whereas all other women were firmly barred at the door.

Another outstanding man of vision and strange ideas was Alfred Ely Beach, editor of the *Scientific American* magazine and patent lawyer, but best known as the creator of the underground pneumatic railway. The two shared an interest in engineering and a lifestyle regulated to the smallest detail. Ericsson and

Beach had a similar view on scientific matters and politics; they admired the liberally thinking practical man who looked to utility as a measure of value and was opposed to elitism. Like Ericsson, Beach spent no time on vacations but loved exercise, which he believed promoted good health.

In November 1861 prior to her launch, Beach published an article in his magazine with a description of the *Monitor*, something that was not appreciated in Washington because it was suspected that this would alert the enemy to speed up repair and reconstruction of their *Merrimack*. He invented a typewriter, his "literary piano," and adapted it to printed raised letters which the blind could read. Beach built the first underground tube-transportation systems, a progenitor of the modern subway. (Previously Isambard Brunel, the father of Ericsson's friend Marc I. Kingdom Brunel, in London tried a suction pump to pull wagons in a tunnel under the Thames.) Beach dug a nine-foot-wide tunnel twenty feet below Broadway and in 1870 installed a huge 100 horse-power rotary blower to propel passenger cars from one end of the tunnel to the other. Beach sought the advice of Ericsson for the construction of his blowers and John in turn asked his help as a patent rights advocate. When invited to the opening of the "Beach Pneumatic Subway" Ericsson was impressed by what he saw. Before entering the elegant subway car he walked through a waiting room with frescoed walls, a grand piano, bubbling fountain and a goldfish tank. After the Civil War Alfred Beach founded the Beach Institute in Savannah, Georgia, for the education of freed slaves.[23]

Business associates and close friends also were John Griswold, John Winslow and Cornelius Bushnell, who in 1861 despite advice to the contrary undertook, at great financial risk, to fund the construction of the *Monitor*. These men also later contributed to the building of the expanded monitor program.

Music Lover

As we have seen, John was fascinated by the visit of Jenny Lind in 1850 and Kristina Nilsson in 1873. Being a music-lover Ericsson "would whistle at his work like a blackbird." Therefore he greatly admired the Norwegian violin virtuoso Ole Bull, who performed many times in New York. Bull became very dear to him and this happened surprisingly when he through a trick was introduced on Franklin Street. Mrs. Stoughton, one of the few friends allowed to enter his house, managed to get permission to admit Ole Bull and his wife. Ericsson's attention was aroused by wonderful sounds and there being no vagrant violinist in the street, he rushed downstairs and embracing his fan exclaimed: "My God! It is Ole Bull!"

Bull, besides being the world's most famous violinist, was a man of many passions and strange ideas and whom William Thackeray called "the mad-cap fiddler." In 1868 on one of his many visits to America he devoted much time to an idea to build a special piano. He wanted to create an instrument that could produce some tone qualities of the violin by incorporating the principle of the violin-bar on the sounding board. The first attempt cost Bull fifteen thousand dollars. When he failed with his "improved piano," Ericsson offered to help and constructed for him a special metal frame of the right weight and strength, insisting on one condition only, that it should be accepted as a present. With this efficient help, Bull finally succeeded in completing the new piano to his satisfaction. Only two pianos of this type were ever made; one of them can be seen at Bull's house in Bergen, Norway. "No friendly service ever touched Ole Bull more deeply than the generous helpfulness of John Ericsson, whom he admired and loved."

Equally strange as his taste for musical instruments was Bull's visionary scheme to create a Norwegian colony called "Oleana" in Pennsylvania, "consecrated to liberty, baptized in independence and protected by the Union's mighty flag." He spent a fortune to buy 125,000 acres and build three hundred homes, an inn, a store and a church but in the end he discovered that he only owned a bogus deal of sale.[24, 25]

Inner Circle

In later years after a time full of turmoil, the bloodiest war in American history, with uncertainty over whether the nation would survive, Ericsson became more and more isolated in his own world he had created around him. His independent research absorbed him to the extent of making him a recluse. He distanced himself from the outside world and withdrew to the sphere of his house and drawing table. He became what we today in psychiatric terms would call a "social phobic." He rarely sought the company of other people, although when together with friends he knew well, he was still very much liked and known as a kind, generous, and gentle person.

At this stage in life John Ericsson had few friends with whom he kept in contact, but to these he stuck and showed his loyalty. His favorite companion was Henry ("Harry") Cornelius Delamater, whom he met soon after his arrival to the U.S. Harry became the owner of the Phoenix Foundry on the North River where he built most of Ericsson's new engines — steam, hot air, and solar. The two became inseparable business partners. Delamater was of Irish descent, an honest man, tolerant and well-known for his generous and kind personality. He believed in the positive sides of people and had great confidence in Ericsson's ability, although their relations became strained at times. "Owing to Ericsson's hasty temper, there was a solid foundation of good will to settle down upon after the tempest had blown over, wrote biographer W.C. Church."[26]

Harry was not only a good business associate but also a close personal friend. Collaboration and friendship of the two men continued for the rest of their lives. Harry and an admiring neighbor, Charles Harris, were the only people he saw to the end. Samuel Taylor described the situation as follows: "He frequently visited Capt. Ericsson and was the only person living who was allowed to enter Capt. Ericsson's presence unannounced. He dined with Capt. Ericsson for years, never less than once a week."[27]

His best Swedish friends were Count Adolf Eugène von Rosen (1797–1886) and Axel Adlersparre (1812–1879). Ericsson already knew von Rosen when he in 1826 traveled with him to London. Based on his previous British experience and friends von Rosen introduced Ericsson to many influential people in business and society. After Ericsson's transfer to the U.S. von Rosen was responsible for his patent rights in Europe. They stayed in close contact by mail until von Rosen's death in 1886.

Ericsson met Adlersparre for the first time when he in 1862 arrived in New York as commander of the Swedish frigate *Norrköping* and made a visit at Franklin Street. Here he was impressed by the design of the *Monitor,* copies of which he took with him to Stockholm. Later Ericsson through his friend tried in vain to promote the *Destroyer* with the new torpedo. Over the years the friendship between the two was truly consolidated, although a glitch in their relationship happened in 1876 when Ericsson severely criticized his friend for a review he had written in a newspaper about the monumental book *Contributions to the Centennial Exhibition*. He objected to the statement that "now the engineers of England and America unanimously agree that Captain Ericsson exceeds them all." Ericsson's response was:

> Your emphasizing the word "now" proves that you are wholly ignorant on the subject. A few years ago England (not America) possessed mechanical men who might, with some show of reason have been put forth as my equals, but they are all dead, hence *now* no mechanical man can be named in either country who has accomplished one half, or even one fourth, of what I have affected. No well informed engineer questions this fact, and why should he? My labors take in the whole range of mechanical philosophy, and that I have solved numerous important problems which had perplexed the greatest men of science of this and former times.[28]

Sometimes, like in this letter, Ericsson realized that he had jumped to conclusions and apologized for his fiery comments, writing: "For God's sake do not judge my letters too severely."

He certainly did not forget his childhood friends in Värmland, like Erik Holm and Sven Carlsson, to whom he sent money, and to his best pal, a gold pocket-watch with the inscription: "To Jonas Olsson from his childhood playmate, John Ericsson."

Sam Taylor

Samuel W. Taylor was a person who certainly deserves special mention. He had been Ericsson's personal secretary for 27 years starting in 1862 as a copying clerk and from 1864 as his private secretary. When asked what he had done in Ericsson's office, he said:

"My duties were principally of communicating to him what was going on that was personally interesting to him in the world outside his house. Capt. Ericsson had withdrawn from personal intercourse with nearly everyone. I took charge of all his domestic affairs and other matters personal to him. I assisted him in experimental work of a scientific nature. I looked at things with his eyes, as I knew he never went out anywhere. All letters written by Capt. Ericsson himself were copied by me."[29]

Taylor was not only a loyal secretary, but his best personal friend who stood by his master at all times — good and bad — and he watched over him in his final days.

26

Home Again

For the soldier who gives all,
for the workshop man who gives all,
for these is the red bar on the flag.
— Carl Sandburg, *"John Ericsson Day Memorial,"* 1918

John Ericsson was blessed with a long, healthy life. As he grew older he fought disease by keeping body and mind active with a rigorous lifestyle of simple food, cold baths and long evening walks in Manhattan. John also liked to take short cat-naps in his study and was proud of his continued ability to make designs of new machines. As time passed, he was no longer able to sit on a piano stool at his drawing table for uninterrupted hours. When tired he refused to go to bed but would stretch himself on a short table near his desk, with his legs hanging uncomfortably over the end until he had the bright idea to lengthen the table. When taking a nap, instead of using a cushion he put a dictionary under his head. His habits and his genius are very much like that of Thomas A. Edison who all the time, only with short interruptions of sleep on a cot in his laboratory, continued tireless work both in New Jersey and Florida.[1]

Frailty and Death

In the beginning of 1889 it became apparent to those close to John Ericsson that he was a very ill man. Ericsson fought off increasing weakness, but insisted that he must be up and dressed during the day, although in the end he needed assistance to get his clothes on. Hoping to coax him out of his habit of resting on the dreadful table in his study, Sam Taylor arranged to have a reclining chair brought to his office. He initially refused to use it because he said that "it was made on a wrong mechanical principle." One slight concession he agreed to was to substitute a hard pillow for the dictionary, and a blanket was spread over the table on which he continued to nap. Ericsson still did not want to be idle and Taylor reported that he had "conceived a new motive engine, the drawings for which he made with his own hands within seven days and he proudly alluded to the achievement as proof of his good physical vigor and undiminished construction energy. Those around him, however, noticed his fatigue and feared that he had overtaxed himself. The engine was built and delivered at Captain Ericsson's residence by February 1st."[2]

This happened at the time of the unexpected death of his very intimate friend Harry Delamater, whom he looked upon as a younger brother. John was devastated and did not want to carry on. It was a terrible shock to him, however much he tried to deny it. On February 18 he could not resist the temptation, ordered the new engine to be operated on the third floor and climbed the stairs to see it running. When it worked he was again in excellent spirits but that did not last long and soon his health deteriorated visibly.

One morning he informed Taylor that he had passed an uncomfortable night and complained that he was exhausted, having been dreaming all night about "mechanical contrivances." Now it was realized that something seriously was happening because he never admitted suffering from anything. From this time on Taylor did not leave his master for twelve days and nights. He kept a diary about what was going on with his boss, making detailed observations about room and body temperature, his diet, fluid intake and urine output by catheter and vital signs, such as breathing frequency.

Once when he obtained permission to remain with him during his usual pre-bedtime naked exercise, he was "painfully made aware that the Captain's body was greatly emaciated," and saw that he had a swelling on one leg and "became somewhat lame." Ericsson implied that he had injured his ankle during previous "gymnastic exercise"—an unlikely explanation in view of the fact that just a day later a similar swelling developed on the other leg. With all that he refused to see a doctor but asked Taylor to look in a dictionary for the cause of dropsy. According to this information there were two possibilities, either heart or kidney failure.[3]

When Taylor detected an irregular pulse on his master the comment was that "my heart is not doing complete duty." After a self-check Ericsson gave an engineering description of his condition: "A diagram of my pulse would resemble a saw with every sixth & tenth tooth broken off." This to him was only a slight abnormality that could be taken care of with proper medication, but to imagine that anything could be wrong with his kidneys was "exceedingly disagreeable," claiming that they were in perfect order.

Now Ericsson finally agreed to be treated by a neighboring physician, Dr. Boullet. He received prescriptions for his heart with digitalis and quinine pills but he gave strict instructions that no mention should be made to anyone about his condition. When he became weaker and had difficulty sleeping, breathing 30 times a minute and running a temperature, he finally agreed to have a urine test done. The result was positive for albumin and therefore a diagnosis of "Bright's disease," an inflammatory kidney disorder, was made.[4] This was a serious condition, named after the famous London physician, Dr. Richard Bright, who in 1827 described the disease that bears his name.

Finally Ericsson was worried and consented to call his good friend and physician, Dr. Markoe. When he appeared in the bedroom, the patient with a loud, firm voice asked: "Markoe, can a man who has Bright's disease of the kidneys do any more work?" To this he got the reply: "Captain, a man who has got Bright's disease of the kidneys has no right to do any more work."[5] This was a devastating verdict and Taylor commented: "I felt [it] to be the final dissipation of any hope the Captain entertained of again being useful to his fellow man, and that now he would not make an effort to live."[6]

Ironically, it was the same ailment that two years earlier had caused his son Hjalmar's death. Ericsson therefore must have been very concerned about the diagnosis. In letters Hjalmar had described the symptoms to his father, who disagreed with the medical treatment he received in Sweden because he was convinced that his disease was due to enlargement of the prostate gland causing mechanical urinary obstruction and should be treated accordingly, like a plumbing problem. He had given advice about the condition and possible cure, but Hjalmar did not improve. After his death he wrote a very uncompassionate letter to his daughter-in-law, complaining: "His constitution was evidently completely destroyed by physician's ignorance and his own senselessness. The fact is that your husband, who was an unusually strong man, was simply murdered by ignorance." In reality the disease was the result of enlargement of the prostate gland, a problem of which Ericsson himself had suffered for "a dozen years " and his bladder had to be emptied by a silver catheter.[7, 8]

The Monitor Man

In the end weakness forced him to leave his work table altogether and stay in bed. Now he was attended by a nurse who detected a fever of 102 degrees, therefore it is very likely that he had a severe urinary tract infection. Every effort was made to keep him alive until the coming Saturday, the anniversary of the battle at Hampton Roads, but one day before he peacefully passed away.

Taylor recalled: "At 11,30 P.M. on my arranging his pillow and speaking to him, he looked at me with a smile and said: 'I am resting, this rest is magnificent — more beautiful than words can tell.' I feel certain that he was perfectly conscious to the last moment. At 12,39 he breathed three times, the lips moving perceptibly and the great good man ended his work."[9]

To a good friend of his master Taylor wrote: "He knew that his end was approaching and viewed it with stoical calmness, simply repeating 'Give me rest.' It may be truly said that his illness was of short duration and without bodily pain, emphatically insisting that he was 'very comfortable' and had 'never felt a pain in his life'; but complained at one time that turpentine application burnt his skin a little."[10]

Ericsson died on March 8, 1889, at the age of eighty-six. Funeral services were held on March 11 in Trinity Church, New York. The beautiful building at the end of Wall Street was the tallest structure in the city when in 1846 it was first erected in Gothic Revival style. The Episcopal congregation was originally founded in 1696 and some of its prominent members were Robert Fulton and John Jacob Astor. Swedish compatriots in America and a few personal friends still living arranged a simple funeral service and laid his remains in the receiving vault of the small Marble Cemetery on East Second Street waiting for the final burial.[11]

Ericsson's death stirred old memories. There were long obituary notices in newspapers and technical magazines, mentioning him as "The Monitor Man" and listing his many inventions. The final resting place was still to be agreed upon. Various suggestions were being considered. One of these was in response to a petition by the Swedish government to transfer his body to the country of his birth, another suggested burying Ericsson beside Robert Fulton in Trinity Church.

Ericsson did not like ostentatious ceremonies and funerals and he once declared that "grand funerals are objectionable in my opinion." "The best thing they can do with my body is to throw it into a retort, convert it into matter and let it mingle with the atmosphere."[12]

He never clearly expressed his opinion as to where and how he wished to be buried. He merely once alluded to his housekeeper that he "thought he might be buried under the stone marking his birthplace." Ericsson's faithful secretary for 28 years, Samuel Taylor, expressed the wishes of most Americans when he said: "My own preference and that of thousands is that he rest for all time to come in the land whose prosperity and freedom he more than any single man benefited and blessed by his creative genius and wonderful achievements."[13]

Departure

After eight months the government suggested the Navy consider "if practical," a transfer of John Ericsson's remains to Sweden. After some haggling about which warship should carry Ericsson's body, the new USS *Baltimore* was chosen for the honor. Now preparations started for the ceremony to transfer Ericsson's remains in New York Harbor.

On August 23, 1890, large crowds had assembled to watch the procession when Ericsson's body was being transferred to Battery Park. It was a moving memorial, remembering the past of a great man who had left an imprint on American history. At the cemetery the coffin was covered with the shot-riddled battle flag of the *Monitor* and placed on a gun carriage with uniformed guards of a Marine Battalion slowly marching beside it through streets thronged with curious onlookers. Rear Admiral John L. Worden, who had commanded the *Monitor* on her famous battle, led the procession. Behind him marched members of the *Monitor's* crew who were still living.

Orders from the White House were: "In recognition of the debt we owe to Sweden for the gift of Ericsson, whose genius rendered us the highest service in a moment of grave peril and anxiety the flag of Sweden shall be saluted by the squadron."

The ceremony attracted many people, not only on Manhattan but also in New York Harbor. On Pier A, North River, on Battery Park the coffin was embarked on the naval tug *Nina* for transfer to the USS *Baltimore*. In New York Harbor a large fleet of warships was ordered to participate but it became impossible to keep up the planned line of sailing because "of the great number of private yachts, tugs, and steamers assembled and crossing the line, but the imperfect formation did not appear to detract from the impressiveness of the ceremony for it seemed to be a tribute to the memory of the well known great inventor, that such a large mass of onlookers should desire to witness the last scene attending the removal of his remains from his adopted country."[14]

On board the *Baltimore* the coffin was draped with the United States Flag and the Swedish flag lying beside it. As anchorage ground a location near the Statue of Liberty had been chosen. In a ceremony aboard the *Baltimore*, John Ericsson's body was surrounded by officials and an honor guard. The secretary of the Navy and the Ministers of Sweden and Norway were present.

The last words of farewell were spoken by George H. Robinson, a son-in-law of Ericsson's best friend, Harry Delamater: "We send him back crowned with honors, proud of the life of fifty years he devoted to this nation, and with gratitude for the gifts he gave us.— Was he a dreamer? Yes. He dreamed of the practical application of screw propulsion ... he dreamed of the sun's rays in sandy deserts where water was hard to get, and the solar engine came."[15]

The Swedish flag waved brightly in the hot August sun, and a 21-gun salute shook the deck of the steamship as it glided swiftly through the Narrows—past schooners, sloops, ferryboats, tugboats and warships, all flying their flags at half-mast. Never before had the United States awarded such an honor with a grand ceremony to a private citizen. Ericsson would have described the occasion as "unnecessary pomp" but he probably could not help being pleased by the recognition of his work and affection that was shown to him.

Back Home

The *Baltimore* reached Stockholm on September 14. Young Elias Grip, an eye-witness of the event and later a biographer of John Ericsson, tells us: "The day started with bright sunshine over the festivity decorated capital. I remember clearly that day. I had just started high school and with my brothers and sisters I came in good time to witness the festive occasion. Already early in the morning formally dressed crowds had assembled in the Royal Garden near the harbor and along the path of the procession. Here buildings were decorated with flags and black veils. Near the river and the harbor were a large number of vessels decorated with flags and all the way in the background we could see the stately white *Baltimore*."[16]

There the ship was boarded by a reception committee of Ericsson's relatives and high ranking naval officers. Sailors of the *Baltimore* transferred the coffin to a Swedish naval barge which landed at Karl XII's Square, near the Royal Castle. All vessels in the harbor lowered their flags to half-mast, and the cannons of Stockholm roared a continuous salute. On shore, the American minister, Mr. W.W. Thomas, received John Ericsson's remains with an address which ended with the words: "We return Ericsson's body to you, but we love to keep his memory to ourselves, or rather we share it with you and the whole world."

In town, bells tolled, and the American marines from the *Baltimore* formed the guard of honor escorting the remains of Ericsson through streets lined with bareheaded citizens to the railroad station where the Crown Prince and other dignitaries received the cortege. Following a brief service, the coffin was placed on a special train that carried John Ericsson on the final stage of his journey back to his Värmland home in Filipstad. Here, on August 15 twelve miners bore him on their shoulders to the church for a burial ceremony. Interment took place on September 15 in a preliminary mausoleum designed by my ancestor Georg Ringström and specially erected at the new cemetery near Lake Daglösen.

During the following years in a campaign, money was collected to build a permanent vault and in 1892 a competition was announced for the best architectural design. Three years later a grandiose mausoleum was completed on a height overlooking the beautiful lake Daglösen. It was built of two types of light gray and dark granite with Ericsson's coffin inside resting on a fundament of green Swedish marble. This became Ericsson's final resting place where an American flag was draped across the sarcophagus, and placed at its foot was his screw propeller, an emblem of the maritime field in which he had won lasting fame.[17]

The final burial ceremony took place in 1895 and started in May with a popular musical recital by the Fish Jubilee Singers, African American men and women who had specially come from the U.S. They paid their homage by placing a wreath with the inscription: "From former slaves and the children of slaves to the memory of John Ericsson, one of the great champions of freedom."

The official opening of the mausoleum took place on Ericsson's birthday, July 31, 1895. Flowers were placed at the coffin, in the center a laurel wreath with palm-leaves and blue and yellow silk ribbons had the inscription "Sophie Elworth."[18]

27

Ericsson Remembered

His inventions were not the result of waking dreams, but the studious application of engineering.
— William C. Church, 1890

John Ericsson is best remembered for his *Monitor,* the turreted ironclad warship which after the battle at Hampton Roads created a "*Monitor* craze" that swept the Union with cartoons, advertisements and other expressions of popular culture. But during the decade after the great war the formidable wartime military force was reduced by more than 80 percent and ironclads rusted in navy yards while the navy returned to ships of canvas and wood.[1] Everybody was pleased that the murderous conflict was finally over and most people wanted to forget the horrible time.

But all that changed in the 1880s and '90s when there was a period of sentimental Civil War revival in which Ericsson and his ship again for a short time entered center stage.

Voices

John Ericsson was a very private man who shunned publicity. After the battle at Hampton Roads he could have been in the limelight if he had visited the *Monitor* like President Lincoln, Gustavus A. Fox, Nathaniel Hawthorne and newspaper reporters, but he preferred solitude and continued his work designing new warships for the Union at his house on Manhattan.

During the following years and until his death isolation became even more pronounced and only his 1890 funeral procession in New York Harbor and a two volume biography by William C. Church published in New York and London the same year brought his name again to public attention. Now people began to look back at the life of a great man and tried to commemorate his achievements both in Europe and the United States. He became a symbol of national pride and an interesting part of the history of the industrial revolution.

During his lifetime John Ericsson had to fight much opposition and sometimes even justified criticism. To this his long-time former collaborator on Manhattan, Professor Charles W. MacCord, expressed the view: "It is safe to say that the memory of John Ericsson will be green in the minds of men long after not only carping criticism, but the critics themselves, with their records, their achievements and all, shall have been sunk fathoms deep in the everlasting limbo of things forgotten."[2]

Much later, in England he was not forgotten. John M. Kenworthy, lieutenant commander of the Royal Navy and member of Parliament, said in 1930: "John Ericsson was one of the greatest marine engineers and architects the world has known. He was the pioneer of the screw propeller and, but for the bad luck of a broken ventilating fan, his railway steam engine, the *Novelty*, might have beaten Stephenson's *Rocket*." Even Winston Churchill in 1939 praised Ericsson's *Monitor*, a ship that finally led to a reconstruction of the British Navy.[3]

It is understandable that Swedish-Americans were particularly proud of their countryman. One of them was Carl Sandburg, who in his memoirs *Always the Young Strangers* gives us a funny glimpse of what happened when he as a boy became interested in small biographies found in cigarette boxes.

> In the list I noticed John Ericsson, the inventor of the *Monitor*, the Swede who helped the North win the war. I tried but couldn't scare up a copy of the John Ericsson. A Swede boy pulled one out of his vest pocket one day and grinned at me. He knew I wanted it. I offered him a penny for it and went as high as a nickel and he shook his head. Then he let me borrow it to read and I let him borrow my Sarah Bernhardt. He had heard she kept a coffin in her bedroom and liked to stretch out in it to rest. I showed him where the book told about that and what kind of woman she was. "They say she is the world's greatest actress," I told him, and then read to him from the book, how "she recites her lines as the nightingale sings, as the wind sighs, as the waters murmur." "Gee I like to hear her," said the Swede boy, and I went on reading so as to get to the coffin.
> "Gee!" said the Swede boy. "I sure want to read that book." I offered to trade him the Sarah Bernhardt for his John Ericsson. He said maybe and the next day said he talked it over with his Swede father and mother and they said, "No keep the John Ericsson. He was a great man and this French actress is a bad woman."[4]

Proud Memories

When new interest surged for the historic battles of the Civil War a "*Merrimack* and *Monitor* Naval Battle Panorama" opened in Manhattan on Madison Avenue. It was a huge round building where the walls displayed the battle scene of Hampton Roads and which became a tourist attraction. Similar displays were made in St. Paul, Minnesota, Chicago and Washington, D.C. In Baltimore, it was called a "Cyclorama"; here according to the pamphlet advertising the event, it was "a vivid reproduction of the celebrated naval engagement between the *Merrimac* and Monitor." In Denver, Colorado, a big building with rotating gun turrets on the roof was opened in Elitch's Gardens.[5]

A wave of memoirs and publications swept the country and veterans of the war celebrated memorials. The best known is the collection of illustrated articles in the *Century* magazine called "Battles and Leaders of the Civil War." It contained a section about the Union and Confederate navies and a review of the battle at Hampton Roads. During his lifetime John Ericsson was asked to contribute. Issued four times, the latest in 1894, it became immensely popular. Until this day John Ericsson and his ship are an American icon of the machine age.[6]

We should, however, not forget that the "*Monitor* Man" did much more than build warships; he also designed many practical things such as small energy saving hot-air engines and above all he was the visionary pioneer of solar energy. The remains of these inventions attracted public attention much later and a few remaining constructions and models now are on display at the American Swedish Museum in Philadelphia and the Technical Museum in Stockholm.

In 1888 the creator of the Stockholm outdoor museum Skansen, Arthur Hazelius, wrote to Ericsson asking for some personal belongings to be included in this collection. As soon as the letter was received in New York, Ericsson's telegraphic answer was that he took no interest in museums that preserve relics that show "crudity and imperfect knowledge of previous generations. Time will soon convert such relics into heaps of mould."[7] Ericsson probably also was annoyed by somebody who anticipated his approaching death.

Shortly after Ericsson's passing Hazelius again tried his luck with a request to obtain some memorabilia. To this Samuel Taylor replied that he was greatly surprised at Ericsson's refusal and wrote: "Personally it will give me pleasure to aid you in securing mementoes of the great and good man."[8] This new approach resulted in the transfer of furniture of Ericsson's study to Stockholm and now there is an Ericsson Room at Skansen in the old Hazelius-House. But unfortunately the new administration does not properly appreciate the gift and the collection was not open to the general public in 2003.

In 1889 New York decided to commemorate John Ericsson with a monument. The legislature of New York City by an unusual act appropriated ten thousand dollars to erect it to the memory of the great inventor. It was to be the first statue ever erected at the expense of the municipality. Colonel William Conant Church, the biographer of Ericsson, was elected chairman of a committee in charge of necessary preparations to select an artist.[9]

It took a long time to chose the proper place, but in 1893 a bronze statue showing the inventor standing on a granite pedestal was erected on lower

Manhattan. On the morning of April 27 a great crowd of members of various societies gathered at Union Square before marching down Broadway to Battery Park to celebrate the dedication ceremony. The *New York Times* wrote: "Miss Esselinda Andersson, a young Swedish beauty selected specially for her personal charms by the Swedish societies from among all the other pretty girls to haul the drawstring and unveil the statue of Ericsson. She was dressed in a silk costume of the Swedish national colors, and carried a bunch of fresh wild flowers which were neither so white nor so red as she." After orations, cheering, clapping and songs the double-turreted monitor *Miantonomah*, which lay at anchor off Battery Park boomed a national salute of twenty-one shots in honor of the inventor of her prototype. (The *Miantonomah* was the only monitor that crossed the Atlantic in 1866 and visited Sweden with Assistant Secretary of the Navy G.V. Fox).

Ten years later, on August 2, 1903, a new version of the statue with Ericsson holding a model of the *Monitor* in his left hand was unveiled and dedicated by New York Mayor Seth Low, who said in his speech: "May Ericsson's statue stand here in Battery Park, where it shall overlook the waters of the proud harbor which his genius did so much to develop. The beat of every propeller that lashes the waters of the bay into foam will bring to him its song and praise." The present statue in Battery Park is a refurbished version with a new pedestal and bronze plates which was unveiled in 1952.[10] There also is a *Monitor* and *Merrimack* monument in Battery Park. It is a sculpture which was created by the Italian-American sculptor Antonio de Filippo (1900–1993) and was dedicated in 1938. The statue depicts a heroic male nude pulling a rope attached to a capstan, symbolizes Ericsson's role in military-maritime technology, and honors the memory of the men of the *Monitor*. There is another statue of Ericsson in West Potomac Park in Washington, D.C. It was earected in 1926.

In the Swedish settlements in America people were justly proud of their famous fellow countryman and they took every opportunity to celebrate not his birthday, but the anniversary of the battle of Hampton Roads, March 9 when the *Monitor* met the *Merrimack* in history's first battle of armored warships.

In Chicago, on March 9, the Swedish-American Republican League introduced the John Ericsson Day to commemorate "the single greatest achievement of a Swedish American, the construction of the *Monitor*." These events sometimes were "brilliant affairs at which the President, members of cabinet, governors, senators and famous wits and orators of the nation and even rival candidates for high offices, have talked and fraternized under the intertwining colors of the U.S. and Sweden." In 1896 the league also published a little paper, *The Monitor News*. The most notable event was the 50th anniversary of the battle in 1912.[11]

In 1926 another monument honoring John Ericsson was erected in Washington's Potomac Park, near the huge Lincoln Memorial. The unveiling

John Ericsson statue in Battery Park, New York City (courtesy Janice Lauletta-Weinmann, Greenpoint Monitor Museum, Brooklyn, New York).

ceremony was performed by President Calvin Coolidge and Crown Prince Gustav Adolf of Sweden. The event was commemorated by the issue of a 5-cent U.S. postage stamp showing the statue and the shields of the United States and Sweden. A contemporary author praised the event with the words: "Thus the Savior of the Nation from his gleaming temple of marble will salute the silent Swede whose mechanical genius saved for him the sea."[12]

In 1907 the John Ericsson Society of New York was founded with the aim "to perpetuate the memory of Captain John Ericsson and to disseminate information concerning the life and works of him." The Swedish American Museum in Philadelphia has a valuable collection of Ericsson memorabilia and an archive of his correspondence.

The people of Greenpoint, Brooklyn, in many ways have honored John Ericsson and his *Monitor*. In November 5, 1938, they dedicated in Winthrop Park a fourteen foot bronze monument to commemorate the naval engagement at Hampton Roads. There also is a street named Monitor Street and two schools honoring the memory of the great inventor, one called The Monitor School and the other the John Ericsson Intermediate School.

In the U.S. three warships were named after Ericsson, the first in 1890, the second in 1912 and finally in 1941 the destroyer *Ericsson*, which actively participated in combat in the second World War.[13]

Ericsson in Sweden

In his homeland there are two statues of John Ericsson, in Stockholm and another in Gothenburg. Värmland, the birthplace, is particularly proud of their famous son and yearly there are a birthday celebrations in Filipstad on July 31 with a colorful re-enactment of the battle of the ironclads on Lake Daglösen. It takes place close to the Ericsson mausoleum overlooking the water near two big cannon from a Swedish monitor.

In 1937 the Swedish film industry produced a one and a half–hour movie entitled *The Victor at Hampton Roads*. It is the idealized story of the great inventor, produced by Gustaf Edgren, with Victor Sjöström in the leading role as the great inventor.

Dr. Mark D. Hirsch of New York in 1954 wrote: "John Ericsson's stage was the *world*. To associate him alone with our city, or State, or even the nation, is to demean him, to make parochial his boundless mental endowment and indomitable spirit. He was a selfless, devoted servant of mankind."[14] Mark Twain once said: "I think we never become really and genuinely our entire and honest selves until we have been dead years and years. People ought to start dead and then they would be honest so much earlier."[15]

Today we have to ask the critical question whether it is worthwhile to continue admiring him. Ericsson's personal friend and biographer, William

Kjell Lagerström, former chairman of the John Ericsson Society of New York, in front of the John Ericsson monument in Washington, D.C. (courtesy Kjell Lagerström).

John Ericsson monument, Nybroviken, Stockholm, Sweden (photograph courtesy Leif Brisfjord, chairman, John Ericsson Society of New York).

C. Church, the year after his death asked the critical question: "When we erect a statue to a private citizen we must justify ourselves to posterity, for we challenge the approval of the future for the personal estimates of today."[16] I think the question is justified and we still can remember Ericsson as a great visionary of his time.

In a 2004 critical evaluation of the *Monitor* discovery and rescue operations, Dr. Robert Sheridan makes the following comment after the recovery of the Monitor turret: "The *Monitor* display will honor John Ericsson, the genius inventor of this extraordinary vessel. There are many statues of Ericsson already in the United States, but when viewers see the major artifacts, and realize what was involved in saving them, then they will realize how much our nation appreciates and treasures innovative thinking skills."[17]

28

Lost and Found

There was the overpowering sense of majesty when this great iron wreck, at once both monument and living document, emerged from the gloom.
— William C. Davis, 2000

Lost but never forgotten, for many years the wreck of the *Monitor* was the object of search in the "Graveyard of the Atlantic" on the coast of North Carolina, the stormy meeting place of northern and southern currents, near Cape Hatteras. From 1526 to 1900 at least 409 vessels perished there with 1000 deaths. Most of the ships were never found again and although the search for the *Monitor* began soon after the Civil War the wreck remained an enigma until 1973.

Shipwrecks

What was the attraction of shipwrecks? Finding lost friends or family, tracing history or money? In the nineteenth century shipwrecking on the Carolina coast actually was a profitable business and there many had steady jobs as crewmen on wrecking schooners. At one time almost every community had a wreck commissioner and there was ample opportunity for a man with business acumen to make a good profit buying and selling salvaged material. The ships recovered in those days were close to the shore and sometimes the cargo was worth a lot.[1]

After the Civil War the most lucrative offer to find a warship came when the showman Phineas T. Barnum of New York City without success offered a staggering $100,000 for retrieval of the Confederate submarine the *Hunley*, which in 1864 mysteriously foundered outside Charleston after sinking the USS *Housatonic*. Barnum was eagerly looking for a big attraction to his new museum on Broadway. Finally, in 1995, after many failed attempts the wreck was spotted four miles off Fort Sumter and raised five years later after years of technical planning.

Even today a dramatic recovery operation at Cape Hatteras of the SS

Central America promises to become a valuable enterprise expected to yield $100 million of a cargo that at the time was worth $2 million. The vessel was a side-wheeler carrying 600 passengers on her return from the gold fields of California when she in 1857 went down in a hurricane off the Carolinas, claiming more than 400 lives and 21 tons of gold. In 1988, after a long and adventurous search, a consortium of investors was able to recover a huge bounty of gold coins to be sold piecemeal.[2]

But so far the best example of a shipwreck as big business is the affair of the British luxury liner *Titanic* which in 1912 hit an iceberg and sunk off the coast of Newfoundland, killing more than 1,500 people. Since 1985, when the wreck was discovered, a company, the RMS Titanic Inc., was formed to conserve the historic wreck. Six trips have been made to the remote spot with the recovery of nearly 5,000 artifacts, including coins, suitcases, chandeliers and engine parts to be sold at auctions. The gross revenue of the company through 1999 was $23 million.[3]

The immense interest that was devoted to finding and recovering the *Hunley* and Ericsson's historic *Monitor*, where nobody could expect to make a penny, may seem surprising. Thankfully, other attractions besides profitable treasures can interest people of today.

The Monitor*'s Gravesite*

Since the loss of the *Monitor* many unsuccessful attempts have been made to find the elusive ship. The search was not only for recovery of the wreck but also directed at details of her construction and to solve the question of why she sank. Was it only progressive flooding or did the upper and lower part of the hull separate due to heavy impact in the high waves, as suggested by some?

The first serious attempt was made in 1955 by Marine Corporal Robert Marx in shallow waters only two miles offshore, northeast of Cape Hatteras. The location was chosen because it was reported that in 1863 five bodies from the *Monitor* had been washed ashore near the old lighthouse at the cape. Marx thought that he had found the wreck. He repeatedly dived to the wreck in 45 feet of water. At one of his dives, to insure his claim for the supposed wreck he scribbled his name on a piece of paper and tucked it in a Coca-Cola bottle, which he placed in what he thought to be one of the gun ports of the *Monitor's* turret. Unfortunately he was not a winner and repeated searches, the last in 1974, could not confirm Marx's initial finding.[4]

In the early 1970s Mr. John G. Newton, the superintendent of the Duke University Marine Laboratory, organized geological studies off the North Carolina coast with the research vessel *Eastward*. Operations in 1973 had dual objectives: geological study of the continental shelf off Cape Hatteras, and a search for the USS *Monitor*. It became a joint venture of Duke University, the

U.S. Army Reserve, the National Geographic Society and the National Science Foundation. This time it was decided to go further offshore to deep waters in an area where the *Monitor* was last sighted in 1862. The operation was guided by a track chart reconstructed after the tug *Rhode Island*'s log. The *Eastward* and her crew spent two weeks at sea using the latest technology of side-scan sonars and cameras. The first promising target was photographed at 300 feet of water, but after three days of intensive labor it was realized that it was the wreck of a fishing trawler with a semicircular pilot-house which looked deceivingly like the *Monitor*'s turret.

The next discovery proved to be the real hit when traces of a suspicious wreck were found. It happened on 27 August 1973, the last day of the planned search. Fred Kelly, who acted as a liaison officer between the scientists and the *Eastward* crew, came to the geophysics lab and told Dr. Robert Sheridan, who was on watch, about a side-scan contact on a recorder. He immediately recognized its significance and when looking at it he said: "There it was — the most beautiful sonar contact we had recorded yet on the cruise. It was a dark, crisp, black mark on the otherwise grey recorder paper. Clearly we had found another wreck."[5]

Now it was decided to make another serious attempt at identifying the interesting object and therefore the *Eastward* and her crew spent three more days scanning the area with a TV camera. Even though the pictures were blurred, in the end many interesting details emerged, such as a flat structure with a circular protrusion that could possibly be the turret. After the ship returned to its base a lengthy puzzle started to put all the bits together from reels of video tape. Thank God, all the efforts had not been in vain and finally it was realized that the wreck of the *Monitor* had been found. Underwater photographs showed the wreck 230 feet below sea level with the turret resting under the hull, being detached when the ship sunk. Obviously the *Monitor* had rolled over when she sank, landing upside-down. The wreck had suffered considerable structural damage.[6]

On January 30, 1975, the National Oceanic and Atmospheric Administration (NOAA) designated the wreck of the *Monitor* as the nation's first National Marine Sanctuary. This means that the wreck is protected from anchoring, trawling, salvage or recovery operations without the permission of NOAA. In 1987 on March 9, the 125th anniversary of the *Monitor-Virginia* battle, the *Monitor* also was selected as a National Historic Landmark and the Mariners' Museum in Newport News, Virginia, as the principal repository and permanent exhibit of salvaged parts of the vessel and other items.

Recovery?

Some objects were saved. In July 1977 a brass navigation lantern with a red Fresnel lens inside was recovered, suggesting that it was a signal lamp, probably the lantern that was lit to signal distress before the *Monitor* sank. Six years later a unique four-fluked anchor emerged from the depth.[7]

The question of raising the *Monitor* has been debated since she was located in 1973 but at the time no final decision of her recovery was made. Recordings of the outline of the *Monitor* from 1974 to 1999 showed that the precious wreck was rapidly deteriorating and at one time it was wrongly believed that in addition to natural decay caused by the sea, it also had been damaged by depth charges during World War II. It was quite clear, something had to be done without delay if anything should be saved. Therefore the consensus called for a partial recovery with conservation and museum

Remote-operated vehicle over the wreck of the *Monitor* (courtesy *Monitor* Collection, NOAA, Newport News, Virginia).

display. NOAA finally proposed a plan to lift parts of the wreck, including the engine, the propeller and the massive iron turret with its two guns. In 1995 the navy joined the recovery efforts to provide training for its divers.

On November 1997 a proposition for the *Monitor* recovery was presented to Congress and the following year, the four-bladed, 4,600-pound propeller was lifted from the bottom of the sea. It is the only surviving original ship's screw by the man who invented the technology. Today the nine-foot screw is in the Mariners' Museum for preservation.[8] In 2000 the *Monitor's* hull was stabilized by shoring up the wreck with cement bags and sinking a 90-ton steel recovery structure deployed to support the steam engine. The following year the 30-ton engine was successfully lifted.

The last scheduled major recovery operation was to lift the turret. For that purpose, divers cut away deteriorated parts of the vessel and clamped on an eight-armed "spider-grip" over it. The turret was then placed on a support platform so that it could be raised intact. On August 5, 2002, Mr. John Broadwater, the Manager of the Monitor National Marine Sanctuary, and his crew finally recovered the 160-ton revolving tower with its two 11-inch Dahlgren cannons, that had rested on the bottom of the sea for 140 years. The coral-encrusted turret was hoisted with a huge crane aboard a barge the size of a football field. It took two days for divers to remove the remains of a human skeleton from under a cannon.

The Cat Mystery

After the salvage of the turret in 2002 came the opportunity to make some important investigations in the rubble of the turret. At the time a reporter of the *Daily News* addressed a less serious issue: "One of the many mysteries that might be solved by the turret's excavation is the fate of the black cat crewman Francis Butts stowed in a cannon barrel to keep dry as the ship floundered. Butts escaped; no one knows what became of the cat."[9]

Francis B. Butts came on board the *Monitor* just before leaving the Washington Navy Yard in November 1862. A native of Rhode Island, Butts eventually wrote about his experience aboard the *Monitor* and this later was printed in *Century* magazine as sensational news in 1885. One researcher with the Monitor National Marine Sanctuary had always been doubtful of the claim that a ship's cat had been stuffed inside one of the ironclad's 11-inch Dahlgren guns shortly before the vessel sank. The most recent news about the mysterious cat came on August 29, 2005, telling us: "No howling cat on board when the Monitor went down." That was the result of two years of carefully sifting the contents of the guns and it was concluded that not only didn't a cat go down with the ship, but there was probably never such a mascot aboard the most famous Union ship of the Civil War.[10]

In retrospect, the story was reasonable. In 1861 in New York Harbor there had been a mascot cat on board the *Monitor*, although not kept by Francis Butts.[11] Mascots on a warship used to be fairly common, and the era of the American Civil War was no exception. Many surviving photographs show crewmembers proudly posing on the decks of their warships with a loyal dog lying in front of them, or a cat crooked in a sailor's arm. There are even two photographs of the crew of the USS *Monitor*, posing on deck with one seaman holding a cat while another on the monitor *Lehigh* holds a fighting cock.[12] Therefore, the story of the cat on the sinking *Monitor* remains a legend.

Face-to-Face History

The turret and the previously lifted screw propeller are being restored at the Mariners' Museum in a slow, painstaking process by immersion in a 93,000 gallon steel tank, containing a mixture of fresh water and chemicals. During the "electrolytic reduction process" visitors can watch the submerged parts from a platform around the tank. Scientists hope to find artifacts when they clean out the tons of silt that remain in the turret. The many precious *Monitor* relics will finally be on display in the museum's $30-million USS *Monitor* Center, a special wing set to open in 2007. Experts are looking forward to the final display of the individual parts because Ericsson was a tinkerer and made last-minute changes that, in the rush to finish the ironclad, were never recorded and may now be revealed.[13]

The decision for recovery had been much easier with the CS submarine *Hunley*, which in 1864 sank in Charleston Harbor. Since then several efforts were made to find the famous sub and in 1995 finally the wreck was located at a depth of only 26 feet, four miles off Fort Sumter. At the millennium, after five years of technical planning and legal maneuvering, the *Hunley* was finally placed in a specially designed cradle and carefully lifted to the surface by a huge crane. The recovered sub is now preserved at the former Navy Yard in North Charleston in a specially designed container. After a stabilization process that can take up to ten years, the submarine will go on display at the Charleston Museum outside of which there already stands a replica.[14]

Why Sinking?

Motivation for the long search of the wreck of the *Monitor* by the research team and midshipmen-volunteers of Project Cheesebox was not gold or money, but is an example of admirable idealism, patriotism, youthful enterprise and quest for knowledge. For the ambitious young team it was not enough to have detected the wreck of the *Monitor*, no, they wanted to dig further into the mysteries of their "cheesebox." So, they started to test all aspects of the historic vessel such as its sea-worthiness. Why did she have such big problems in heavy seas, both on the way to Hampton Roads and on her last voyage? Did big waves induce pounding movements that separated the hull from the upper overlapping raft?

Intensive efforts soon gave some exciting results. The team prepared a miniature model of the *Monitor* and took it to the Naval Research Laboratory for stability tests. In order to study the sea-worthiness of new ships "Towing Tank Tests" are conducted. This involves subjecting ship's models in a water tank in which artificial waves are created while recording the vessel's motions in two directions. In a series of experiments a model of the *Monitor* was tested to check its stability at variety of waves corresponding to actual sea conditions. Eighteen runs at increasing wave heights were made to determine motions of pitch and heave.

The results were unexpected and very different from a modern ship. Usually a vessel's motion increases with wave height, meaning the higher the waves, the more severe the vessel's motion. Not so with the *Monitor*, which was very stable each time the bow submerged; a large amount of water was picked up and dampened the motion because the additional weight of the water caused the bow to plow *through the wave rather than over it.* Therefore it could be concluded that the *Monitor* must have been remarkably stable even in rough seas. Lt Edward M. Miller reasoned: "Though designed for smooth waters, with low freeboard, the upper raft portion of the hull acted as a scoop when the seas increased, supplying the additional mass which dampened out the oscillating motion. *The ride aboard the Monitor may have been wet, but it was relatively smooth!*"[15]

These experiments support the credo John Ericsson expressed in front of the Ironclad Board in 1861: "The sea shall ride over her, and she will live in it like a duck."[16] Later we have a confirmation of this tenet by a newspaper reporter who described his experience from the trial run of another monitor, the *Passaic:* "The waiter held a glass full of water in his hand, while white caps were breaking over the deck, and a particle of the liquid never trembled."[17]

In order to better understand of how the *Monitor* reacted during the storm before she sank, additional investigations were done at the David Taylor Model Basin in Carderock, Maryland. Here conditions were created where the model was put in tow at high seas with wave heights corresponding to twenty feet. When the ship's motion was tested at conditions of a storm, another surprising finding was that the bow and stern emerged from the water in every pitching cycle, with no slamming of the bow. The superstructures such as the turret and smokestack were subjected to heavy impact of water and it became clear that the oakum packing around the turret must have been washed out by the great force of water. At the time the investigators noted a unique historical coincidence: the test with the *Monitor* gave the same result as that of the Navy's newest submarine, the *Trident*.[18]

The question of whether there was a separation of the upper and lower hull was a major issue that the recovery operations of the wreck might solve. When the remains of the *Monitor* were found, unfortunately, the lower part of the vessel was nearly completely disintegrated. But Mr. Broadwater told me that "there is no firm evidence that a separation actually took place."[19]

We now can conclude that the un-seaworthiness and weak point of Ericsson's unorthodox flatboat was not her alleged instability at heavy seas, presumably verified by the foundering of the *Monitor,* but was mainly due to water leaks at the turret, the ventilation shafts and the anchor-well. The real problem of monitor vessels was their low freeboard and therefore, despite stability, they were unseaworthy for ocean travel and had little reserve buoyancy, so that a leak could be fatal.[20]

Today, looking back at the great interest in the *Monitor*'s wreck with many people watching the recovery operations and visiting the Mariners' Museum in Newport News, John Ericsson would have been very pleased to see his little ship receiving so much attention.[21] On March 9, 2007, exactly 145 years after the historic clash between the Civil War ironclads USS *Monitor* and CSS *Virginia*, the Mariners' Museum and its partner, the National Oceanic and Atmospheric Administration (NOAA) will open the doors to one of the premier Civil War attractions across the nation — the USS *Monitor* Center. Another site of interest is the American Swedish Historical Museum in Philadelphia. Dedicated to preserving the contributions of Swedish-Americans in the United States, it has a permanent John Ericsson exhibition, and then there is the Greenpoint Monitor Museum in Brooklyn.

Chronology

1803	Johan (John) Ericsson was born July 31, at Långbanshyttan, near Filipstad, Sweden.
1810–19	Move to Forsvik, where John goes to school and works at Göta Canal.
1820	Ericsson joins the army.
1821	Designs his first steam and "fire"-engines.
1824	John Ericsson's and Carolina Lilljeskold's son, Hjalmar Elworth, is born in Stockholm.
1826	To London.
1827	Promoted to captain in the Swedish army.
1829	Ericsson's locomotive, the *Novelty,* participated in a competition at Rainhill with Stephenson's *Rocket.*
1832	On May 2, 1832, jailed at King's Bench prison for debt.
1834	October 10, moves to 8 Albany Street, Regent's Park, London NW1.
1836	May 31, British patent for screw propeller.
1836	July 13, moves to Brook Street, London W1. Oct. 15, marries Amelia Jane Byam.
1837	Launch of the twin propeller vessel *Francis B. Ogden*, also called the *Flying Devil*. Applies through Francis B. Ogden for an American patent for his screw propeller.
1838	SS *Stockton* launched. The first propeller vessel to cross the Atlantic, in 1839.
1839	July 6, moves to Cambridge Terrace, Hyde Park, London NW1.
1839	November 23, arrives in New York.
1840	Amelia comes to New York in May and leaves in October. The last time she came was in the winter of 1842 and left the following year.
1843	Moves from the Astor House to 95 Franklin Street, Manhattan.
1843	First screw propeller war-vessel, the *Princeton*, launched at the Philadelphia Navy Yard.
1846	Designs ironclad with engine below deck for U.S. Navy.
1848	John Ericsson becomes a U.S. citizen.
1850	Elected a member Royal Academy of Sciences, Stockholm. Alfred Nobel comes for his first visit. Jenny Lind sings at Castle Garden, they meet in Ericsson's house.
1852	Caloric-engine vessel, the *Ericsson*, launched; trial runs the following year.

1854	Submits plan for armored cupola vessel to Napoleon III.
1861	October 4, contract signed for *Ericsson's Battery*.
1861	October 25, keel laid for *Ericsson's Battery*.
1862	January 30, USS *Monitor* launched at Greenpoint, Long Island.
1862	March 9, battle with the *Merrimac* (CSS *Virginia*) at Hampton Roads.
1862	May 13, Ericsson awarded the Rumford Medal for his heat engines.
1862	May 15, *Monitor* in battle at Drewry's Bluff on the James River, near Richmond.
1862	October 3, *Monitor* to the Washington Navy Yard for repairs.
1862	November 8, *Monitor* to Newport News.
1862	December 31, *Monitor* founders and sinks off Cape Hatteras.
1863	Draft riots in New York City cause the death of over 1200 people.
1864	Moves to his own house on 36 Beach Street, Manhattan.
1866	Awarded an honorary doctorate for his work on solar energy at the University of Lund, Sweden.
1867	Amelia Byam Ericsson dies on July 20 at the age of 50 in London.
1867	Second visit of Alfred Nobel to the U.S.
1876	*Contributions to the Centennial Exhibition* published. John Ericsson's son, Hjalmar Elworth, visits his father.
1878	Starts work on his torpedo boat, the *Destroyer*.
1887	Hjalmar Elworth dies.
1889	March 8, John Ericsson dies.
1890	The body of John Ericsson brought to Sweden on board the U.S. cruiser *Baltimore,* buried in Filipstad.
1895	The Ericsson mausoleum unveiled in Filipstad.
1926	Ericsson Memorial unveiled in Potomac Park, Washington, D.C.
1973	The wreck of the *Monitor* found off Cape Hatteras.
1975	U.S. government establishes the *Monitor* National Marine Sanctuary.
1999	Recovery of the *Monitor's* propeller.
2002	Recovery of the *Monitor's* gun-tower.

Chapter Notes

Abbreviations: NYHS—John Ericsson Papers, N.Y., New-York Historical Society; ASHF—John Ericsson Papers, Philadelphia, American Swedish Historical Foundation; RLS—John Ericsson Papers, Royal Library, Stockholm; GUL—John Ericsson Papers, Gothenburg University Library; DAB—Dictionary of American Biography, New York; DNB—Dictionary of National Biography, British Library, London.

Preface

1. Thulesius, O. *Edison in Florida.* Gainesville: University of Florida Press, 1997.

1. Miner and Canal Boy

1. The genealogy of John Ericsson described in: Goldkuhl, C. *John Ericsson, Mannen och Uppfinnaren.* Stockholm: Bonniers, 1961, and www.genealogi.se.
2. O'Brien, R. *Machines.* New York: Time Inc., 1964. pp. 76–77.
3. Sahlin, C. *Mårten Triewald.* Stockholm: Steam Engine Library, 1928.
4. Hedin, M. and Carlsson, U.-B. *Nils & John Ericsson i Forsvik.* Mariestad: Forsviks Industriminnen, 4: 12–13.
5. Goldkuhl, C. pp. 9–22.
6. Hedin, M. and Carlsson, U.-B. 4: 21.
7. Letter by John Ericsson to his son, Hjalmar Elworth, on May 23, 1879. In Adelsköld, C.L. *John Ericsson, Biografiska Teckningar.* Stockholm, 1894. RLS.
8. Church, W.C. *The Life of John Ericsson.* London: Sampson Low, Marston, Searle, & Rivington, 1890. Vol. I, p. 18.
9. Lindvall, G. *Ingenjören vid Beach Street.* Stockholm: Ahlen and Soner, 1937. p. 36.
10. Church, W.C. Vol. I, p. 15.
11. Jonsson, Runvik, M. *John Ericsson, Resan mot Solen.* Karlstad: Källan, 1996. pp. 26–34.

2. Soldier and Inventor John

1. Church, W.C. *The Life of John Ericsson.* London: Sampson Low, Marston, Searle, & Rivington, 1890. Vol. I, pp. 23–35.
2. Jönsson Runvik, M. *John Ericsson, Resan mot Solen.* Karlstad: Källan, 1996. pp. 31–32.
3. Ibid., p. 33.
4. Örback, A. *Lantmätaren John Ericsson.* Stockholm: Lantmäteriet, September 1987. RLS.
5. Hirsch, M.D. "John Ericsson: His Influence on My Community and Beyond." *The Swedish Pioneer* V (1), 1954.
6. The exact nature of the pumping engine used in Jämtland is based on speculation. It could simply have been the post-heating generated vacuum in an enclosed tubing system or it might have been the first piston operated hot-air engine. cf. Lindvall, G. *Ingenjören vid Beach Street.* Stockholm: Ahlen & Soner, 1937. pp. 51–53.
7. In Sweden *privilegia exclusica* were granted by the *Kommerskollegiet,* the Department of Trading. The term *patent* was introduced in 1836.
8. Hedin, M. and Carlsson, U.-B. *Nils & John Ericsson i Forsvik.* Mariestad: Forsviks Industriminnen, 4: 21.
9. Data on Thomas Telford from the DNB. London: Smith Elder & Co., 1808.
10. Goldkuhl, C. *John Ericsson, Mannen och Uppfinnaren.* Stockholm: Bonniers, 1961. pp. 34–35.
11. Jönsson Runvik, p. 49.

3. To England

1. Lindwall, G. *Ingeniören vid Beach Street*. Stockholm: Åhlen & Söner, 1937. p. 63.
2. Ibid., pp. 343–347. In his table of John Ericsson's patents in England, Lindwall listed dates of submission: No. 5398, April 1, 1826, and No. 5437, April 22, 1826, but the correct dates of registration were August 16 and December 20, 1826, respectively.
3. Ibid., p. 343 and pp. 96–102.
4. Ross, M.J. *Polar Pioneers*. Montreal: McGill-Queen's University Press, 1994. pp. 121–122.
5. Fleming, F. *Barrow's Boys*. New York: Atlantic Monthly Press, 1998. pp. 325, 245, 249.
6. Ross, M.J. p. 140.
7. Church, W.C. *The Life of John Ericsson*. London: Sampson Low, Marston, Searle, & Rivington, 1890. Vol. I, pp. 40–44.
8. Ibid., pp. 44–48.
9. Lindwall, G. p. 343.
10. Thurston, R.H. *A History of the Growth of the Steam-Engine*. New York: D. Appleton & Co., 1878. pp. 31–38.
11. Jönsson Runvik, M. *John Ericsson, Resan mot Solen*. Karlstad: Källan, 1996. p. 51.
12. Lindwall, G. pp. 346–347.
13. Schütz, F. *Samuel Owen: British-born Pioneer of Mechanical Engineering in Sweden*. Stockholm: Daedalus, 1975. 45: 93–145.
14. *Minutes of Proceedings of the Institution of Civil Engineers*. London: 1853, Vol. 12, p. 351.
15. Lindwall, G. p. 343.
16. British Patent 6409, April 4, 1833. London, British Library.

4. Locomotion

1. Tute, W. *Atlantic Conquest: The Men and Ships of the Glorious Age of Steam*. Boston: Little Brown & Co., 1962. p. 5.
2. Thurston, R.H. *A History of the Steam-Engine*. New York: D. Appleton & Co., 1893. pp. 193–94, 219.
3. Lindwall, G. *Ingenören vid Beach Street*. Stockholm: Ahlen & Söner, 1937. p. 343.
4. Reder, G. *The World of Steam Locomotives*. New York: G.P. Putnam's Sons, 1974. pp. 39–45.
5. Walton, H. *The How and Why of Mechanical Movement*. New York: E.P. Dutton & Co., 1968. p. 154.
6. Rolt, L.T.C. *The Railway Revolution: George and Robert Stephenson*. New York: St. Martin's Press, 1962. p. 168.
7. The report of the *Times* as quoted by E. Grip in: *John Ericsson, En Livsbild*. Uppsala: J.A. Lindblads, 1920. p. 47.
8. Loxton, H. *Railways*. London: Paul Hamlin, 1963. pp. 17–18.
9. www.spartacus.schoolnet.co.uk.
10. Church, W.C. *The Life of John Ericsson*. London: Sampson Low, Marston, Searle, & Rivington, 1890. Vol. I, p. 62.
11. Furnas, J.C. *Fanny Kemble: Leading Lady of the Nineteenth-Century Stage*. New York: Dial Press, 1982. p. 69.

5. John Bull

1. Quotation from Punsch. In: Weinreb, B. and Hibbert, C. *The London Encyclopaedia*. London: Macmillan, 1987.
2. Letter of John Ericsson to M.F. Gussander, November 26, 1826. John Ericsson Papers, RLS.
3. Weinreb, B. and Hibbert, C. p. 9.
4. J.E. to Gussander, 1826. RLS.
5. Dugan, J. *The Great Iron Ship*. New York: Harper & Brothers, 1953. p. 26.
6. Lindwall, G. *Ingeniören vid Beach Street*. Stockholm: Ahlen & Söner, 1937. p. 127.
7. Weinreb, B. and Hibbert, C. pp. 433–434.
8. Letter of Nils Ericsson to N.E. Hesselborg, Oct. 30, 1833. John Ericsson Papers, GUL.
9. Church, W.C. *The Life of John Ericsson*. London: Sampson Low, Marston, Searle, & Rivington, 1890. Vol. I, p. 92.
10. Ibid., p. 82.

6. Propulsion

1. Lindwall, G. *Ingenioren vid Beach Street*. Stockholm: Ahlen & Söner, 1937. pp. 138–140.
2. The 1831 venture with F.B. Ogden was based on Ericsson's patents No. 5398 (1826) and No. 5763 (1829), cf. Church, W.C. *The Life of John Ericsson*. London: Sampson Low, Marston, Searle, & Rivington, 1890. Vol. I, pp. 91–92.
3. Ericsson and F.B. Ogden on November 14, 1835, obtained a British patent, No. 6928, for an "Instrument for ascertaing the depth of waters in seas and rivers." cf. Lindwall, G. p. 343.
4. Ross, M.J. *Polar Pioneers: John Ross and James Clark Ross*. Montreal: McGill-Queen's University Press, 1994. p. 263.
5. Carlton, J.S. *Marine Propellers and Propulsion*. Oxford: Buttherworth-Heinemann, 1994. p. 6.
6. Ross, M.J. p. 264.
7. Church, W.C. Vol. I, pp. 93–95.
8. Thurston, R.A. *A History of the Growth of the Steam-Engine*. New York: 1893, 3rd ed. p. 294.
9. Canney, D.L. *Lincoln's Navy: The Ships, Men and Organization, 1861–65*. Annapolis: Naval Institute Press, 1998. p. 13.

7. The New World

1. White, R. *Yankee from Sweden.* New York: Henry Holt & Co., 1960. pp. 68–69. According to John Ericsson's first biographer, William C. Church, the passage from England to New York was on the *Great Western,* but Ruth White reports that it happened on the *British Queen,* an opinion shared by John H. Finley of the *New York Times* in an article on November 23, 1839.
2. Dunshee, K.H. *As You Pass By.* New York: Hastings House, 1952. p. 157.
3. Church, W.C. *The Life of John Ericsson.* London: Sampson Low, Marston, Searle, & Rivington, 1890. Vol. I, pp. 106–138.
4. Still, W. *Monitor Builders: A Historical Study of the Principal Firms and Individuals Involved in the Construction of USS* Monitor. Washington, D.C.: National Maritime Initiative, Div. of History, 1988. p. 20.
5. Jardin, A. *Tocqueville: A Biography.* New York: Farrar Strauss Giroux, 1988. p. 116.
6. Thulesius, O. *Edison in Florida: The Green Laboratory.* Gainesville: University Press of Florida, 1997.
7. White, R. p. 134.
8. Church, W.C. Vol. I, p. 113.
9. From: *New York: A Collection from Harper's Magazine.* New York: Gallery Books, 1991. pp. 124–25.
10. McCabe, J.D. *Lights and Shadows of New York Life.* Philadelphia: National Publication Co., 1872.
11. Church, Vol. II, p. 302.

8. The Princeton Disaster

1. Schneller, R.J., Jr. *A Quest for Glory: A Biography of Rear Admiral John A. Dahlgren.* Annapolis, Md.: Naval Institute Press, 1996. pp. 23–27.
2. White, R. *Yankee from Sweden.* New York: Henry Holt & Co., 1960. pp. 76–77.
3. Schneller, R.J., Jr. p. 26.
4. Letter of John Ericsson to A. von Rosen, September 1, 1840. John Ericsson Papers, NYHS.
5. Church, W.C. *The Life of John Ericsson.* London: Sampson Low, Marston, Searle & Rivington, 1890. Vol. I, p. 119.
6. Ibid., pp. 119–120.
7. Ibid., p. 117.
8. Miller, E.M. *U.S.S.* Monitor: *The Ship that Launched a Modern Navy.* Annapolis, Md.: Leeward Publications, 1978. pp. 8–9.
9. Church. Vol. I, p. 118.
10. Ibid., p. 125.
11. White, R. p. 97.
12. Beach, E.L. *The United States Navy 200 Years.* New York: Henry Holt & Co., 1986. pp. 196–222, 513.
13. Webster, D.B., Jr. "The Beauty and Chivalry of the United States Assembled." *American Heritage.* December 1965. 17 (1), 50.
14. Greene, J. and Massignani, A. *Ironclads at War.* Conshohocken, Pa.: Combined Publishing, 1998. pp. 88–89.
15. Church. Vol. I, p. 141.
16. Beach, E.L. pp. 217–218.
17. Letter of John Ericsson to the secretary of the Navy, George Bancroft. John Ericsson Papers, ASHF.
18. Letter of John Ericsson to Congressman Bishop, New York, February 18, 1857. John Ericsson Papers, ASHF.
19. White, R. pp. 117–118.
20. Hammar, H. *John Ericsson's* Monitor *och drabbningen på Hampton Roads.* Stockholm: H. Gebers, 1937. p. 18.

9. The Age of Caloric

1. Cardwell, D. *The Norton History of Technology.* New York: W.W. Norton, 1994. pp. 240–242.
2. Ferguson, E.S. *John Ericsson and the Age of Caloric.* Washington, D.C.: U.S. National Museum Bulletin 228, 1961. pp. 52–54.
3. Lindwall, G. *Ingenioren vid Beach Street.* Stockholm: Ahlen & Söner, 1937. p. 157.
4. Philip, C.O. *Robert Fulton: A Biography.* New York: Franklin Watts, 1985. p. 29.
5. Canney, D.L. *Lincoln's Navy: The Ships, Men and Organization, 1861–65.* Annapolis: Naval Institute Press, 1998. p. 167.
6. White, R. *Yankee from Sweden: The Dream and the Reality in the Days of John Ericsson.* New York: Henry Holt & Co., 1960. p. 154.
7. Report of Samuel Taylor at U.S. District Court, N.Y., 1890. p. 13. John Ericsson Papers. ASHF, reel 7.
8. White, R. pp. 152–154.
9. Lamm, M. "The Hot Air Era." *American History Illustrated* IX, October 1974. pp. 18–23.
10. Ericsson, J. Letter to John O. Sargent. May 1, 1854. John Ericsson Papers, ASHF, Reel 7.
11. McKay, R.C. *South Street: A Maritime History of New York.* New York: G.P. Putman's Sons, 1934. p. 340.
12. Church, W.C. *The Life of John Ericsson.* London: Sampson Low, Marston, Searle & Rivington, 1890. Vol. I, pp. 191–192.
13. Report of Samuel Taylor at U.S. District Court, N.Y., 1890. p. 13. John Ericsson Papers, ASHF, reel 7.
14. Brown, C.H. *William Cullen Bryant.* New York: Charles Scribner's Sons, 1971. p. 369.

15. John Ericsson in a letter to John B. Kitching, June 27, 1857. Ericsson Papers, NYHS.
16. S.W. Taylor's witness report at N.Y. District Court, 1890. John Ericsson Papers, ASHF.
17. Ibid. John Ericsson to the *New York Times*, October 22, 1857.
18. Ibid. Letter from Peter Dahlberg, August 29, 1859, and from Edward Lish, Dec. 11, 1860.
19. Still, W. *Monitor Builders: A Historical Study of the Principal Firms and Individuals Involved in the Construction of USS Monitor.* Washington, D.C.: National Maritime Initiative, Div. of History, 1988. p. 21.
20. Church. Vol. I, pp. 217–219.
21. Horsford, E.N. *Address on the Occasion of Presenting to John Ericsson the Rumford Medal of the American Academy.* New York: Hard & Houghton, 1866.
22. White, R. p. 181.
23. Letter of John Ericsson to G.V. Fox, May 17, 1866. John Ericsson Papers, ASHF, reel 7.
24. Ibid.

10. Naval Blockade

1. Elliot, C.W. *Winfield Scott: The Soldier and the Man.* New York: Macmillan Co., 1937, p. 722.
2. Spears, J.R, *The History of Our Navy.* New York: Charles Scribner's Sons, 1899. Vol. IV, 30–36. Nash, H.P., Jr. *A Naval History of the Civil War.* New York: A.S. Barnes & Co., 1972. p. 25.
3. Porter, D.D. *Naval History of the Civil War.* New York: Sherman Publishing Co., 1885. pp. 17–18.
4. Hoggenboom, A. "Gustavus Vasa Fox." *American National Biography.* New York: Oxford University Press, 1999. pp. 340–342.
5. Miller, E.M. *USS Monitor: The Ship that Launched a Modern Navy.* Annapolis, Md.: Leeward Publications Inc., 1978. p. 22.
6. Anderson, B. *By Sea and by River: The Naval History of the Civil War.* New York: A Knopf, 1962. pp. 41–43.
7. Canney, D.L. *Lincoln's Navy.* Annapolis, Md.: Naval Institute Press. pp. 58–59. Murphy, R.W. *The Blockade: Runners and Raiders.* Morristown: Time-Life Books, 1983. p. 22.
8. Ibid., pp. 76–81.
9. Miller, E.M. *USS Monitor: The Ship that Launched a Modern Navy.* Annapolis, Md.: Leeward Publications Inc., 1978. p. 22.
10. Wise, S. "Stephen Russell Mallory." *American National Biography.* New York: Oxford University Press, 1999.
11. Coski, J.M. *Capital Navy: The Men, Ships and Operations of the James River Squadron.* Campbell: Savas Publishing Co., 1996. p. 3.
12. Ibid., p. 26.
13. Ibid., pp. 121–123.
14. Church, W.C. *The Life of John Ericsson.* London: Sampson Low, Marston, Searle & Rivington, 1890. Vol. I, p. 245.

11. The New Merrimack

1. Still, W.N., Jr. "Technology Afloat." In: *Raiders and Blockaders.* Dulles, Va.: Brassey's, 1998. pp. 44–45.
2. Coski, J.M. *Capital Navy: The Men, Ships and Operations of the James River Squadron.* Campbell: Savas Publishing Co., 1996. p. 24.
3. Church, W.C. *The Life of John Ericsson.* London: Sampson Low, Marston, Searle & Rivington, 1890. Vol. I, p. 246.
4. Jones, V.C. *The Civil War at Sea.* New York: Holt, Rinehart Winston, 1960. Vol. I, pp. 156–58.
5. Greene, J. and Massignani, A. *Ironclads at War: The Origin and Development of Armored Warships, 1854–1891.* Conshohoken, Pa.: Combined Publishing, 1998. p. 58.
6. Porter, D.D. *Naval History of the Civil War.* New York: Sherman Publishing Co., 1885. p. 121.
7. Ibid., p. 123.
8. Musicant, I. *Divided Waters.* New York: Harper Collins, 1995. p. 218.
9. Jones, V.C. pp. 404–406.

12. Lincoln's Raft

1. Niven, J. *Gideon Welles: Lincoln's Secretary of the Navy.* Baton Rouge: Louisiana State University Press, 1994. p. 364.
2. White, R. *Yankee from Sweden.* New York: H. Holt & Co., 1960. pp. 131–32. Archives Report No. 681 of 29th Congress. Hansen, H. *The Civil War: A History.* New York: Mentor/Penguin, 1991. p. 147.
3. Church, W.C. *The Life of John Ericsson.* London: Sampson Low, Marston, Searle & Rivington, 1890. Vol. I, p. 240.
4. Ibid., p. 241.
5. Craven, E. Memorandum for Captain Knox. May 12, 1931. Library of Congress, Washington, D.C.
6. *Congress Letter Book No. 14*, pp. 442–450. Library of Congress, Washington, D.C.
7. Church, W.C. Vol. I, pp. 246–247.
8. Niven, J. p. 365.
9. Anderson, B. *By Sea and River: The Naval History of the Civil War.* New York: Da Capo Press, 1989. p. 68.
10. White, R. p. 195.

11. According to a printed document, the cupola vessel was an elaborate ship, equipped with "reflecting telescopes, capable of being protruded or withdrawn at pleasure, afford a distinct view of the surrounding objects. This new system of naval attack will place an entire fleet of sailing ships, at the mercy of a single craft. Alas for the 'wooden walls' that formerly 'ruled the waves.'" The John Ericsson Papers, NYHS.
12. Church, W.C. Vol. I, pp. 248–252. Hammar, H. *John Ericsson's Monitor och Drabbningen på Hampton Roads*. Stockholm: Hugo Gebers, 1937. pp. 20–25. Paraphrasing the Bible: Exodus 20:4. Burnett, C.B. *Captain John Ericsson: Father of the Monitor*. New York: Vanguard Press, 1960. p. 200.
13. Letter of Joseph Smith to John Ericsson, Washington, September 21, 1861. John Ericsson Papers, ASHF.
14. Letter of Joseph Smith to John Ericsson, March 3, 1853. The John Ericsson Papers, NYHS.
15. Davis, W.C. *Duel Between the First Ironclads*. New York: Doubleday & Co., 1975. p. 42.
16. Abraham Lincoln, Patent No. 6,469, "Manner of Buoying Vessels," May 22, 1849.
17. Catton, B. *This Hallowed Ground*. New York: Doubleday, 1975. p. 160. West, Jr., R.S. *Gideon Welles: Lincoln's Navy Department*. Indianapolis: Bobbs-Merrill, 1943. p. 148.
18. Hirsch, M.D. "John Ericsson: His Influence on My Community and Beyond." *The Swedish Pioneer* V (1), 1954, p. 7.
19. Schneller, R.J., Jr. *A Quest for Glory: A Biography of Rear Admiral John A. Dahlgren*. Annapolis, Md.: Naval Institute Press, 1996. pp. 180–189.
20. Paymaster William F. Keeler to his wife, May 7, 1862. Quoted by Mindell, D.A. *War Technology and Experience on Board the USS Monitor*. Baltimore: Johns Hopkins University Press, 2000. p. 79.
21. West, R.S., Jr. *Gideon Welles: Lincoln's Navy Department*. Indianapolis: Bobbs-Merril, 1943. p. 224.
22. Neely, M.E., Jr. *The Best Hope of Earth: Abraham Lincoln and the Promise of America*. Cambridge: Harvard University Press, 1993. p. 182.

13. The Monitor

1. Catton, B. *This Hallowed Ground*. New York: Pocket, Simon & Schuster, 1975. p. 160.
2. Canney, D.L. *Lincoln's Navy: The Ships, Men and Organization, 1861-65*. Annapolis: Naval Institute Press, 1998. p. 82.
3. Anderson, B. *By Sea and By River: The Naval History of the Civil War*. New York: Knopf/DaCapo, 1962. pp. 70–71.
4. Peterkin, E. "Building a Behemoth." *Civil War Times*. 20 (4), 1981.
5. Letter by John Ericsson to G.V. Fox, January 20, 1862, and letter of John A. Griswold, January 22, 1862, to John Ericsson. John Ericsson Papers, NYHS.
6. Porter, D.D. *Naval History of the Civil War*. New York: Sherman Publishing Co., 1885. p. 121.
7. Letter of J. Smith to John Ericsson, January 25, 1862. Ericsson Papers, SAHF. West, Jr., R.S. *Gideon Welles: Lincoln's Navy Department*. Indianapolis: Bobbs-Merril, 1943. p. 153.
8. Wade, P.F. U.S. Senate, *Congress Letter Book No. 14*, pp. 442–450. Library of Congress, Washington, D.C.
9. Greene, S.D. *In the* Monitor *Turret*. http://www.civilwarhome.com/monitorturret.htm.
10. MacCord, C.W. "Ericsson and His 'Monitor.'" *North American Review*. October 1889. p. 144.
11. Ibid.
12. Davis, W.C. *Duel Between the First Ironclads*. New York: Doubleday & Co., 1975. p. 47.
13. Musicant, I. *Divided Waters: The Naval History of the Civil War*. New York: Harper Collins, 1995. pp. 163–164. For further details about the crew see: Davis, W.C. *Duel Between the First Ironclads*. New York: Doubleday & Co., 1975. pp. 48–49. For a full list of all men fighting at Hampton Roads see: Miller, E.M. *USS* Monitor: *The Ship that Launched a Modern Navy*. Annapolis, Md.: Leeward Publications, 1978. p. 111.
14. Musicant, I. p. 159. DeKay, J.T. *Monitor*. New York: Ballantine Books, 1997. p. 110.
15. Still, Jr., W.N., Taylor, J.M. and Delaney, N.C. *Raiders and Blockaders: The American Civil War Afloat*. Washington: Brassey's, 1998. pp. 18–20.
16. Musicant, p. 162.
17. Campbell, R.T. *Gray Thunder: Exploits of the Confederate Navy*. Shippensburg: Burd Street Press, 1996. p. 43.

14. The Right Track

1. Greene, J. and Massignani, A. *Ironclads at War*. Conshohocken, Pa.: Combined Publishing, 1998. p. 27.
2. Eisenschiml, O. and Newman, R. *The American Iliad*. Indianapolis: Bobbs-Merrill Co. p. 127.
3. Burnett, C.B. *Captain John Ericsson: Father of the Monitor*. New York: Vanguard Press, 1960. p. 211.
4. Mindell, D.A. *War, Technology, and*

Experience Aboard the USS Monitor. Baltimore: Johns Hopkins University Press, 2000. p. 67.
    5. Davis, W.C. *Duel Between the Ironclads.* Garden City, N.Y.: Doubleday & Co., 1975.
    6. Eisenschiml, O. and Newman, R. pp. 136–137.
    7. Welles, G. "The First Ironclad Monitor." In: *Annals of the Civil War.* New York: Da Capo, 1994. pp. 24–25. Leech, M. *Reveille in Washington 1860–1865.* New York: Harper & Brothers, 1941. pp. 131–132.
    8. Davis, W.C. *Duel Between the First Ironclads.* Garden City, N.Y.: Doubleday.

15. Happy Experience

1. Still, W.N., Jr. *Iron Afloat.* Columbia: University of South Carolina Press, 1985.
2. Churchill, W.S. *The American Civil War.* New York: The Fairfax Press, 1985. p. 72.
3. Greene, J. and Massignani, A. *Ironclads at War: The Origin and Development of the Armored Warship, 1854–1891.* Conshohocken, Pa.: Combined Publishing, 1998. pp. 80–81.
4. Delbano, A. *The Portable Abraham Lincoln.* New York: Penguin Books, 1993. p. 233.
5. Stodder, L.N. "Aboard the USS *Monitor.*" *Civil War Times* 1 (9) 35.
6. Greene, S.D. *In the* Monitor *Turret.* http://www.civilwarhome.com/monitorturret.htm.
7. Maccord, C.W. "Ericsson and his '*Monitor.*'" *North American Review,* October 1889.
8. Sandburg, C. *Abraham Lincoln: The War Years.* New York: Harcourt, Brace & World, 1939, Vol. 1.
9. Mindell, D.A. *War, Technology, and Experience Aboard the* Monitor. Baltimore: Johns Hopkins University Press, 2000. p. 90.
10. Letter of F.H. Gregory to John Ericsson. Dec. 10, 1862. John Ericsson Papers, ASHF, reel 7.
11. Mills, E. *Chesapeake Bay in the Civil War.* Centreville, Md.: Tidewater Publishers, 1996. pp. 144–145.
12. DeKay, J.T. *Monitor.* New York: Ballantine, 1997. pp. 119–120.
13. Davis, W.C. *Duel Between the First Ironclads.* New York: Doubleday & Co., 1975. p. 156.
14. Fort Monroe, at the mouth of the Chesapeake Bay, is also referred to as the "Gibraltar of Virginia."
15. Coski, J.M. *Capital Navy.* Campbell: Savas Publishing Co., 1996. pp. 41–56. Jones, V.C. *The Civil War at Sea.* New York: Holt, Rinehart, Winston, 1961. pp. 30–40.
16. West, R.S., Jr. *Gideon Welles: Lincoln's Navy Department.* Indianapolis: Bobbs-Merril, 1943. pp. 216–217, 219. Davis, W.C. p. 159.

17. Davis, W.C. p. 158.
18. Ibid., p. 159.

16. The Monitor Boys

1. Still, W.N., Jr. *Raiders and Blockaders.* Dulles, Va.: Brassey's, 1998. pp. 54, 57.
2. Nash, H.P., Jr. *A Naval History of the Civil War.* New York: A.S. Barnes & Co., 1972. p. 85.
3. Davis, W.C. *Duel Between the First Ironclads.* New York: Doubleday & Co., 1975. p. 58.
4. Grattan, J.W. *Under the Blue Pennant, or Notes of a Naval Officer.* R.J. Schneller Jr., ed. New York: Wiley & Sons, 1999. pp. 40–41.
5. Musicant, I. *Divided Waters: The Naval History of the Civil War.* New York: Harper Collins, 1995. p. 165.
6. Grattan, p. 42.
7. Mindell, D.A. *War, Technology, and Experience Aboard the USS* Monitor. Baltimore: Johns Hopkins University Press, 2000. pp. 65, 98.
8. Coski, J.M. *Capital Navy: The Men, Ships and Operations of the James River Squadron.* Campbell: Savas Publishing Co., 1996. p. 180.
9. Hammar, H. *John Ericsson's* Monitor *och drabbningen på Hampton Roads.* Stockholm: H. Gebers, 1937. pp. 45–46.
10. Canney, D.L. *Lincoln's Navy: The Ships, Men and Organization.* Annapolis, Md.: Naval Institute Press, 1998. p. 125.
11. Turner, A. *Nathaniel Hawthorn: A Biography.* New York: Oxford University Press, 1980. p. 369. Quote from: Mindell, D.A. pp. 5, 82, 84.
12. MacCord, C. "Ericsson and his '*Monitor.*'" *North American Review.* October 1889. p. 151.
13. Quarstein, J.V. *The Battle of the Ironclads.* Charleston: Arcadia, 1999. p. 104.
14. Greene, S.D. "I Fired the First Gun." *American Heritage* 8 (4), 1957.
15. Marvel, W. (ed.). *The* Monitor *Chronicles: One Sailor's Account.* New York: Simon & Schuster, 2000. p. 56.
16. Davis, W.C. pp. 159–60.
17. Marvel, W. pp. 111, 200.

17. Tragic End

1. Marvel, W. (ed.). *The* Monitor *Chronicles: One Sailor's Account.* New York: Simon & Schuster, 2000.
2. Davis, W.C. *Duel Between the First Ironclads.* New York: Doubleday & Co., 1975. p. 160.
3. Butts, F.B. "The Loss of the *Monitor* by

Survivor." *Century Magazine,* 1885, 31: 299–302.
 4. Miller, E.M. *USS* Monitor: *The Ship That Launched a Modern Navy.* Annapolis, Md.: Leeward Publications, 1978. pp. 70–78.
 5. Ibid., p. 74, 80–84.
 6. Marvel, p. 231.
 7. Davis, pp. 168–169.
 8. Mills, E. *Chesapeake Bay in the Civil War.* Centreville, Md.: Tidewater Publ., 1996. pp. 144–145.

18. Monitor Craze

 1. Details about her dimensions, fittings and machinery have been described by S.B. Besse in *U.S. Ironclad* Monitor. Newport News, Va.: The Mariners' Museum. Publication No. 2, 1936.
 2. DeKay, J.T. *Monitor.* New York: Walker & Co., 1997. p. 214.
 3. Gibbons, T. *Warships and Naval Battles of the Civil War.* New York: Gallery Books, 1989. p. 65.
 4. Canney, D.L. *Lincoln's Navy: The Ships, Men and Organization, 1861–65.* Annapolis, Md.: Naval Institute Press, 1998. pp. 69–73.
 5. Church, W.C. *The Life of John Ericsson.* London: Sampson Low, Marston, Searle & Rivington, 1890. Vol. II, p. 21.
 6. Ericsson, J. Letter to G.V. Fox, Dec. 31, 1864. John Ericsson Papers, ASHF, Reel 7.
 7. Hansen, H. *The Civil War: A History.* New York: Penguin Press, 1961. p. 156.
 8. Letter of John Ericsson to G.A. Fox, New York, May 17, 1866. John Ericsson Papers, ASHF, Reel 7.
 9. Church, W.C. Vol. I, p. 80. Greene, J. and Massignani, A. *Ironclads at War: The Origin and Development of the Armored Warship, 1854–1891.* Conshohocken, Pa.: Combined Publishing, 1998. pp. 199–200.
 10. West, R.S., Jr. p. 233. Anderson, B. *By Sea and River: The Naval History of the Civil War.* New York: Knopf, 1962. p. 164.
 11. Gibbons, T. *Warships and Naval Battles of the Civil War.* New York: Gallery Books, 1989. pp. 38–39.
 12. Osborn, P.R. *The American Monitors.* U.S. Naval Inst. Proc., February 1937, pp. 235–238.
 13. Paist, P.H. *Monitors: Ships that Changed War.* Naval Inst. Proc., June 1961. pp. 76–89.

19. The Destroyer

 1. Thurston, R.H. *Robert Fulton: His Life and its Results.* New York: Dodd, Mead & Co., 1891. Chapter V.
 2. Church, W.C. *The Life of John Ericsson.* London: Sampson Low, Marston, Searle & Rivington, 1890. Vol. I, pp. 237–239.
 3. Letter of John Ericsson to Nils Ericson, April 10, 1875. Quoted in Church, W.C. Vol. II, p. 154.
 4. Church, W.C. Vol. II, p. 166.
 5. Ibid. White, R. *Yankee from Sweden.* New York: H. Holt, 1960. p. 244.
 6. Letter of John Ericsson to his son, Hjalmar Elworth. February 10, 1885. John Ericsson Papers, RLS.
 7. Letter of S.W. Taylor to Captain W. Arthur, November 23, 1880. John Ericsson Papers, ASHF, Reel 7.
 8. Letter of A. Swinton to S.M. Taylor, September 29, 1886. John Ericsson Papers, ASHF. Reel 7.
 9. Brophy, A. *John Ericsson and the Inventions of War.* Englewood Cliffs: Silver Burdett Press, 1991. pp. 112–113.
 10. Church, W.C. Vol. II, p. 176.

20. Solar Energy

 1. Ericsson, J. *Om Solvärmens användande som mekanisk drifkraft.* Lund's Universitets Andra Secularfest. Lund: Berlingska, 1868. p. 3. Lund University Library.
 2. Roberts, P. *Running Out of Oil and Time.* Los Angeles Times, quoted in St. Petersburg Times, March 14, 2004.
 3. Yellott, J.I. "Captain Ericsson: Pioneer in Solar Energy." *The Sun at Work, 1956–1957.* Phoenix: Association for Applied Solar Energy.
 4. Daly, R.W. (ed.) *Aboard the USS* Monitor: *1862.* Annapolis, Md.: Naval Institute Press, 1964. p. 205.
 5. Strand, S. *Solmaskiner, varmluftmotorer och kanoner.* Stockholm, 1962. p. 3.
 6. Ericsson, J. 1868. pp. 3–4.
 7. *Van Nostrand's Engineering Magazine.* 1868, p. 170.
 8. Letter of J.E. to his son, Hjalmar Elworth, February 10, 1885. John Ericsson Papers, RLS.
 9. *Van Nostrand's Engineering Magazine.* 1869, p. 171.
 10. Ericsson, J. 1868. pp. 7–8 (supplement, 1869).
 11. Church, W.C. *The Life of John Ericsson.* London: Sampson Low, Marston, Searle & Rivington, 1890. Vol. II, p. 238.
 12. Smith, C. *Journal of Solar Energy Engineering,* 1995. pp. 5–6.
 13. Church, W.C. Vol. II, pp. 266–267.
 14. Grip, E. *John Ericsson, en Livsbild.* Uppsala: J.A. Lindblads, 1920. p. 129. Church, W.C. Vol. II, p. 274.

15. Lindwall, G. *Ingenjoren vid Beach Street.* Stockholm: Ahlen & Soner, 1937. p. 294.
16. Church, W.C. Vol. II, p. 266.
17. Ibid., p. 282.

21. Centennial Exhibition

1. White, R. *Yankee from Sweden.* New York: Henry Holt & Co., 1960. pp. 239–240.
2. Devens, R.M. *The Great Events of the Greatest Century.* Chicago: Hugh Heron, 1883. pp. 689–706.
3. McCullough, D. *The Great Bridge.* New York: Simon & Schuster, 1982. pp. 351–353.
4. Post, RC. *1876: A Centennial Exhibition.* Washington, D.C.: Smithsonian Institute, 1976. pp. 11–43.
5. Church, WC. *The Life of John Ericsson.* London: Sampson Low, Marston, Searle & Rivington, 1890. Vol. II, pp. 278–279.
6. Post, R.C. pp. 163–165.

22. Alfred Nobel

1. Sohlman, R. and Schuck, H. *Nobel, Dynamite and Peace.* New York: Cosmopolitan Book Corp., 1929. p. 91.
2. Browaldh, T. "Alfred Nobel som multinationell företagare." In: *Nobel och hans tid.* Stockholm: Atlantis, 1983. p. 49.
3. *Alfred Nobel och Hans Släkt.* Minnesskrift utgiven av Nobelstiftelsens Styrelse, Stockholm, 1926, p. 197–216.
4. Sohlman, R. and Schuck, H. pp. 91–92.
5. Tolf, R.W. *The Russian Rockefellers: The Saga of the Nobel Family and the Russian Oil Industry.* Stanford: Hoover Institution Press, 1976.
6. Feldman, B. *The Nobel Prize.* New York: Arcade Publishers, 2000. p. 46.
7. Strandh, S. "Alfred Nobel som fri forskare." In: *Nobel och hans tid.* Stockholm: Atlantis, 1983. pp. 113–114.
8. Sohlman, R. and Schuck, H. pp. 114–141.
9. Church, W.C. *The Life of John Ericsson.* London: Sampson Low, Marston, Searle & Rivington, 1890. Vol. II, p. 162.
10. Anderson, B. "How to Live Forever." *Attaché Magazine*, March 2001. p. 52.
11. "The Old Year's Progress." *Scientific American.* December 28, 1861.
12. Feldman, B. p. 46.
13. Goldkuhl, C. *John Ericsson: Mannen och uppfinnaren.* Stockholm: Bonniers, 1961. p. 240.
14. Ibid., p. 238.
15. Sier, R. *Hot Air Caloric and Stirling Engines.* Chelmsford: L.A. Mair, 1999. p. 53.
16. Tägil, S. "Krig och fred i Alfred Nobels föreställningsvärld." In: *Nobel och hans tid.* Stockholm: Atlantis, 1983. pp. 25–46.
17. Quote from: Mindell, D.A. *War Technology and Experience Aboard the USS* Monitor. Baltimore: John Hopkins University Press, 2000. p. 2.
18. Ibid., p. 145.

23. Manhattan

1. Smith, M.H. *Sunshine and Shadow in New York.* Hartford: J.B. Burr, 1868.
2. Dix, M. *A History of the Parish of Trinity Church in the City of New York.* New York: Putnam's Sons, 1906. pp. 235–236.
3. Philip, C.O. *Robert Fulton.* New York: Franklin Watts, 1985. pp. 47, 76–77.
4. Burrows, E.G. and Wallace, M. *Gotham: A History of New York City to 1898.* New York: Oxford University Press, 1999. pp. 457–459.
5. McCabe, J.D. *Lights and Shadows of New York Life.* Philadelphia: National Publication Co., 1872.
6. Burrows and Wallace, p. 944. Grip, E. *John Ericsson, en Livsbild.* Uppsala: J.A. Lindblad, 1920. p. 140.
7. Church, W.C. *The Life of John Ericsson.* London: Sampson Low, Marston, Searle & Rivington, 1890. Vol. II, p. 313.
8. Ibid., p. 306.
9. Ibid., p. 312.
10. Ericsson, J. Letter to Carl Ekenstam, New York, January 26, 1877. John Ericsson Papers, RLS.
11. Letter of John Ericsson on July 2, 1859. John Ericsson Papers, NYHS.
12. White, R. *Yankee from Sweden.* New York, H. Holt & Co., 1960. p. 123.
13. Jackson, J.T. *The Encyclopedia of New York City.* New Haven: Yale University Press, 1995. p. 690, see: "Ann Lohman."
14. Cavanah, F. *Jenny Lind's America.* Philadelphia. Chilton Book Co., 1969.
15. Carlsson, B. *Kristina Nilsson, Minnen och Upplevelser.* Stockholm: Ahlen & Akerlunds, 1921. p. 202.

24. The Man

1. Church, W.C. *The Life of John Ericsson.* London: Sampson Low, Marston, Searle & Rivington, 1890. Vol. I, pp. 112–113.
2. Lindwall, G. *Ingeniören vid Beach Street.* Stockholm: Åhlen & Söner, 1937. p. 63.
3. Church, W.C. Vol. II, p. 216 and Vol. I, p. 194.
4. Davis, W.C. *Duel Between the First Iron-*

clads. New York: Doubleday & Co., 1975. pp. 42–43.
  5. MacCord, C.W. "Ericsson and his '*Monitor.*'" *North American Review.* October 1889 (Reprinted in the *Stevens Indicator,* pp. 144, 149).
  6. Church, W.C. Vol. I, p. 67.
  7. Church, W.C. Vol. II, pp. 249–259.
  8. Samuel Taylor to Miss A.J. Smith, August 6, 1887. John Ericsson Papers, ASHF, Reel 7.
  9. Thulesius, O. *Edison in Florida: The Green Laboratory.* Gainesville: University Press of Florida, 1997. p. 100.
  10. Samuel Taylor to A.S Gardiner, March 29, 1889. John Ericsson Papers, ASHF, Reel 7. Church, W.C. p. 230.
  11. Dahlman, P.R. *Om Nils Gabriel Djurklous boksamling och dess öde.* Samfundet Örebro Stads-och Länssbiblioteks Vänner. Nr. IV. RLS.
  12. Church, W.C. Vol. II, pp. 229–
  13. Aftonbladet, Stockholm, March 4, 1936.
  14. MacCord, C.W. "Portraits for the Institute Library." *Stevens Indicator* 8: 7, 1890. p. 147.
  15. At the time Sweden was very francophilic with their new French Royal dynasty, the Bernadottes. Church W.C. Vol. I, p. 241.
  16. Laurentz, P. *Visit of Russian Squadrons in 1863.* United States Naval Institute Proceedings 61 (387) pp. 692–696.
  17. Cook, A. *The Armies of the Streets: The New York City Draft Riots of 1863.* Lexington: University Press of Kentucky, 1974.
  18. Bernstein, I. *The New York City Draft Riots.* New York: Oxford University Press, 1990. p. 18. Grip, E. *John Ericsson, En Livsbild.* Uppsala: J.A. Lindblads, 1920, p. 131.
  19. Church, W.C. Vol. I, p. 219. "Ericsson's Revolving Turreted War Ship." *Scientific American* 63 (6 September 1890).
  20. Churchill, W.S. *The American Civil War.* New York: The Fairfax Press, 1985. p. 30.
  21. Clinton, C. *Fanny Kemble's Civil Wars.* New York: Simon & Schuster, 2000.
  22. Church, W.C. Vol. I, p. 229.
  23. Thulesius, O. *Harriet Beecher Stowe in Florida: 1867 to 1884.* Jefferson, N.C.: McFarland, 2001. pp. 15–18.
  24. Church, W.C. Vol. II, p. 220.
  25. Letter of John Ericsson to Axel Adlersparre, New York, November 1, 1867. John Ericsson Papers, RLS.
  26. McCullough, D. *The Great Bridge.* New York: Simon and Schuster, 1982. p. 40.
  27. Mindell, D.A. *War Technology, and Experience Aboard the USS* Monitor. Baltimore: Johns Hopkins University Press, 2000. p. 90.
  28. Church, W.C. Vol. I, p. 67 and Vol. II, p. 313.
  29. Rodgers to his wife, quoted by Mindell, D.A. p. 122.
  30. Lindwall, G. *Ingeniören vid Beach Street.* Stockholm: Åhlen och Söner, 1937. p. 294.
  31. Philip, C.O. *Robert Fulton: A Biography.* New York: Franklin Watts, 1985.
  32. Thulesius, O. *Edison in Florida: The Green Laboratory.* Gainesville: University of Florida Press, 1997. p. 118.
  33. Grip, E. p. 135. Boorstin, D. *The Americas.* New York: Vintage Books, 1974. p. 527.
  34. Musicant, I. *Divided Water: The Naval History of the Civil War.* New York: Harper Collins, 1995. p. 158.
  35. McPherson, J.M. *Battle Cry of Freedom: The Civil War Era.* New York: Oxford University Press, 1988, p. 374.
  36. Sheridan, R.E. *Iron from the Deep: The Discovery and Recovery of the USS* Monitor. Annapolis, Md.: Naval Institute Press, 2004. p. 242.

25. Family and Friends

  1. White, R. *Yankee From Sweden.* New York: H. Holt, 1960. pp. 222–223.
  2. Letter by John Ericsson to A.E. von Rosen, New York, Sept. 1, 1840. John Ericsson Papers, GUL.
  3. Letter of J.E. to his mother, Nov. 30, 1842 (stamped March 17, 1843). Technical Museum, Stockholm.
  4. Church, W.C. *The Life of John Ericsson.* London: Sampson Low, Marston, Searle & Rivington, 1890. Vol. I, p. 82.
  5. White, R. p. 236.
  6. Letter of J.E. to his mother, Nov. 30, 1842.
  7. White, R. p. 237.
  8. Letter of H. Elworth to J.E., Nov 22, 1872. In: Lindwall G. *Ingeniören vid Beach Street.* Stockholm: Åhlen & Söner, 1937. pp. 302–305.
  9. Goldkuhl, C. *John Ericsson, Mannen och Uppfinnaren.* Stockholm: Bonniers, 1961. p. 234.
  10. Church, W.C. Vol. II, p. 215.
  11. Letter by H.E. to J.E. in: Lindwall, G. *Ingeniören vid Beach Street.* Stockholm: Åhlen & Söner, 1937. p. 306.
  12. Thulesius, O. *Edison in Florida: The Green Laboratory.* Gainesville: University Press of Florida, 1997. p. 123.
  13. White, R. pp. 267–270.
  14. Letter of J.E. to Axel Adlersparre, New York, November 1, 1867. John Ericsson Papers, RLS.
  15. Note of S.W. Taylor in a letter of March 24, 1889, from J. Zortman. John Ericsson Papers, ASHF, reel 7. Here he disclosed that the oil painting of a woman is not that of his wife, nor of any relative.
  16. Morris, L. *Incredible New York.* New York: Random House, 1951. pp. 44–49.

17. Church, W.C. Vol. I, p. 113.
18. Chilström Meixner, E. *The John Ericsson Collection of the American Swedish Historical Foundation.* Philadelphia: ASHF Yearbook 1969–70. p. 34.
19. Church, W.C. Vol. II, pp. 247–248.
20. Ibid., Vol. I, p. 194.
21. Ibid., p. 191. Goldkuhl, C. pp. 206–207.
22. Goldkuhl, C. pp. 220–221.
23. Data on Alfred Ely Beach from J. Colldeweih, in DAB pp. 381–382 and *Scientific American*, Suppl. 764, Aug. 23, 1890.
24. White, R. p. 145.
25. Haugen, E. and Cai, C. *Ole Bull: Norway's Romantic Musician and Cosmopolitan Patriot.* Madison: University of Wisconsin Press, 1993. pp. 163–165. Church, W.C. Vol. II, p. 242.
26. Church, W.C. Vol. I, p. 226.
27. Report of Samuel Taylor at U.S. District Court, N.Y., 1890. John Ericsson Papers, ASHF, p. 11, reel 7.
28. Letter of J.E. to A. Adlersparre, New York, November 16, 1877. John Ericsson Papers, RLS.
29. Report of Samuel Taylor at U.S. District Court, N.Y., 1890. John Ericsson Papers, ASHF, pp. 2–3, reel 7.

26. Home Again

1. Thulesius, O. *Edison in Florida: The Green Laboratory.* Gainesville: University Press of Florida, 1997. p. 20.
2. Samuel W. Taylor describing John Ericsson's final disease. John Ericsson Papers, ASHF, reel 7.
3. Ibid.
4. Ibid.
5. Church, W.C. *The Life of John Ericsson.* London: Sampson Low, Marston, Searle, & Rivington, 1890. Vol. II, p. 322.
6. Samuel W. Taylor's description as above.
7. Church, W.C. Vol. II, pp. 217–219. Bright's disease, or nephritis, originally described as an inflammatory disease confined to the kidneys, was diagnosed by detection of albumin (a protein) in the urine and a low specific gravity of the urine. It also can be caused by chronic urinary obstruction like prostate hypertrophy causing an ascending kidney infection.
8. Thulesius, O. "Uppfinnaren John Ericsson fälldes av Brights sjukdom." *Läkartidningen*, 99: 297, 2002.
9. Samuel W. Taylor's description as above.
10. Letter of S. Taylor to Professor Colin, March 17, 1889. John Ericsson Papers, ASHF, reel 7.
11. Church, W.C. Vol. II, pp. 323–324.
12. Samuel Taylor to Baron John Ericsson, Ostersund, New York, April 23, 1889. John Ericsson Papers, ASHF, reel 7.
13. Ibid.
14. Letter of Rear Admiral D.L. Braine to the secretary of the Navy, August 25, 1890.
15. Burnett, C.B. *Captain John Ericsson: Father of the Monitor.* New York: The Vanguard Press, 1960. pp. 247–251.
16. Grip, E. *John Ericsson, en Livsbild.* Uppsala: J.A. Lindblads, 1920. p. 145–148.
17. *Teknisk Tidskrift för Byggnadskonst*, Stockholm. 5th release, 1895.
18. *Filipstads och Bergslags Tidning*, August 2, 1895.

27. Ericsson Remembered

1. Mindell, D.A. *War, Technology, and Experience Aboard the USS Monitor.* Baltimore: John Hopkins University Press, 2000. p. 135.
2. MacCord, C.W. "Ericsson and his 'Monitor.'" *North American Review*, October 1889 (reprinted in the *Stevens Indicator*).
3. Kennworthy, J.M. *New Wars, New Weapons.* London: Elkin Matthews & Marrot, 1930. p. 49. Churchill, W.S. *The American Civil War.* New York: The Fairfax Press, 1985. p. 72.
4. Quote from Sandburg, C. *Always the Young Strangers.* New York: Harcourt, Brace & Co., 1993. p. 260–261.
5. Harlowe, J.L. *Monitors: The Men, Machines and Mystique.* Gettysburg, Pa.: Thomas Publications, 2001. pp. 96–99.
6. Ibid., p. 136.
7. Church, W.C. *The Life of John Ericsson.* London: Sampson Low, Marston, Searle & Rivington, 1890. Vol. II, p. 308.
8. Samuel Taylor to Arthur Hazelius, Stockholm, April 10, 1889. John Ericsson Papers, ASHF, Reel 7.
9. Letter of W.C. Church to S.W. Taylor. New York, May 14, 1890. John Ericsson Papers, ASHF, Reel 7.
10. Eliasson, E. *Captain John Ericsson in New York.* New York: John Ericsson Society, 1988.
11. Olson, E.W. *The Swedish Element in Illinois.* Chicago: The Swedish American Biographical Association Publisher, 1917. pp. 235–237.
12. Dagens Nyheter, Stockholm, May 22, 1926. *John Ericsson: ett äreminne över svensk ras.*
13. Eliasson, E. 1988.
14. Hirsch, M.D. "John Ericsson: His Influence on My Community and Beyond." *The Swedish Pioneer* V (1), 1954, p. 5.
15. Blount, R., Jr. "The Mark Twain That Exists Today. *St. Petersburg Times*, Jan. 26, 2002.
16. William C. Church, 1893.
17. Sheridan, R.E. *Iron from the Deep: The Discovery and Recovery of the USS Monitor.*

Annapolis, Md.: Naval Institute Press, 2004. p. 242.

28. Lost and Found

1. Stick, D. *Graveyard of the Atlantic*. Chapel Hill: University of North Carolina Press, 1952.
2. Kinder, G. *Ship of Gold*. New York: Vintage Books, Random House, 1998.
3. Barancik, S. "Return to *Titanic*." *St. Petersburg Times*, July 16, 2000.
4. Tise, L.E. "Off Carolina Searching for the *Monitor*." *Civil War Times*, 1981, Vol. 20 (4).
5. Sheridan, R.E. *Iron From the Deep: The Discovery and Recovery of the USS* Monitor. Annapolis, Md.: Naval Institute Press. pp. 59–60.
6. Newton, J.G. "How We Found the *Monitor*." *National Geographic Magazine* 147, pp. 48–61, January 1975.
7. Miller, E.M. *USS* Monitor: *The Ship That Launched a Modern Navy*. Annapolis, Md.: Leeward Publications, 1978. p. 108.
8. Monitor National Marine Sanctuary Activities Report, ("Cheesebox") Vol. X, No. 1, December 1998.
9. Rose, D. "160-ton Gun Salute: Civil War *Monitor*'s Turret Raised From Sea." *Daily News*, August 6, 2002.
10. Lee Bowman, Scripps Howard News Service. Monday, August 29, 2005.
11. Musicant, I. *Divided Waters: The Naval History of the Civil War*. New York: Harper Collins, 1995. p. 165.
12. Detail of the four crew men of the monitor USS *Lehigh* (National Archives photo).
13. Marvel, W. *The Monitor Chronicles*. New York: Simon & Schuster, 2000. pp. 254–256.
14. Brennan, P. Raising of the *Hunley*. *North & South* 4 (1): 73.
15. Miller, E.M. pp. 87–104.
16. Foot, S. *The Civil War*. New York: Random House, 1958. p. 259.
17. West, R.S., Jr. *Gideon Welles: Lincoln's Navy Department*. Indianapolis: Bobbs-Merril, 1943. pp. 240–242.
18. Miller, E.M. p. 94.
19. Personal communication by Mr. John Broadwater, Monitor National Marine Sanctuary, The Mariners' Museum, Newport News, Va., February 1, 2002.
20. Still, W.N., Jr. in: *Raiders and Blockaders*. Dulles, Va.: Brassey's, 1998. p. 43.
21. Allen, F.E. "The '*Monitor*' Rises." *Invention and Technology*, Winter 2003.

Bibliography

Primary Sources

Forsviks Industriminne (The Forsvik Industrial Museum, Forsvik, Sweden). Drawings by John Ericsson and documents.

Göta Kanal Arkiv (Gota Canal Archives, Motala, Sweden). Drawings by John Ericsson and documents.

John Ericsson Papers, Gothenburg. Gothenburg University Library. Letters and documents to and from John Ericsson and Count von Rosen (Göteborgs Universitetsbibliotek).

John Ericsson Papers, New York. Letters and documents. New-York Historical Soceity, New York.

John Ericsson Papers, Philadelphia. A collection of original letters from and to John Ericsson and Samuel Taylor, and documents. The American Swedish Historical Foundation, Philadelphia, Microfilm, edited by Ester Chilstrom Meixner, 1970.

John Ericsson Papers, Stockholm. Letters to and from John Ericsson and documents in the Royal Library, Stockholm (Kungliga Biblioteket).

John Ericsson Papers, Washington. Library of Congress, Washington, D.C.

Linköping City Library (Linköping, Sweden). Letters from John Ericsson.

Lund University Library (Lund, Sweden). John Ericsson documents such as related to his doctoral promotion and letters.

Stevens Institute of Technology, Hoboken, N.J. Documents and drawings about the USS *Monitor*.

Tekniska Museet (Technical Museum, Stockholm, Sweden). Letters to and from John Ericsson, documents and illustrations.

Västeras Municipal Archives (Västeras, Sweden). Letters by John Ericsson and Johan Edström.

Secondary Sources

BIOGRAPHIES. For description of persons: *The National Cyclopaedia of American Biography*, *The Dictionary of American Biography*, *Dictionary of National Biography* (London), *Chambers Encyclopaedia* (London), *Svensk Uppslagsbok* (Malmö). Some of the main secondary sources are books directly connected with the life and work of John Ericsson: biographies by Ericsson's contemporary, William Conant Church and later biographies by Gustaf Lindwall, Ruth White and Carola Goldkuhl, which also contains a complete list of John Ericsson's 600 letters in libraries and private collections in Sweden. The most recent with some new documents from Ericsson's life in Sweden: Margaretha Jönsson Runvik. Other important biographies are those about John A. Dahlgren, John Ross, Robert Fulton, Alfred Nobel, Gideon Welles and Fanny Kemble.

CIVIL WAR. The engagement between the *Monitor* and the *Virginia* is described by

William C. Davis and James T. DeKay. The history of the *Monitor* and the detection of its wreck, by Edward M. Miller. Recently William Marvel published an account of a crew member and David A. Mindell gave an interesting description of the technology. Angus Constam recently published a color-plated popular book about ironclads and the battle at Hampton Roads. Civil War history: Bruce Catton, Ivan Musicant and Sir Winston Churchill.

MONITOR. DeKay, James T., and Edward M. Miller. For the technical details: William N. Still. Development of ironclads: Donald L. Canney, Thomas Gibbons, Jack Greene and Allesandro Massignani. The 1884 Century Magazine edition of *Battles and Leaders of the Civil War* gives a vivid description to which John Ericsson himself contributed. The recovery of the wreck: Robert E. Sheridan.

CALORIC ENGINES. A good source about steam and "caloric engines" is Robert Sier's account on *Hot Air Caloric and Stirling Engines*, S. Lindqvist's *Technology on Trial*, Sadi Carnot's *Reflexions*, D. Cardwell's *The Norton History of Technology* and Eugene S. Ferguson's *John Ericsson and the Age of Caloric*.

MANHATTAN. For information about New York City a good source is Burrows and Wallace's *Gotham: A History of New York City to 1898*. John Ericsson's places of interest on Manhattan are reviewed by Erik Eliasson in his *Captain John Ericsson in New York*.

Books

Burrows, E.G., and Wallace, M. *Gotham: A History of New York City to 1898*. New York: Oxford University Press, 1999.
Canney, D.L. *Lincoln's Navy*. Annapolis, Md.: Naval Institute Press, 1998.
Cardwell, D. *The Norton History of Technology*. New York: W.W. Norton, 1994. pp. 240–242.
Carnot, S. *Reflexions on the Motive Power of Fire*. New York: Lilian Barber Press, 1986.
Catton, B. *The American Heritage Short History of the Civil War*. New York: Dell Publishing, 1975.
_____. *This Hallowed Ground*. New York: Doubleday, 1956.
Church, W.C. *The Life of John Ericsson*. London: Sampson Low, Marston, Searle & Rivington, vols. I-II, 1890.
Churchill, W.S. *The American Civil War*. New York: Fairfax Press, 1985.
Clinton, C. *Fanny Kemble's Civil Wars*. New York: Simon & Schuster, 2000.
Constam, A. *Duel of the Ironclads USS* Monitor *& CSS* Virginia *at Hampton Roads, 1862*. Oxford: Osprey, 2003.
Davis, W.C. *Duel Between the First Ironclads*. New York: Doubleday, 1975.
DeKay, J.T. *Monitor*. New York: Ballantine Books, 1997.
Eliasson, E. *Captain John Ericsson in New York*. New York: John Ericsson Society. 1988.
Ferguson, E.S. *John Ericsson and the Age of Caloric*. U.S. National Museum Bulletin 228, 1961.
Gibbons, T. *Warships and Naval Battles of the Civil War*. New York: Gallery Books, 1989.
Goldkuhl, C. *John Ericsson, mannen och uppfinnaren*. Stockholm: Bonniers, 1961.
Greene, J., and Massignani, A. *Ironclads at War*. Conshohocken: Combined Publishing, 1998.
Jönsson Runvik, M. *John Ericsson: resan mot solen*. Karlstad: Källan, 1996.
Lindqvist, S. *Technology on Trial: The Introduction of Steam Power Technology into Sweden*. Stockholm: Almqvist & Wiksell, 1984.
Lindvall, G. *Ingenjören vid Beach Street*. Stockholm: Ahlen & Söner, 1937.
Marvel, W., ed. *The Monitor Chronicles*. New York: Simon & Schuster, 2000.

Miller, E.M. *USS* Monitor: *The Ship That Launched the Modern Navy.* Annapolis, Md.: Leeward Publications, 1978.
Mindell, D.A. *War Technology and Experience Aboard the USS* Monitor. Baltimore: Johns Hopkins University Press, 2000.
Musicant, L. *Divided Waters.* New York: Harper Colllins, 1995.
Niven, J. *Gideon Welles.* Baton Rouge: Louisiana State University Press, 1973.
Philip, C.O. *Robert Fulton: A Biography.* New York: Franklin Watts, 1985.
Ross, M.J. *Polar Pioneers.* Montreal: McGill-Queen's University Press, 1994.
Schneller, R.J., Jr. *A Quest for Glory: A Biography of Rear Admiral John A. Dahlgren.* Annapolis: Naval Institute Press, 1996.
Sheridan, R.E. *Iron from the Deep: The Discovery and Recovery of the USS* Monitor. Annapolis, Md.: Naval Institute Press, 2004.
Sier, R. *Hot Air Caloric and Stirling Engines.* Chelmsford: L.A. Mair, 1999.
Sohlman, R., and Schuck, H. *Nobel, Dynamite and Peace.* New York: Cosmopolitan Book Corp., 1929.
Still, W.N. *Monitor Builders: A Historical Study of the Principal Firms and Individuals Involved in the Construction of USS* Monitor. Washington: National Maritime Initiative, Division of History, National Park Service, 1988.
White, R. *Yankee from Sweden.* New York: H. Holt, 1960.

Index

*Numbers in **bold italics** refer to pages with illustrations.*

Adams, John Q. 63
Ambinavigator (ship) 70
Amphitrite (ship) 145
Anaconda Plan (Naval Blockade) 81–86
Archimedes screw 46
Astor House 50, 52

Baltimore (ship) 215
Bankhead, John 134
Barnum, Phineas Taylor 52
Battery Park 73
Battle of Hampton Roads 116, 117
Bayam, Amelia 40, 41, 52
Beaufort, Francis 45, 46
Beech Street residence 152, 173–***177***, 178; boy tramp Willie ***186***; rat trap 176
Bigelow, John 75
Booth, Felix 22
Braithwaite, John 21, 26, 31, 38, 40
Bremer, Fredrika 50
Broadwater, John 234
Brooke, John 87, 88
Brooklyn Navy Yard 49
Brunel, Marc Isambert K. 41, 62
Buchanan, Franklin 88, 120
Bull, John 37
Bull, Ole 207, 208
Bushnell, Cornelius 96, 97
Butts, Francis 134

Caloric engines 28, 67–***69***
Cape Hatteras 133
Carl XIV Johan, King 17, 37
Carnot, Sadi 67
Catton, Bruce 100
Centennial Exhibition 160–165
Century (magazine) 131
Charleston 141, 142

Chase, Salmon 121
Church, William C. 15, 69
Churchill, Winston 219
Clermont (ship) 70
Coles C.P. 47
Cooper, Peter 55
Cornwall mine project 26–28
Crimean War 92
Cupola vessel 81, 92, ***93***

Dahlgren, John 17, 56, 84, 94
Dana, Charles A. 73
Davis, Jefferson 88
Delamater, Harry C. 50, 57, 65, 96
Depth recorder 43
Destroyer (ship) 146–***148***, 149
Dictator (ship) 141
Drewry's Bluff 123

Eads, James B. 83
Edison, Thomas A. 52
Edström, Johan 10, 11, 20
Elworth, Hjalmar 17, 200–***201***, 202
Ericsson, Amelia Byam ***40***, 52, 184, 198, 199
Ericsson, Britta Sophia 5, 17
Ericsson, John ***2***, ***103***; America 49–180; birthplace ***6***; character 181–190; daily life, health 178, 191, 192; death and burial 211–217; England 19–48; family and friends 196–210; remembered 218–226; soldier ***13***; statues ***222***, ***224***, ***225***; Sweden 5–18
Ericson, Nils 5
Ericsson, Olof 5–9
Ericsson (caloric ship) 70–***72***, 73–75

Faraday, Michael 28, 79
Filipstad 5, 150

Index

Fillmore, Millard 74
Fire, hot-air engines 14, 16, 19, 20, 69, 77
Fitch, John 70
Fleet Prison 40
Flying Devil 45
Forbes, Robert B. 51
Fort Monroe 137
Fox, Gustavus 79, 83, 89, 92, 97, 99, 120, 143
Fulton, Robert 42, 56, 70

Galena (ship) 84, 96
Geer, George 132, 133
Gosport Navy Yard 85, 89
Göta Canal 7, 9, 10, 14
Great Western (ship) 62
Greene, Samuel 107, 115, 130
Griswold, John 102, 106

Hampton Roads, Va. 114
Hawthorne, Nathaniel 100, 129
Hazelius, Arthur 220
Hot air engine (caloric engine) 14
Hunley (ship) 131, 142

Ironside (ship) 84, 96
Irving, Washington 50, 53, 74
Isherwood, Benjamin 96, 104

Jeffers, William 130
Joule, James P. 28, 79

Keeler, William 101, 127, 129, 131, 135
Kelvin W. Thomson 79
Kemble, Fanny 36
King's Bench Prison 39
Kitching, John B. 71

Lamar, Gazaway B. 71
Liljesköld, Carolina 17
Lincoln, Abraham 81, 119; *Monitor* project 91–101; visits the *Monitor* 131
Lind, Jenny 180
Ling system 14
Locomotives 29–36

Mallory, Stephen 66, 84–88, 90
Manhattan 173–178
Mariners' Museum 234
Maury, Matthew F. 84, 85
McClellan, George 121, 122
McCord, Charles W. 103, 108, 140
Mechanic's Institute 51
Melville Herman 19, 101

Merrimack alias *Virginia* (ship) 66, 85, 87–**88**, 89–90
Miantonomah (ship) 141, 143
Monitor 61; crew 109, 110, *117*, 130; design 84, 89, 102–109, *110*; interior 128; launch *107*; rescue *136*; sinking 131–138; Swedish *150*; waste disposal 128, 129; wreck found 227–***230***, 231–234
Monitor Center 234
Morse, Samuel 71
Mouchot, Auguste 152
Munn, Orson 73

Napoleon III 144
Newton, Isaac 115, 129
Newton, John G. 228
Nilsson, Kristina 180
Nobel, Alfred 166–***169***, 170–172
Novelty (locomotive) 31, ***32***, ***35***
Novelty Iron Works 50, 103

Ogden, Francis B. 40, 43, 47
Orator (gun) 61
Oregon (gun) 61
Östersund 13
Owen, Samuel 16

Passaic (ship) 125, 134, 137, 140
Patents 16, 20, 21, 27, 28, 30, 43, 165
Paulding, James K. 57
Peacemaker (gun) 64, 65
Phoenix Foundry 50, 103
Pierce, Franklin 74
Polar Ventures 21–24
Polhem, C. 6
Porter, John 87, 88
Princeton (ship) 53, 54, 58, ***59***, 60, 66, 85, 94
Propeller 25, 42–***44***, 45–49
Pyrometer 68, 152

Ram 86
Rhode Island (ship) 134, 137
Rider, Alexander 76, 77
Risley, Samuel 50, 52, 54
Roanoke, (ship) 116
Robert F. Stockton (ship) 70
Ross, John Scott 21–23, 39
Rumford, Benjamin 68, 78, 79
Russia 143

Sandburg, Carl 67
Sargent, John 45, 50, 54, 74
Scientific American 72–74, 76, 104
Scott, Winfield 81, 122

Index

Seidler, Charles 19, 21, 41
Slavery 190
Smith, Francis P. 43, 46
Smith, Joseph 94, 104
Solar calorimeter *161*
Solar energy 151–159
Solar hot-air engine *155*
Sölve (ship) 145
Stanton, Edwin 121
Steam engines *15*, 20, 22, 43
Steam fire engines 24, *25*, 51
Stephenson, George 30, 31, 34
Stevens, Robert 130
Stimers, Alban 105, 115, 120
Stirling motor 78
Stockton, Robert 47, 48, 57, 58, 62

Taylor, Samuel 165, 210
Telford, Thomas 8, 11, 16, 20
Thermodynamics 79
Torpedoes 147–149

Trevithick, Richard 5, 30
Triewald, Marten 7
Tyler, John 58, 63, 64

Union Club, NY 54, 71
Upshur, Abel P. 58, 64

van Buren, Martin 56, 57
Victory (ship), polar sail 23, 42
Virginia (ship) 86
von Platen, Baltzar 8, 9, 11, 12
von Rosen, Adolf 18, 19, 21, 38, 40, 57, 158

Watt, James 20, 26, 43, 68, 70
Weeks, Grenville 134, 135, 138
Welles, Gideon 83, 89, 90, 94, 97, 99
Whitman, Walt 118, 126
Williamson, William 87, 88
Winslow, John 102
Worden, John L. 119, 120, 127, 130, 134

www.ingramcontent.com/pod-product-compliance
Ingram Content Group UK Ltd.
Pitfield, Milton Keynes, MK11 3LW, UK
UKHW041935140426
5217IPUK00014B/493